IN AN ABUSIVE STATE

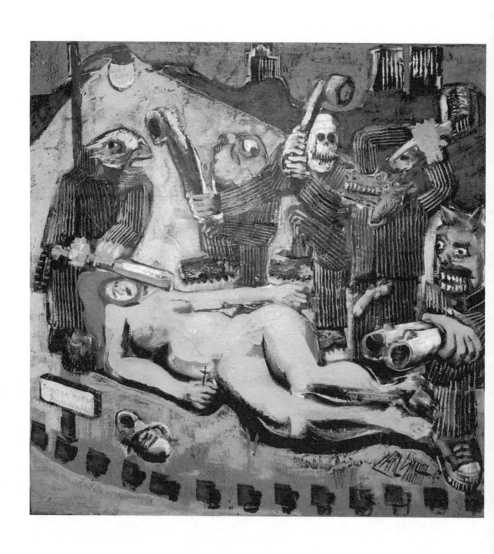

KRISTIN BUMILLER

In an Abusive State

HOW NEOLIBERALISM APPROPRIATED

THE FEMINIST MOVEMENT AGAINST

SEXUAL VIOLENCE

Duke University Press   Durham and London   2008

© 2008 Duke University Press
All rights reserved.
Printed in the United States of America
on acid-free paper ∞
Designed by C. H. Westmoreland
Typeset in Scala by Keystone Typesetting, Inc.
Library of Congress Cataloging-in-Publication Data
appear on the last printed page of this book.

frontispiece: Central Park Jogger (16″ x 16″, acrylic on wood),
© Carl Smith, 1997.

for **Gabriel**

CONTENTS

ACKNOWLEDGMENTS

During the many years it took for this body of empirical and theoretical work to coalesce into a book, I received the support and encouragement of many friends and colleagues. From start to finish, this project benefited from the feminist legal theory community organized by Martha Fineman. I deeply appreciate Martha's generosity of spirit and time and her efforts to make the Feminist Legal Workshops a productive intellectual arena for many feminist scholars of my generation. Another vital source of support for many years was an informal Boston-Amherst reading group that brought together supportive friends and colleagues, including Alice Hearst, Martha Umphrey, Vicky Spelman, Martha Minow, Molly Shanley, Jill Frank, Susan Silbey, Martha Ackelsberg, and Patty Ewick. The mentorship of Murray Edelman is greatly missed, but his scholarship still has enormous resonance in this project. Many colleagues at Amherst College offered ideas, suggestions, or encouragement along the way, including Amrita Basu, Margaret Hunt, Martha Saxton, Uday Mehta, Stephanie Sandler, Mary Renda, Pavel Machala, and Karen Sanchez-Eppler. Karen was a strong source of inspiration as my long time co-teacher in our course "Representing Domestic Violence." In addition to presentations of this work at Feminist Legal Theory Workshops at Columbia Law School and Cornell Law School, I benefited from feedback from presentations to Vicki Schultz's Feminist Theory Seminar at Yale Law School, John Brigham's Political Science graduate seminar on the Legal Process at the University of Massachusetts–Amherst, and the

American Bar Foundation Socio-Legal Studies Seminar. Other scholars have offered valuable comments, although not always in agreement with my analysis, including Christine Harrington (who provided extensive comments on an earlier version of the manuscript), Boaventura de Sousa Santos, Elizabeth Schneider, Laura Woliver, Lois Bibbings, and Risa Liberwitz. I would particularly like to thank Patricia Williams, who was my "trial-watching" companion during the Central Park Jogger trial—her insightful reactions were crucial to stimulating my interpretations of the case.

The observational research on rape trials and interviews with participants and lawyers was supported by the National Science Foundation. Permission to reproduce artwork was generously granted by Arcady Kotler. The ethnographic research on battered women was supported by an Amherst College Faculty Research Grant. The research in chapter 5 was based upon interviews with women who experienced domestic violence and received assistance from shelters. I am indebted to these remarkable women for taking the time to tell me their stories and being candid about their disappointments and dreams for a better future. While analyzing the interview material, I found a hospitable home and a quiet environment to work as a visiting fellow at the Law School at the University of Bristol.

I also received the fantastic assistance of Cecelia Cancellaro in the publication process. Cecelia provided editorial assistance on the entire manuscript and found a home for the book at Duke University Press. Her encouragement and wisdom were critical to the completion and publication of this project. I would also like to thank the anonymous reviewers for the Duke University Press; their constructive criticism and extensive suggestions were instrumental to my refashioning of the book. Students and staff at Amherst College assisted with transcribing interviews and compiling bibliography information; thanks to Donna Simpter, Leena Valge, Assia Dosseva, and Priyanka Jacob.

Finally, I would like to thank my family, Jack, Gabe, and Josh. Jack not only has been my greatest source of personal support but he carefully and thoughtfully edited the entire manuscript many times over. This book is dedicated to my son Gabe. His childhood brought many challenges and rewards to my life. Oftentimes being his advocate distracted me from my life as a scholar, but it also brought sweet victories—this most important: seeing him become an adult filled with happiness and full of hope for a bright future.

PREFACE

The recent reversal of the convictions in the 1991 Central Park Jogger trials[1] redresses a shameful example of American injustice analogous to the infamous Scottsboro Boys trial, in which a group of black teenagers was convicted of raping two white women on a railroad train between Chattanooga and Memphis in March 1931.[2] Both events were accompanied by a public outcry for immediate "justice," the incompetent legal defense of young, vulnerable boys, the failure of prominent national organizations to draw attention to their innocence, and long delays in the overturning of wrongful convictions.

Historians have long debated the reasons behind this dramatic miscarriage of justice in 1930s America. Many see the events as an outgrowth of racism in the Deep South that created circumstances that made it nearly impossible for black men accused of raping a white woman to get a fair trial. Others have cited the slowness of the NAACP to realize that these boys were innocent and to provide resources and draw national attention to the situation. And as was shown in the lengthy appeal process and retrials, these defendants were subjected to the vagaries of local politics and a corrupt local criminal justice system.

These are all undoubtedly important factors, but the Scottsboro Boys Trial and the modern equivalent in the conviction of the "Central Park Five" are agonizing examples of what Hannah Arendt called the "banality of evil"; injustices that come about when ordinary people, often acting as agents of state power, become indifferent to their participation in violence and their role in the perpetuation of racism.[3] In both cases, it is important not only to raise questions about the actual trials but also to investigate the role of ordinary conditions of culture, bureaucracy, and government that create the conditions for injustice.

In this regard, this book formulates an understanding of the contemporary political environment that produced the Central Park Case and, more generally, the increasingly coercive state reactions to crimes involving sexual violence. In part, this has arisen from a dominant construction of sexual violence as a "social problem" that emerged in the early 1970s.[4] In the United States, awareness of the problem of sexual violence was accompanied by a phenomenal growth in the crime control apparatus, including increased prosecutorial power, mandatory sentences, and an unprecedented rise in prison populations. At the same time, sexual violence became important to the agenda of the "therapeutic state," a network of professionals, social workers, and government agents providing service delivery to the poor and disadvantaged. These clients of the welfare state are predominantly women and their children who are afflicted with a high incidence of troubles that are of concern to therapeutic professionals, including domestic violence, child abuse, addiction problems, and other "dependencies." As a result, the feminist movement became a partner in the unforeseen growth of a criminalized society, a phenomenon with negative consequences not only for minority and immigrant groups of men but also for those women who are subject to scrutiny within the welfare state.

This does not mean that either state power or feminist activism is monolithic in form. In an analysis of the politics of state action, it is important to differentiate between political ideology, governmental practices, instrumental policies, and the actions of individual actors. The power of the state emerges through highly diffuse forms of authority that influence people in everyday life and become constituted in citizens' political consciousness. Likewise, the influence of feminism is found in grassroots movements, professional ideologies, academic thinking, and popular consciousness. In all these facets, feminist knowledge and practice is greatly contested and constantly in flux. There has been, however, an amalgamation of forces that has produced a dominant understanding of the problem of sexual violence and its causes and consequences. This prevailing understanding has solidified in cultural representations and has been ratified in a range of governmental and nongovernmental institutions.

Recently there has been increased concern among feminist activists about their problematic alliance with the state. There are three likely responses. The first and the most politically vehement is to call attention to state repression. From this perspective, the unjust verdicts in the Central Park case are simply another example of racist justice, media conspiracies, and police misconduct. Although this response correctly draws our attention to the fundamental importance of racism in American culture and criminal justice policy, it fails to look systematically at how the growth in the crime-control sector is part of a larger scheme of bureaucratic control over women and groups of threatening "outsiders."

The second response is focused on reclaiming personal autonomy for women. This view can be seen either as a powerful argument for women's agency, even under conditions of extreme duress, or, regrettably, in terms that contribute to the backlash against feminism. The social work theorist Linda Mills, for example, advances a forceful argument about the need for women to exercise absolute choice over decisions affecting their safety and their lives in order to protect themselves from all forms of professional intrusiveness.[5] She calls for the end of mandatory arrest policies in the case of domestic violence and moving away from policies that isolate perpetrators from victims. Her alternatives, which rely on community-based dispute resolution, are based upon a fundamental presumption of the universality of violence in relationships. She points to evidence indicating that women are as violent as men in intimate relationships and concludes that the feminist victim/perpetrator model doesn't accurately describe the dynamics of domestic violence.

Although Mills carefully avoids presenting her work as an across-the-board attack on feminism, her scheme is not compelling in the face of overwhelming evidence about the distinctiveness and extreme brutality of violence against women. Mills's portrayal of the intrusiveness and often counterproductive role of therapeutic professionals finds strong support in this book; however, it is also important not to glorify women's opportunities for choice and ability to exercise autonomy given unequal power relations with perpetrators and the influence of therapeutic knowledge. Putting the dilemmas encountered by victims in a broader perspective is necessary to make clear how the professional treatment of battered women is endemic to contemporary conditions of citizenship and often arises in the context of women's dependency on the welfare state.

And finally, the loose coalition of feminists most involved with programs and policies, including academics, activists, and service providers, clearly sees contradictions and failures in practice but is not well positioned for self-criticism. Already overwhelmed by women's need for safety and redress, the movement devotes much of its energy to keeping their current services operational in the face of declining support for all social welfare programs. Nonetheless, it has been feminist policymakers and researchers who have conducted most serious studies of the effectiveness of programs. Yet much of this work remains silent about the overall negative consequences of criminalization. Within mainstream feminism and its activist organizations there is also little critical reflection about how feminists pose sexual violence as a "social problem." In particular, the early efforts to make clear that rape, battering, and other forms of sexual abuse are "violence" and "not sex" has led to entrenched understandings of the causes of violence, the social dynamics of racism and gender, and the potential solutions.

This book takes another tack. *In an Abusive State* examines the ways in which society has defined sexual violence as a social problem and how this creates policies that reinforce stereotypical assumptions about women's dependency and the character of intimate violence. In part, this analysis stems from interpreting the symbolic representations of sexual violence in contemporary society and how these representations are reinforced in some of the most well-known rape cases of the recent past. This book also shines a critical light on how the large-scale expansion of legal and governmental efforts to counteract the threat of sexual violence has transformed the everyday relationships between the state and women as both actual and potential victims. It reveals how the now commonplace practices of responding to cases of rape and domestic violence promote *problematic* state control over the disrupted lives of victims. In this regard, strategies employed to help victims of sexual violence are narrowly focused on individualistic forms of problem solving rather than seeking a more comprehensive understanding of this phenomenon or counteracting other forms of domination in women's private and public lives.

This "new" look at this issue is largely made possible by an ability to examine the movement in *retrospect*—from a historical perspective, the motivations and actions of reformers can be seen in terms of the larger political forces that defined their engagement with the state. Despite contestation from both within and outside the movement, the feminist campaign against sexual violence was driven by the logic of social reform; it pushed for new legal definitions of crime, swifter and surer processing of cases by courts, the investment of resources by social welfare bureaucracies, and ultimately the transformation of public attitudes. From this perspective, the lack of progress along the way was often viewed as the unanticipated consequence of social change. This book, however, calls for a reevaluation of the reformist goals of the movement and also examines how its prospects were changed by the growth of neoliberal state policies. It shows how the contemporary campaign against sexual violence is fundamentally shaped by dramatic shifts in welfare policies, incarceration rates, and the surveillance role of social service bureaucracies over recent decades.

The analysis presented in this book may not satisfy the reader looking for a pragmatic solution to narrowly framed policy questions; however, it offers much broader prescriptions for how to address the real threat of violence against women while building more vibrant, inclusive, and democratic communities. One clear piece of advice is that it no longer makes sense to single out violence against women as a specific issue for policymaking because there are advantages to seeing it as part of a larger project of enabling women to be more effectual citizens. It is critical to "protect" women by removing the economic and social obstacles they regularly encounter rather than by expanding the capacity of the state to reproduce violence. The best means to counter a range of encroachments caused by the growth of bureaucracies and police power is by sustaining all citizens' fundamental rights and dignity.

Chapter 1 provides an overview of the argument presented in this book. It describes from a historical perspective how the feminist campaign addressing sexual violence has evolved in alliance with the state. Chapter 2 considers how feminist ideology has transformed in the context of cultural anxieties associated with sexual terror. It shows how the issue of sexual violence, once placed on the public agenda, polarized gender- and race-based interests and fueled notions about the sadistic nature of this violence.

Chapter 3 looks at how the modern crime control apparatus has developed in response to demands on the state to assert control over sexual violence. The focus of this chapter is political trials involving high-profile crimes, in particular, the New Bedford and the Central

Park Jogger gang-rape trials. This analysis demonstrates how prosecutors' narratives about the crimes epitomize forms of expressive justice, where the trial becomes a forum to publicly affirm the law's capacity to maintain order.

Chapter 4 examines the routine forms of state control over sexual violence, particularly the development of a professional cadre of doctors, therapists, and social workers who increasingly assert responsibility for diagnosis, treatment, and prevention of sexual assault and family violence. It shows how these expanding forms of expertise about rape victims and battered women have the dual effect of transforming sexual violence into a treatable social problem, or medical condition, amenable to the norms of professional practice, while rationalizing the anxiety associated with often brutal and persistent violence between intimates.

In Chapter 5 the consequences of increased state involvement in the containment of sexual violence are considered from the "victim's" perspective. The analysis is based upon testimonies of rape victims and interviews with battered women. In the face of the expansion of regulatory authority, women negotiate their status vis-à-vis the state. This chapter chronicles their complex responses to the protection offered by state actors and shows how women sometimes challenge professional depictions of themselves and their problems.

Chapter 6 examines the expansion of feminist concerns about sexual violence into the international human rights arena. It raises concerns about the appropriation of the rhetoric of human rights, particularly the degree to which it is used to buttress the coercive apparatus of state or international organizations. The book's conclusion assesses the movement to combat sexual violence as it has developed over the past forty years. The significant law reforms pertaining to rape and domestic violence are shown to have had limited impact in terms of their desired objectives. Even though recent studies have demonstrated the limits of reform and in some cases the counterproductive effects, such evidence rarely has led to a questioning of the value of using the punitive power of the state in countering sexual violence. The conclusion puts forward suggestions for the redirection of feminist activism.

THE SEXUAL VIOLENCE AGENDA

feminists and the state

Neoliberalism . . . is hostile to concessions to the popular classes (social and economic rights) and to the state as a promoter of non-mercantile interactions among citizens . . . [D]emocratic struggles for inclusion in the social contract . . . have been suppressed, illegalized, criminalized, while organizations that conducted them have been under attack and often dismantled. A new virulent counter-reformism emerged, determined to erode or eliminate social and economic rights, expanding the market economy in such a way as to transform the whole society into a market society. Since whatever is being proposed as a reform (of education, health, social security, etc.) is definitely for the worse, the left is often forced to defend the status quo.
—Boaventura de Sousa Santos

For almost forty years a concerted campaign by feminists has transformed popular consciousness and led to the widespread growth of organizations designed to address the problem of sexual violence. This campaign is often seen as the core component of the contemporary feminist movement and fundamental to the feminist agenda of promoting autonomy, equality, and social justice. The movement's primary objective has been the recognition of the harm of sexual violence and the consistent sanctioning of perpetrators. Undeniably, this work has been extremely important; it has called attention to the effects of sexual violence on women's lives and demanded a large-scale public commitment to stopping this violence. However, feminists have not been in total command of the "sexual violence agenda"; much of it has transpired through an explicit or implicit reliance on the coercive power of government to ensure women's safety.

This feminist alliance with the state is to a large extent unavoidable. Concerning violent crimes against women, it is difficult to imagine policies that would not ultimately rely upon the carceral capacities of the state. Clearly, there are some instances of grave harm that require the segregation of offenders for the protection of society. Yet in the United States and other national contexts, it is important to be aware of both the potentialities and limitations of using state power to advance the interests of women. The growth of neoliberal politics has provided even more reason for skepticism as feminists find their innovations incorporated into the regulatory and criminal justice apparatus.[1] In this regard, it is essential to consider how the feminist campaign against sexual violence evolved in alliance with the state, and even more critically how this campaign enabled countervailing state interests.

foundational feminism

In the late 1960s "radical" feminists focused the movement's attention on rape as a political problem.[2] Radical activists initiated a series of small grassroots campaigns throughout the United States that called attention to the realities of violence in women's lives and particularly to how rape was used as a tool to subordinate women to men.[3] For these feminists the focus on rape was connected to new self-help approaches to support women's health and safety. At the same time, the issue of sexual violence reached mainstream feminist organizations and was seen as a core concern linked to equal rights and women's full participation in the public sphere. By 1971, the National Organization for Women (NOW) organized task forces to transform existing rape statutes and to promote model rape laws.

By focusing on law reform, mainstream organizers promoted objectives consistent with the broad agenda of the women's movement. They called on the state to fulfill its obligations to protect all its citizens equally and identified the lack of enforcement of sexual crimes against women as a major obstacle to women's freedom within the public sphere. Most activist groups named the problem as the failure of the state to recognize and protect women; in fact, the often flagrant denial of violence against women was characterized as state-sanctioned violence and was seen as complicit with other forms of patriarchal control that oppressed women. Giving rapists a mere "slap on the wrist" and considering women's battering a "domestic disturbance" reinforced cultural presumptions that did not take violence against women seriously. These reformist objectives have been and remain an important element in the campaign against sexual violence. From this perspective, an alliance with the state is essentially a nonissue, except in terms of compelling the state to follow through on its promises for more aggressive enforcement of the law.

The battered women's movement began from similar ideological roots in terms of its theory of patriarchy, power, and violence. The goal of the movement was to bring into the public realm an everyday event that had been hidden by the ideology of privacy surrounding the patriarchal family. The term "battered woman" had no public significance before the feminist movement politicized the issue by defining it as a form of violence produced by a system of male domination.[4] An essential part of the movement against wife battering was the creation of shelters; these were not institutions but houses formed through collective action to provide a safe haven from male violence.[5] The shelters were centers of consciousness raising and were staffed by feminist volunteers, some of whom were previously battered women. Part of the core beliefs of the grassroots movement was that the shelter was both a physical and symbolic boundary between women's space and the violence of the male world. Within these homes women could exercise their own strength and autonomy outside relationships of domination.[6] Shelters were built to be homes, albeit temporary, in which women would feel free to come and go as they pleased. It was hoped that battered women's lives would "intersect" with these houses, and that their continued connection with this protected space would vary over time according to their needs and contributions.[7] The core philosophy of the shelter movement was anti-state.

This early history was influential; most shelters and rape crisis centers formed as distinctive "feminist organizations" that explicitly recognized the need for less hierarchy, democratic decision making, and women working with women. This meant that women came to understand the violence they experienced as a collectivity and that there were no rigid boundaries between organizers and women who sought help.[8] Shelters and crisis centers provided a place for women to become whole again after the experience of violence, an experience they learned to see not simply as a series of injurious acts but as a shattering condition that affects many women's lives. Beyond a spiritual component, which stressed the interconnectedness of women's problems, was a practical mission of providing the basic resources needed by the women and their children. The volunteer staff utilized the government service network (although not exclusively) in assisting women in their search for housing, jobs, and childcare.

As these organizations matured, they encountered numerous challenges in carrying out their purpose and meeting women's needs.[9] The imposition of regulations and the desire for stable funding sources pushed these organizations onto the "terrain of the state."[10] Studies of these organizations show that although state power was actively contested, shelters and rape crisis centers had to make compromises and structural changes to remain in compliance and to take advantage of available resources. Over time, this led to rape crisis centers and shelters functioning bureaucratically and relying on professionals in order to secure reliable funding.[11] Institutionalization also brought internal conflict and contestation over fundamental questions of theory versus practice.[12] Organizational turmoil was not driven by state involvement alone; over time shelter and crisis center workers gained a greater appreciation for the necessary scope of individual and system-wide transformation and struggled to gain more realistic assessments of the political, economic, and personal challenges facing women.

The consequences of moving onto the terrain of the state are still widely debated: some see these transformations as a betrayal of grassroots sensibilities, while most see these changes as an inevitable outcome of growth and stability. Overall, the majority of these organizations have been successful at maintaining their feminist identity. The foundational goal of empowering women was not lost; rather, new strategies were developed as the conditions for this empowerment changed.[13] Yet the internal evolution of these organizations reveals only part of the story. While battered women's shelters and rape crisis centers maintained their quasi-autonomy from the state, other organizations whose primary purposes were not treating rape and domestic battery and which did not ascribe to feminist ideology were increasingly being called upon by the state to address the problem. The growing recognition of sexual violence as a public health crisis brought legitimacy to the work of feminist organizations, but it also resulted in the broad-scale expansion of the instrumental capacities of the state to address sexual violence. The state's terrain reached far beyond feminist organizations and their agendas.

growth of neoliberalism

By the late 1970s, the tenets of neoliberalism began to influence American public policy at home and abroad. Ronald Reagan's first term as president marks the shift to neoliberal principles of governance which are associated with less restraint on free-market policies, pro-corporatism, privatization, and in particular, the transfer of public services to private organizations. This shift significantly affected the already established feminist anti-violence movement in its attempts to reform the criminal justice programs and build up victim services. The call for state responsibility for preventing and treating victims was in direct contrast to the new ethics of personal responsibility that was the cornerstone of the neoliberal agenda. This contradiction was resolved, but the cost was the incorporation of the feminist anti-violence movement into the apparatus of the regulatory state.

For example, the rationale for providing services for women was transformed by the neoliberal agenda.[14] The organizers of the shelter movement saw the necessity of encouraging women to take advantage of available government benefits, but only as a temporary means to provide for their children. Importantly, seeking government help was part of a growing recognition both within shelter organizations and in the feminist movement more generally of the fundamental insecurity of marriage as an institution. Now, in many battered women's shelters women are required to apply for all appropriate state benefits as part of a process of showing that they are taking all necessary steps to gain self-sufficiency. These requirements entangle women in an increasingly value-laden welfare program tied to the promotion of the traditional nuclear family, fear of dependency, and distrust of women as mothers.[15] These ties, moreover, come with fewer benefits as the "devolution" of welfare systems has brought about cutbacks in services and rescaling to the local level.[16] At the same time, the welfare system has become more linked to other forms of state involvement, including probate court actions concerning custody, paternity hearings, child protective services, and relationships with school officials. As a result, when women seek help from shelters, it now produces an inevitable dependency on the state.

Another outgrowth of neoliberalism has been the expansion of the regulatory functions of the state. This expanded role of the state as a manager of personal lives has been described as the growth of governmentality. This concept is drawn from the political theorist Michel Foucault, whose analysis of power in modern societies demonstrates how coercive forms of authority are manifested through quasi-governmental instruments and other "softer" forms of power. This growing presence of the state is seen within feminist organizations, as discussed above, but it also emerges as more state and quasi-state actors become part of a network of responders to sexual violence. With the growth of the regulatory apparatus, crisis centers and shelters are now a small segment of a service sector for which intimate violence is one of a long list of social problems to which they respond. Some of these organizations are central to the policing function of the state, such as sex crime units in police and prosecutors' offices. Others are more ancillary to the state and even private in form. These include hospital emergency rooms, medical doctors in a range of specialties, mental health professionals, community service and religious organizations. As the responsibility for recognizing and treating intimate violence has expanded, so has the use of protocols for defining who is eligible for services, client expectations, and treatment methodologies. These systems often function in conjunction with the welfare regulatory apparatus and are obligated to follow protocols and reporting procedures, even though many are private or quasi-state efforts to manage the large numbers of women who experience relationship violence.

While these changes were occurring in the social service sector, there was a dramatic rise in incarceration rates in the United States beginning in the late 1970s. Some see this swell in incarceration as a direct consequence of neoliberalism—a less regulated economy resulted in increased social stratification and a generalized sense of insecurity that then led to more regulation of the poor and minorities. The criminologist David Garland posits that this dramatic upturn is a multifaceted response to both a changing political climate and an evolving logic of penal reform. This brought about a "culture of control," which was grounded in conceptions of the essential "otherness" of the criminal and highly dependent on mechanisms of social segregation.[17] In this way, crime control emerged as a new form of social exclusion reinforcing other forms of discrimination against minorities and directed against potentially unruly classes of persons.[18]

Mainstream feminist demands for more certain and severe punishment for crimes against women fed into these reactionary forces. This resulted in a direct alliance between feminist activists and legislators, prosecutors, and other elected officials promoting the crime control business. Although the feminist's "gender war" did not have the same impact on incarceration rates as the "war on drugs," it still contributed to the symbolic message. Sex crimes generated diffuse fears that justified more punitive action by the state. Like other issues on the crime control agenda, the link to an actual rise in the crime rate was less significant than how violence against women shaped a generalized fear of disorder and the image of habitual and recalcitrant criminals.[19] The prominence of sexual violence on the crime control agenda led to the creation of specialized sex crime units in large urban police and prosecutors' offices. These units were responsible for many of the most celebrated cases in the latter part of the century.

As the rest of this chapter will show, the impact of neoliberalism was most powerfully seen as the feminist campaign was modified and integrated into state and quasi-state organizations and became part of the routine business of social service bureaucracies and crime control. Once incorporated into this agenda, the campaign against sexual violence had far-reaching effects for the exercise of symbolic, coercive, and administrative power over both men as perpetrators and women as victims. The new awareness about "sex as violence" resulted in a panic over sex crimes that contributed to wrongly directed fears about the omnipresence of predators and to opportunistic prosecutions. At the same time, an ostensibly feminist knowledge about sexual violence informed professional practices and spearheaded the surveillance and management of victims. Through these developments, the progressive ideals of this campaign deferred to the more pressing prerogatives of security, public health, preservation of the family, and other demands to maintain order.

the culture of control

On a cultural level, the new feminist consciousness was incorporated within a broader framework of representation;[20] the rallying cry about women in danger mobilized deep-seated fears about sexual terror. What began as a "gender war" led to more generalized fears about the epidemic of sexual abuse and the pandemic threat of sex criminals. These apocalyptic fears, to some degree, can be attributed to feminist warnings about the pervasive risk of stranger violence and depictions of horrible attacks. Feminists also produced narratives about sadistic violence that took place in the home, often fixated on a primal scene of incest, ripe for appropriation within a larger cultural setting.

Other forces were at work in creating sexual panic, including the mass media, prosecutors, therapists, and law enforcement officials who had a stake in constructing sexual violence as a growing social problem. The last two decades of the twentieth century were also the beginning of a cycle of new fears of societal danger; sex panics were spurred on by fears of AIDS and other sexually transmitted diseases, the war on drugs, increased divorce rates, and shifting gender norms.[21] In this milieu, the feminist concern about rape and domestic abuse merged with a much larger agenda focusing on the sex criminal.[22] The "child abuse revolution" gained momentum through the 1980s furthered by sensationalized accounts and an alliance among diverse interest groups. The feminist campaign against rape also fed a new wave of gender-neutral statutory rape law enforcement. In the context of efforts to reinforce middle-class lifestyles and conventional family forms, especially as seen in the new welfare reforms of the 1990s, prohibitions against statutory rape targeted mostly poor, young minority women.[23] These moral panics not only led to selective prosecution, and in the case of child abuse to some spectacular witch hunts; they also served to reinforce a dominant narrative about dangerous elements in society (pedophiles, child predators, and sexual deviants) and to crystallize fears about deviant strangers. The most recent additions to sex crimes codes are Megan's Laws, which mandate systems of registration and community notification. Rose Corrigan has argued that these statutes not only reinforce "beliefs that strangers inherently always pose the greatest threat to communities" but ultimately have the effect of nullifying what has been achieved in feminist rape law reform "by . . . increasing emphasis on crimes, victims, and offenders who fit more easily with stereotypes about rape held by criminal justice gatekeepers."[24]

This rise of moral panics set the stage for prosecutors to capitalize on these concerns.[25] As the new consciousness about sexual violence assumed its place on the crime control agenda, prosecutors called for punitive action against the most violent offenders. This brought about a series of celebrated sex crime trials, cases involving celebrity defendants, gang rapes, and interracial crime. The interest in these cases by law enforcement was further stimulated by sensationalized media reports of brutality against women and racial typecasting. The sociologist Lynn Chancer defines these high-profile cases as a distinctive phenomenon of the mid-1980s to mid-1990s that intersected with controversial gender, race, and class issues as they emerged in that time and in their place.[26] In Chancer's terms, these cases and their news coverage "partialized" the stories to arouse and divide public reaction based on identity issues. In this way, these cases reinforced rather than dispelled dominant notions of victims and offenders.

These high-profile cases profoundly influenced the public perception of the causes of sexual violence and raised fears about its potentially cataclysmic effects on society. Prosecutors constructed narratives casting perpetrators as driven by sadistic impulses that led them to target unknown women out of hatred for their gender, ethnicity, or race. These narratives, for the most part, replayed the themes found in feminist scholarly and popular accounts of sexual trauma. Yet in the context of high-profile trials these narratives authorized racialized images of perpetrators and positioned the menace of sexual violence against a backdrop of social disorder. The victim in celebrated cases not only was subjected to public scrutiny but was cast in a role necessary for the prosecutor's ascription of events and motives. The conventions of the rape trial, which made the victim's story relevant only in terms of its verification of injuries to her body, further disabled a more complete and sympathetic portrayal. In effect, celebrated trials either reinforced iconic representations of victims (as innocent, white, and/or angelic) or sacrificed the actual victims for their failure to live up to this idealization.[27] These characterizations of both perpetrators and victims, however, contributed to the crime control mentality by adding force to the belief that the maintenance of social order depended on ruthlessly castigating violent perpetrators who preyed on innocent victims.

When feminists pointed to these cases to reinforce their message about rape, they ended up encouraging an all-or-nothing adherence to the women's side in the gender war. This oftentimes defeated their purposes because victims inevitably failed to fit into the stereotyped conceptions of innocence and worthiness. This rigid defense of a feminist position brought about a small, but vocal, dissent among activists. A few radical feminists criticized the movement for selling out to the establishment and following a path inconsistent with the "revolutionary" mission. Even stronger dissent emerged among black feminists who saw rape reform, with its focus on expanding the role of law enforcement, as primarily driven by the interests of white middle-class women. Yet a deeper set of problems emerged as the threat to women became identified with the risks posed by random criminals. This marking of the rapist was inextricably tied to the history of lynching black men. What had begun as a new feminist sensibility that "any man could be a rapist" was transformed primarily into a campaign driven by fear of dangerous strangers, who were implicitly or explicitly marked as dark-skinned men.

These issues about the racialization of rape were longstanding and did not emerge solely from the capitalization of celebrated rape cases by the law and order forces.[28] In the 1970s, the movement framed the issue of rape without regard to its historical legacy as a tool to control black men. Consequently, insufficient attention was given to how stricter enforcement of sexual assault and women battering would occur within settings fraught with racism as well as sexism. Subsequently, women of color raised concerns about increasing police involvement in their own communities and the disproportionate impact on black and Hispanic men. They pointed out that in urban minority communities where the population of young black males has been eviscerated by incarceration, the framing of sexual violence as a crime problem and external threat made little sense.

The critique based on race, however, did not change the direction of the movement. Many of the core assumptions have remained impervious to revision, for fear of undermining women's precarious claim to state protection. This defensive posture grew in response to a growing backlash campaign. Backlash writers capitalized on the persistence of rape mythologies by attacking victims as benefiting from making claims and pronouncing that real feminists don't cry rape.[29] In the face of this propaganda, feminists solidified their anti–sexual violence agenda. Like other cultural issues at the time, a self-protective stance led to a "normalizing" of the movement.[30] Efforts were made to mainstream a rape and anti-battering consciousness by situating it as part of programs to combat sexism in workplaces, build healthy relationships, and improve communication between men and women. The prevention of rape and domestic violence soon merged into programmatic endeavors designed to lessen institutional liability, including mandated regulation of sexual harassment and internal disciplinary procedures to counteract the prevalence of date rape on college campuses. As the anti–sexual violence movement repositioned itself in response to the culture wars, preventing sexual violence became everyone's concern and was motivated by principles no longer tightly connected to the original feminist analysis.

institutionalizing the agenda

Rape law reforms were swiftly adopted in jurisdictions across the country spurred on by a "tough on crime" sentiment as well as concerted lobbying by mainstream feminist groups. By the end of the 1980s, the anti-rape campaign was successful in initiating major law reform and procuring funding for specialized services for rape victims. These efforts culminated in the adoption of the Violence against Women Act (VAWA) in September 1994, described by some as "perhaps the most significant accomplishment of the anti-rape movement."[31] The legislative proponents of the act clearly supported it as a continuation of other federal crime control initiatives but also as an anti-discrimination measure designed to rectify the injustice that occurs when the criminal justice system fails to protect women from violent crime committed by nonstrangers.

Although mainstream feminists were successful in achieving these formal legal victories, the measures were adopted in the context of the penal-welfare systems of the neoliberal state.[32] Whether or not sexual assault cases are processed by special sex crime units, most cases continue to be diverted. Studies of routine criminal justice processing show that only a small percentage of cases are prosecuted, and the discrediting of victims is a significant factor despite rape law reforms.[33] Prosecutors, motivated by their own presumptions about rape and organizational and political directives for high success rates, selectively bring forth cases involving "good victims," women whose behavior conforms to traditional expectations and whose assaults involve unambiguous circumstances.[34] In order to address the systematic failure of the police to respond to domestic violence, most jurisdictions established mandatory arrest laws and some adopted no-drop prosecution polices by the late 1980s. It is unclear whether changes in arrest and prosecution policies have led to either higher conviction rates or less violence against women.[35] For many women, particularly those who are poor and racial minorities, mandatory policies have made them worse off.[36] These policies may either lead to dual arrests (of women who likely were defending themselves) or to involvement with officials that put women at greater risk of future violence by perpetrators or unwanted interventions by the state.[37] Donna Coker has recently summarized this critique of mandatory policies: "Mandatory domestic violence policies increase the risk of [punitive criminal intervention] . . . when women's (unrelated) criminal offending is exposed, when mandatory arrest practices threaten women's probation or parole status, when undocumented women are made more vulnerable to deportation, or when child welfare departments are prompted to investigate neglect or abuse claims based on a domestic violence incident report."[38] The disappointing track record of mandatory policies has produced a cautionary tale for activists about the precariousness of relying on stepped-up police enforcement and attempting to control prosecutorial discretion.

These tales of counterproductive law reform and unintended consequences are indicative of failures of liberal law reform and its misplaced faith in formal legal equality. Many activists in the anti-rape and domestic violence movement, however, view these setbacks as all the more reason to stay on course in efforts to reform mainstream institutions. Yet if these results are viewed in a historical and cultural context, it is clear that they are actually the "productive" and the "intended" consequences of state policies of social control. One of the major factors creating seemingly more punitive actions toward women is that the programs are often carried out by individuals who are not invested in feminist methodologies. The commitment to eradicating sexual violence, therefore, is not rooted in a collective understanding of this violence or a sense of the interconnectedness of women's problems as expressed by the early grassroots organizers. Even more critically, these programs are implemented according to gender-neutral standards, both formally and in terms of the state's interest in the problem. The most dramatic example of this is dual-arrest policies in domestic violence situations that have led to the criminalization of victims. One study summarizes the consequences: "rather than victims of violence being treated the same regardless of gender, female victims are again subject to discrimination. . . . An arrest policy intended to protect battered women as victims is being misapplied and used against them. Battered women have become female offenders."[39] Although the author of this study views these police actions as simply discrimination against women, this treatment occurs as a direct result of how the sexual violence agenda has been incorporated into state policy. The state's interest in controlling violence is powerfully driven by social control priorities; for example, intimate partnership violence is "of interest" because it unsettles families, harms children, and creates a public health crisis. This mandates intervention for the purposes of containing crises and managing harm, not to address women's systematic oppression.

Moreover, in the context of neoliberalism the state is primarily invested in limiting its responsibility to provide for dependents, including women whose experiences with violence have made them homeless or disabled and their children's lives traumatized and disrupted. The retrenchment of the welfare system means that the state has little to offer these women and children. Those most reliant on government services are the first to suffer as the social welfare state turns toward increased forms of regulation and coercive government control,[40] such as the restriction of benefits and the implementation of policies that treat single mothers as pathological.[41] As a result, poor, homeless, unemployed, and underemployed women have fewer resources available for general or emergency relief.[42] Specifically, in terms of battered women and rape victims, this has meant that their eligibility and priority for services became increasingly linked to their status as victims and their ability to recognize their problems in medical and psychological terms.

By far the broadest reach of state power is found in its transformation of sexual violence into a social, medical, and legal problem. In addition to programs originated by feminists, a large professional apparatus has developed in response to the problem of rape and family violence. The creation of a professional language to account for, intervene in, and prevent rape and domestic violence is a major part of this apparatus and is regularly used as a means by which violence against women is rationalized as a chronic yet treatable problem.[43] The ascendancy of professional expertise is most clearly seen in the limited options for victims outside of the expanding systems of medicalization and criminalization: it has become nearly impossible to understand the causes and consequences of being a victim of violence in terms which do not fit squarely within the purview of medicine or criminal justice. In these frameworks, feminist ideological concepts, like patriarchy or sexual domination, are introduced mainly because of their applicability within the language of surveillance, diagnosis, and social control.

In this highly rationalized form of social control, victims and perpetrators exist in a methodological duality. This duality is at work when perpetrators are turned into a class of dehumanized offenders whose pathologies are beyond treatment.[44] By the same logic, victims become the perfect subject for medical and therapeutic treatments and are rewarded for their adaptability to and compliance with treatment protocols. Through these rationalized processes, victims and perpetrators are divided into two categories: those who can be medicalized, controlled, and reformed and those who must be removed beyond the territory of a civilized society. The routine business of law enforcement also blurs the distinction between victim and criminal, especially when illegal activities are profit-making enterprises within families and supported, sometimes involuntarily, by partners. Moreover, perpetrators are rarely outsiders, and in cases of both rape and battery they are most often spouses, partners, family, or members of one's community. In all situations, prosecutors pursue cases on behalf of the state rather than the victim; but when victims are from criminalized communities (due to poverty, immigrant status, ethnicity, or race) their status as victim may in many cases become the functional equivalent of being a perpetrator in the eyes of the law.

As this analysis makes clear, concerns about rape and domestic violence need to be primarily addressed in the context of communities and in terms of their links to social disadvantage and impoverishment. But by the beginning of the twenty-first century, the sexual violence agenda had become more universalized rather than integrated into other social movements and community-based activism (with some notable exceptions). This means that sexual violence has become everybody's problem not only culturally but administratively. Employers, teachers, lawyers, doctors, therapists, and the like are expected to watch for the signs and symptoms of sexual violence and if they detect such, they are often required to take appropriate action to protect victims, treat clients, and report to authorities. Some feminists have challenged this trend, along with sexual harassment regulations, for its effect of desexualizing the workplace, college campuses, and community settings to the point of inhibiting ordinary social expression and interaction.[45] The evolving logic of this increased surveillance is most dramatically seen in measures taken against victims of violence themselves, who are now being regularly sanctioned for the "failure to protect" children who view domestic abuse.[46] In addition, the sexual violence agenda is being exported abroad and used instrumentally as part of American human rights policy. Its application in other cultural contexts and its focus on a major new target, the international problem of the trafficking of women, renews the energy of feminists and others committed to the cause but also raises the question—is this human rights campaign simply a vehicle to advance the neoliberal agenda around the globe?[47] Moreover, the political uses of "terrorism" in a post–9/11 context provide additional reasons to be concerned about the potential for "sexual terror" to serve as an excuse for the retrenchment of civil liberties or the deliberate destabilizing of society.[48]

The following chapters examine how the feminist campaign against sexual violence evolved in the context of neoliberal state policy. Each chapter raises concerns about the mainstreaming of the sexual violence movement and provides what some might consider counterintuitive conclusions about the desirability of the widespread incorporation of sexual violence prevention and treatment in the public health and social service sectors. Many activists see problems but remain true to the movement and its underlying logic of social change; in this view, the unintended consequences of the alliance with the state are just collateral damage in a gender war.

There is an alternative perspective, however, that raises fundamental concerns about how sexual violence was constructed as a social problem and its evolution into programmatic initiatives. This book chronicles this evolution in five contexts: the production of cultural images, symbolic gang-rape trials, professional discourse on intimate violence, the everyday life of battered women, and international policymaking. This analysis demonstrates that the feminist alliance with the state has produced something far more significant than unintended consequences—a joining of forces with a neoliberal project of social control.

2

GENDER WAR

the cultural representation of sexual violence

We have managed to extricate ourselves from the sacred somewhat more successfully than other societies have done, to the point of losing all memory of the generative violence; but we are now about to rediscover it. The essential violence returns to us in a spectacular manner—not only in the form of a violent history but also in the form of a subversive knowledge.
—Rene Girad

The original intention of the feminist campaign against sexual violence as it emerged in the early 1970s was to dismantle myths about rape victims and battered women. These myths described women as inviting violence, enjoying brutality, deserving of punishment, and easily discredited. These myths were counteracted by a new feminist ideology that clearly identified the root of violence in patriarchy and gender hierarchies and the sexual socialization of women to be passive and men to be aggressive. Feminists hoped to transform social attitudes that condoned violence against women and fight against the oppression of women performed through "sex as violence."

Yet even a passing look at how sexual violence is portrayed in contemporary society reveals other powerful forces at work. Contemporary media is replete with images of violated women. The brutalized bodies of women with blackened eyes, open wounds, and as bloodied corpses are abundantly displayed in media reports about crimes and criminal trials. Examples confront us regularly on front pages of popular magazines (for example, photos of Nicole Simpson), television specials about grisly murders and subsequent trials (especially cases involving multiple murders of wives and children), and in rags and some mainstream newspapers about notorious and celebrity rapists and murderers.[1] The immense attention to the shocking details of crimes against women might be seen as recognition of feminists' message about the seriousness of this violence. But for this to be true, the obsession with these images of battered women would need to reflect a social consensus about the causes of this violence and the threat it poses to the most vulnerable members of society. Violence against women, on the contrary, exacerbates the darkest divisions in modern life.

These narratives exaggerate the potential for all women to become victims and the need for state-exercised social control as well as make it appear that sexual violence is at the root of social disorder. The representation of sexual violence as ever present and cataclysmic grips the social imagination with images often primed to provoke deep-seated animosities and stimulate incomprehensibility rather than foster a compassionate understanding of the situations of either perpetrators or victims. Moreover, the mass production of these images allows everyone to be a consumer who participates vicariously in the horror of being a survivor (by creating an untold number of opportunities to witness the effects of sexual violence toward women). This participation leaves the viewer with a vision of sexual danger as it is visited upon the bodies of seemingly innocent and random victims, but without the necessary explanation to make these painful sights intelligible.

While the viewing of such horrific images has become common-place since the issue of sexual violence reached the public agenda, it has generated little insight about the extent and causes of terror. These public spectacles invite fearful speculation about the vulnerabilities of women as targets and the potential sources of evil, madness, and desire that perpetuate violence toward women. However, the reports rarely provide the kind of information that would make the crime appear less random or as arising from long-term oppressive relationships. For example, for every report of a murder by a spouse there is often a long history of both psychological and physical abuse as well as the woman's frustrated efforts to seek protection and stability. The more complete story might focus on not only the final acts of violence by the perpetrator but the hazards of seeking help within the current welfare system. Instead, the proliferation of images ends up feeding a large-scale social denial of the disturbing nature of this violence and its inexplicability in the context of ordinary life.

Clearly, intensifying a sense of indiscriminate sexual horror was neither the aim of the feminist movement or a desirable outcome of it. This chapter considers how feminists framed their message about sexual violence, and in particular, their use of a war metaphor. It also examines how this message was received in a cultural context and how that reception led to its failure to directly and simply change social attitudes. This feminist message unleashed societal fears linked to race, gender, sexuality, and violence by portraying sex as dangerous. It also set in motion stories about the sources of this danger which led to the polarization of gender and racially based interests and fueled notions about the sadistic nature of this violence. Through the cultural production of images about sex and violence, the movement reinforced and created presumptions about what causes sexual violence, the character of victims and perpetrators, and the capacity of society to contain such violence. These representations are enormously consequential; they not only influence public reaction and often create sexual panic but also produce ways of understanding sexual violence that drive the professional and governmental practices that respond to it.

the gender war

The feminist cause of eradicating sexual violence was characterized by its early proponents as a "gender war."[2] As with other social issues promoted as domestic wars, this metaphor has important implications for the movement's popular representation and its incorporation into larger social agendas. The war metaphor promoted a dominant narrative about sexual violence that framed the issue in terms of men's instrumental use of violence against women as a means to maintain their control. In its initial formulations, the anti-rape movement reinforced a disturbing message: women and children exist in constant fear of encounters with perpetrators and are subjected to the ubiquitous sadism of sexuality under this regime of domination. The battered women's movement also employed the war metaphor and was apt to describe partner violence as a form of domestic captivity or sexual terrorism. These messages warn of a global system of terror in which women are in constant fear of the violation of their bodies. This places the locus of fear on the actions of random male perpetrators driven by insatiable desires to transgress sexual norms and violate social boundaries of appropriate sexuality (by force or abuse of authority).

These messages were, in part, intended to dispel the commonplace assumption that rape and sexual battery was infrequent and only committed by severely pathological men. By suggesting that "every man could be a potential rapist" or "any woman could be a victim of domestic violence" the movement's advocates were attempting to remove a broad range of assumptions that blamed the victim. This launching of a gender war, however, unleashed larger cultural anxieties about security and crime as well as race and class. In doing so, the modern feminist campaign against sexual violence fueled the conditions of sexual panic that reemerged in the late 1970s and opened the door to the routine marketing of violent images of women by the media.

This happened in a society positioned for war: sexual terror threatens civilized societies' ability to contain and respond to violence, particularly when its appearance is seemingly random and it produces devastating effects. Outbreaks of sexual violence are especially feared because they signify the kind of chaotic passions that societies hope to keep at bay. This produces enormous pressures on governments to contain and deny the physical threat of sexual terror because such crimes not only threaten the public's general sense of security but are also warning signs about the breakdown of social conventions that civilize sexual impulses. This denial functions to magnify the threat of violence (especially in public settings and perpetrated by strangers) in producing social disorder, while undermining the recognition of the extensiveness of the harm caused to women by collective and individual acts of violence.

Moreover, war conditions distort the perception of risk. Reports of the most horrific cases generate excessive fears among women about the potential threat of violence from dangerous (usually dark-skinned) strangers. Yet these fears do not conform to the social realities of American life, where women are much more likely to encounter sexual violence from known perpetrators. In this context, women associate danger with public spaces, despite the fact that most physical and sexual assaults take place in private.[3] One study concludes: "despite the clear evidence that the risk of interpersonal violence is overwhelmingly from those near and dear to us, we all seem to worry more about threats from strangers."[4] This perception creates alarm about random violence, and that alarm controls the behavior of many women whose personal freedom is then, paradoxically, limited more by exaggerated threats than by realistic precautions.

Another important facet of a culture of terror is that it brings new urgency to regulate "sexual excess," the forms of sexual behavior that are viewed as being outside social norms. The very nature of sexual terror provokes fears about the rupture of social norms associated with proper sexual relationships. And when horror stories are told, there is often an implicit indication that victims violated sexual norms. For example, victims are frequently seen as inviting violence because of their promiscuous behavior or passivity in response to natural male aggression. Sometimes explicit associations are made between the horrible fate of victims and their involvement in immoral sexual activities, such as prostitution. The vulnerability of the victims may reflect their own failure to follow the social rules that maintain the sexual economy of conventional families. By locating the genesis of sexual violence in sites of excess, such as racial hatred, open borders, and sexual perversion, interpretations of horrific events rarely evoke questioning about the origins of violence in traditional domestic settings. The acts of violence are often scripted so that traditional masculine and feminine role behavior remains unchallenged, despite the dramatic disruption of normal life caused by violence and the complex nature of sexuality that such acts represent.[5] In the everyday context, incest and woman battering occur with remarkable prevalence without fueling mass anxieties about the illicit power of men in familial relationships. Crimes committed by people who remain honored members of their communities frequently go unpunished. The cumulative effect is to contain rather than raise uncertainties about conventional sexual norms, while the focus on horrific spectacles draws attention away from the material and psychic harms experienced by individual victims.

Consequently, the apocalypse of sexual violence is closely linked to more general fears about sexual epidemics.[6] In late capitalist societies, sexual crises, including child abuse, prostitution, gayness, family disintegration, teenage pregnancies, pornography, addictions, and disease, arouse concerns about their excessiveness and anxieties about their pervasiveness. The production of a crisis then serves as a justification for state intervention to regulate sexual practices. By focusing attention on the social problems that arise from these disorders, whole classes of individuals (such as teenage mothers or single women) become subject to either therapeutic treatment or regulation. The naming of the problem as an epidemic also reinforces the public message that sex is deadly. This message, in turn, legitimizes control over the unruly practices of women, homosexuals, and others who depart from the conventions of the nuclear family. In sum, the fear generated by the perception of unrestrained sexual excess has the effect of making women both the source of sexual hostility and the primary subject of regulations that become necessary to protect the social organization of the state and family life from sexual terror.

racialization of sexual violence

One of the most consequential results of the war metaphor is that it affirmed the notion that all acts of violence against women should primarily be seen as an assault on their gender identity. This was based on the supposition that the war against sexual violence was race neutral; that it served to dispel mythologies about black rapists and the danger of the ghetto. Yet portraying rape and other forms of sexual violence as a universal condition affecting women regardless of their racial identity in effect repressed the significance of race and its relation to the American fascination with sexual crime.[7] This denial has enormous significance for the development of different strands of the American feminist perspective on sexual violence in that in many cases women's demands for freedom from sexual oppression have been dissociated from the movement for racial justice.

American rape consciousness evolved from a legacy of race relations in which blacks' threats to Southern white society's property and authority led to excessive countermeasures and, in rape cases, to the disproportionate use of the death penalty for black men. In the antebellum South, the prosecution of rape arose as a tool to sanction blacks selectively while affirming white male property interests. This pattern of excessive punishment for interracial sexual assault continued into the twentieth century, but the differential punishment of black defendants gradually declined. Yet forms of racial violence like slave burnings, and its continuation in the American tradition of lynching mostly black men, have strong repercussions for the cultural understandings of sexual violence. These events reveal how the perception of sexual danger is rooted in the fear of the black man's revenge against systematic white oppression. This history of excessive racial violence is difficult, if not impossible, to reconcile with the norms of modern social life and creates potent reminders of the sexual origins of racial conflict.

Thus, when the war against sexual violence emerged on the public agenda, it revived the specter of black men as sexual predators, while continuing to devalue the safety of black women. In the ongoing crisis of urban danger and increasing crime rates, Toni Morrison has suggested that it is almost predictable that "nonwhites and women figure powerfully, although their presence may be disguised, denied, or obliterated."[8] Under these conditions, black men remain in constant fear that they will be singled out as perpetrators (especially in the rape of white women) and black women are reluctant to report intragroup rape for fear of subjecting black men to discriminatory treatment by the criminal justice system. Interracial cases become especially controversial, particularly those involving gang rapes, because they raise fears about black men retaliating against racism by threatening white men's property interest in white women.[9] Fascination with interracial rape, while leading to the excessive attention to the threat of black men to white women, also contributes to cultural conditions that allow the perpetuation of white-on-black rape without notice or consequence.

By launching a gender war, the feminist campaign against sexual violence instigated a wave of sexual panic that heightened generalized fears of sexual predators and attributed the increased risk to the breakdown of social conventions. In this way, the feminist movement was not unlike other moral crusades that periodically arouse public fear and root out "dangerous" persons. The declaration of a gender war also greatly influenced how contemporary society understands sexual violence both on the street and at home. The rest of this chapter explores two important representational frames that have emerged from this war. The first is the iconographic portrayal of victims, which is a particularly powerful means to propagate racialized imagery. The second is the trauma model, a psychological framework that defines how women and children experience violence as well as how the effects of that violence become known.

the iconography of rape

When feminists raised alarms about sexual terror, they recharged already powerful cultural motifs about sexual danger. The evocation of the sexually violated body, bruised and beaten, dead or alive, opens up a certain kind of cultural fascination. This fascination is the result of a psycho-cultural projection of hatred onto women's bodies.[10] Such theories see not only violence against women but also fears about violence against women driven by "abjection." Abjection is a process, occurring both on the individual and social level, of projecting onto a dreaded object that which is most fearful about human existence. According to this theory, the construction of the abject is a universal element of maintaining a social order and a crucial force in the definition of culture: "Abjection, just like *prohibition of incest*, is a universal phenomenon; one encounters it as soon as the symbolic and/or social dimension of man is constituted, and this throughout the course of civilization. But abjection assumes specific shapes and different codings according to the various 'symbolic systems.' "[11]

Abjection is also the sociopsychological process that leads to the creation of iconic symbols of victims and perpetrators. Accordingly, fear-inspiring images of fallen women, murdering mothers, and other female victims and criminals are focused on to expel and repress the subjects of abjection.[12] The abject appears as a kind of ghost, coming onto the scene as a hallucination at the edge of reality, often marking the boundaries between life and death. This image is found in media reports of murdered women where the condition or positioning of the dead body evokes the ultimate cruelty of the murderous acts. The corpse is an object of abjection because its sight overwhelms us and forces us to confront the universal vulnerabilities created by the thin line between acts of cruelty that leave the victim living and those that turn into the blows of death.[13]

The positioning of the ravaged dead body in itself may convey fixed expectations about the nature of women as dangerous and as subjects of danger. For example, Jane Caputi observes that the fixed iconography of a "nude spread eagle body of a woman" was repeatedly used in media programming about the Hillside Strangler in Southern California as well as other contemporary sex crime cases.[14] She finds recurring images of these flattened bodies arranged in positions that mimic sexual availability and symbolize female submission. That these murders pose a threat to national security becomes known and knowable through how these bodies are viewed in the aftermath of the crime. The reference to the fallen bird suggests the rape and total defeat of a national symbol. The fixed image of the body in the "spread eagle" position is both an intimation of the performance of the murder and harbinger of total defeat. This presentation demonstrates that even while dead, the female still *engenders* her sexual punishment.

In these iconographic images women's bodies signify the essential dangers of femininity as well as the risks posed by outsiders. The sight of a dead body arouses the threat of the breaking down of borders and the possibility of a stranger who poses a potential threat to social identity and safety. The threat of the stranger has a powerful effect on the cultural imagination precisely because apocalyptic stories of rapes and murders are evasive and severed from reality and it is impossible to confirm or disconfirm this threat in the context of everyday life.

The symbolic power of abjection explains how the nearly dead body of the victim and the scene of the rape in Central Park immediately became symbols of a white woman's youth and innocence tragically sacrificed by the uncontainable wildness of black and ethnic gangs in New York City. The public interest in the rape was a conduit for middle-class demands for criminal control measures targeted against young minority men who were seen as dangerous strangers. The conditions under which the victim was found, having been dragged into a remote location and left to bleed nearly to death, contributed to the characterization of the perpetrators as feral beasts that stalked their prey, then left it to die in the wilderness.

Over the years the symbolic representations of the jogger's body, as well as those of the victims of other high-profile sex crimes, have gained the status of icons of sexual sacrifice, in a sense that corresponds closely to the meaning of icon creation in religious art and practice.[15] These icons present a vision of the raped and brutalized body displayed as a figure of sacrifice. The image of the jogger's body, prostrate and bleeding from her wounds, is a replication of a sacred figure who lingers on in a condition between life and death.

The artistic representation of rape and rape victims, in any historical period, often reflects prevailing cultural views of sexual violence. The work of the art historian Diane Wolfthal, who has studied rape imagery in art of the medieval and early modern periods, offers some cogent insights. Her comparison of rape imagery over historical periods reveals a complex and nonmonolithic conception of rape. Some representations depict the raped women obscured by images that eroticize the heroic rapists, while others subvert the heroic ideal by showing the "dark side" of the rapists' heroic behavior or portraying women's energetic resistance and their avenging of violation.[16] In reading these artistic representations we can search for the legacy, as well as the current manifestations, of deeply held beliefs about men's behavior and the nature of victims. These scenes of violation reveal fundamental assumptions about both the experience of individual pleasure and harm and the social meaning of the rape.

One such fundamental assumption is whether rape is conceived of as either hurtful to the victim or a crime against society. To the extent that the recognition of individual or social harm is made comprehensible, it often follows from a projection of how rape violates the ordering of private or public spaces. Wolfthal's analysis shows that as Western art moves toward its more modern forms, the violence of the encounter is less obscured while the architecture of scene circumscribes women within normative visions of domesticity and racial or sexual purity. For example, a lone woman's innocence is often suggested by setting her within more rarefied and orderly surroundings.

In analyzing rape as a contemporary icon there is also significance in how the rape victim is portrayed within her environment, especially in the context of the representation of gang rape. This is seen in the artistic representations of highly publicized gang rapes, in which the essence of the brutality is projected through images of attackers surrounding an immobilized body. These representations have made their way into popular culture through film, music, and avant-garde art. Controversies stimulated by references to gang rapes in popular culture have created a forum for debating feminist views of rape, particularly in response to pornographic cartoons and rap music that condone the violence as an expression of male bonding or race-motivated revenge. Feminist mobilization against rape has taken these antagonistic characterizations as a focal point to raise consciousness about insensitivity toward victims and to stimulate public concern about violence toward women. Notable gang rapes have also been the subject of avant-garde art that explicitly attempts to portray the rapes in ways that promote a feminist consciousness about the event. It is important to consider, however, how feminist artwork, despite its intention to unsettle social convention, may actually conform to popular conceptions of rape.

An artistic depiction of this kind of icon is shown in a mixed media on canvas work by Sue Coe titled *Romance in the Age of Raygun*. This painting, actually inspired by the New Bedford rape trial, graphically depicts the woman as a skeletal figure with outstretched arms, blood emerging from wounds spread over her bodily surfaces, and exposing a bloody crotch.[17] The group of men surrounding her is given a ghostly appearance; some are lurking around the perimeters of a pool table while others are poking her with cues. This artwork features both the Christ-like positioning of the victim's body and the surrealistic exposure of bodily wounds. The representation of the victim suggests a living body despite its evisceration by her attackers, while the ghostly presence of the men is evocative of evil so haunting that it cannot take a human form.[18]

This icon of the Central Park Jogger as it has come to be represented in literature, poetry, and art seeks not only to capture the brutality of the rape scene but to build upon cultural memories that enshrine the brutality of gang rapes. In fact, the actual location of the attack in Central Park is marked with a shrinelike memorial. Another example of enshrinement is found in the contemporary artist Arcady Kotler's figurative sculptures *Jogger* and *Rapist*. These figures enshrine the jogger as translucently white, fleeting, and lithe and show the rapist as dark, militantly posed, and transformed into a weapon. Iconic representations of the jogger bear close similarity to the particular qualities of some Buddhist icons. While the Buddhist icon takes human forms, in its setting it "paradoxically . . . becomes a kind of tomb . . . a container, a recipient, a funerary urn, or stupa."[19] The evolving icon of the raped woman's body, in this tradition, is enshrined in the would-be death chamber of the landscape of Central Park.

This enshrinement also induces a vision of the body being surrounded by phantoms through the projection of the icon as a solid form (such as a statue) within a visual field that includes other realities, such as ghostly "visions."[20] Like the religious icon, the image of the jogger's body is visualized as a sacred figure of a woman against the backdrop of marauders in the park. In this way, the iconic body is a sacred element within the natural order of the landscape. When the icon is then seen within her surroundings, she is set within a "predatory landscape,"[21] a landscape grounded in the visual field of violence (i.e., hunting, war, and surveillance). This setting creates an ideal vantage point for the spectator, so that those who worship the memory of the jogger are able to take on the "eyes of justice" and view the predators as the naturally latent content of the landscape.[22]

Icons are often denounced as false images. The use of religious imagery lends itself to controversies about the image's validity and form of iconic representation.[23] In this way, the icon creates a focal point for reaction to disturbing events and sacred figures. Also, a certain kind of unreality is created by representational motifs that suggest the figure is neither alive nor dead. For example, Bernard Faure

Sue Coe, *Romance in the Age of Raygun*. Courtesy of the artist.

Arcady Kotler,
Jogger.
Courtesy of
the artist.

Arcady Kotler, *Rapist*.
Courtesy of the artist.

has written of iconic Buddhist statues that they evoke the boundaries between life and death, making them appear as "still life" or "suspended animations"; moreover, "when they seem to be on the move, their containment often goes hand in hand with a certain sexualization."[24] This is similar to the iconic figure of the "jogger," which appears captured while being chased and bears a resemblance to a potently sexually attractive Greek goddess (see figure 2). This unreality of the iconic image may, in part, explain why at the time of the trial, and continuing even after the recent revelations about defendant Matias Reyes's confession, authorities have been accused by vocal members of the New York black community of making up the "jogger" in order to justify the rounding up of young black and Hispanic men in Central Park.

Yet the appeal to iconic symbols, more generally, has been an important strategy employed by the American feminist movement for the purpose of unsettling and then hopefully transforming consciousness about violence against women. Iconic images of women as victims have been employed to spur activism and political involvement, and from the perspective of the leaders in these movements, icons have the power to disrupt complacency and uncritical media representations. This kind of appeal has contributed to the overall success of the women's movement and has given structure to the motivating ideologies that incite local activism. Mobilization on issues of violence, in particular, has benefited from "being unashamedly one-sided."[25] Despite this perception of movement success, however, iconic symbols have the potential to mobilize interests in ways that deter rather than promote democratic fluidity and expression. Such symbols may create rigid perceptions about a movement's vision and goals.[26] As the arguments throughout this book will show, such icons and other cultural symbols often reinforce normative assumptions about sexual violence rather than promote new feminist understandings.

Also, the promotion of the iconic images is part of a strategy to create public awareness of the "dead certainty" of rape and is used as a means to counteract false perceptions about the actual risks of victimization.[27] This also allows feminist activism to deny the significance of race, even in situations where interracial aspects of the crime have gained wide attention. A notable example is the assertion by the prosecutor in the Central Park Jogger trial that "race" had no significance in the case; that despite "all these voices that were trying to look at it in terms of race . . . I really felt it was about gender."[28] Her claim that all acts of rape are fundamentally about gender oppression, as will be explored fully in the next chapter, is symptomatic of the pretense of state neutrality when power is exercised in a highly racialized context. Moreover, in the context of this kind of official denial of the significance of race, public reaction becomes more polarized as competing interests seek to frame the situation in ways compatible with their worldviews. Consequently, media reports of such cases draw attention to the inflammatory aspects of race, either by emphasizing racialized motifs of perpetrators or indicting state action as racially motivated. This creates a context for highly polarized cultural representations of sexual violence, particularly in situations where any relevant actor is racially marked. As the next chapter will show, this polarization serves to fuel the spectacle and accentuate the underlying racial conflict.

the war at home

Feminist campaigns against sexual violence have also focused on issues of family violence and have sought to raise consciousness about the cycle of violence that turns intimate relationships into a battleground. Violence within families fuels and confounds apocalyptic narratives about sex and crime. Publicized stories often find the cause of domestic violence in predictable dangers: interracial liaisons, "low-class" behaviors, alcoholism, divorce, and promiscuity in women. But violence in the home, by its very nature, raises the specter of disorder within the bonds of intimate relations. Indeed, domestic violence has far-reaching implications beyond the havoc it creates in the lives of individual women: it threatens the normative order of the family. The very notion of violence perpetuated by intimates shatters expectations about home as a refuge. Fundamentally, sexual violence in the home contradicts the assumption that the domain of the family is a sanctuary from the risks encountered in the public world. This challenge is borne out empirically, in that the statistical prevalence of domestic brutality against women is staggering, and the physical injuries women experience, if not mortal, are often debilitating. For many women, survival often depends on escaping their private lives and submitting themselves to the protection available in the public sphere.

The horror of domestic violence arises from the inevitability of seeing the family as a nexus of dangerous desires. The modern feminist movement gave recognition to the dangers within the family through the popularization and professional application of the theory of sexual trauma. This theory is rooted in Freudian psychoanalysis, although its reinvention by feminists was based on a repudiation of Freud's assertion that incest and childhood sexual abuse were rare and women's claims were a product of fantasies rather than actual violations by male authority figures.[29] Trauma theory has provided the framework to describe the harm of sexual abuse in intimate childhood relationships and to explain why young children are seemingly passive in abusive situations and often repress memories of sexual acts.

Feminist consciousness raising about sexual violence has employed trauma theory to describe the broader cultural significance of violence against women.[30] For example, Catharine MacKinnon describes the prototypical act of sexual violence as the rape of a female child. In *Only Words* she graphically describes a five-year-old girl screaming and struggling on a bed as she is attacked by her father.[31] The nature of the violation is the intrusion on the body of a child who is powerless against such transgressions. In the trauma model, the primary form of resistance is the child's retreat into a psychic sphere, or splitting of consciousness, to escape from the pain of the bodily experiences. The site of desire rests in the perpetrator alone, because the acts are motivated by his impulse to control, indeed to bury the young girl under his body and to keep her interred as a condition of feminine existence. The perpetrators' passions are unfettered by taboo, violating those whom they are entrusted to protect. MacKinnon focuses on this scene to show the damage done to women and to further warn the reader that harassment, abuse, and pornography are repetitions of this atrocity.[32]

In this way, trauma theory is essential to understanding and bearing witness to the harm of sexual violence. For MacKinnon, rape is a real event in all (or almost all) women's lives, and its reality is affirmed through the multiple occasions when pornographic words and images cause its reenactment. Consequently, the recognition of sexual violence involves the "voyeuristic" act of viewing this endless repetition of the sadistic violation of the helpless child. The story of incest can never be wholly reconstructed because a victim's story is constructed from the consciousness of the traumatized child who is unable to become an observer of her own violence.

The trauma model has important cultural resonance and has been employed by feminists to lend impact to accounts of sexual terrorism. Yet as a cultural representation, it also has influence over how professionals who routinely treat survivors of violence view their clients. The therapeutic community advanced this model to replace treatment practices that dismissed women's experiences and devalued survival mechanisms that emerged as productive coping skills in the aftermath of traumatic abuse. The trauma model, as institutionalized in professional practice, became essential to the process of verifying sexual abuse and providing evidence of it for use in the legal process.

In these institutionalized practices, sexual violence is made verifiable through the voyeuristic reimagining of the violation of women's bodies. In an often ironic manner, evidence of sexual violence is produced by the professional assuming the role of perpetrator, in the sense of reenacting the visual violation of the victim's body. This methodology was "invented" by professionals as they became interested in supporting feminists and child welfare advocates in their efforts to document the prevalence of sexual violence. These techniques of investigation, to a large extent, reproduce the cultural representation of trauma within the logic of professional practice.

This can be seen in the description by medical doctors of how they acquired the techniques for the medical examination of suspected sexual assault victims.[33] Determining sexual abuse of children, for example, began to be recognized as the responsibility of the medical profession after the publication of Henry Kempe's seminal paper "Sexual Abuse: Another Hidden Pediatric Problem."[34] As pediatricians evaluated children clinically to identify signs of sexual abuse, they also set into motion a process of criminal prosecution of child abusers. Physicians took on the challenge of looking for violence after the fact, which required them to look closely at children's bodies for signs of "healed trauma." As a practitioner explains: "For the first time physicians began to look at the genitalia of nonabused and abused children with a critical eye and fervor not seen previously. . . . The hymen began to take on a significance not previously seen except in the ethnologic literature regarding virginity. . . . Each and every nuance of the female genital structures was observed and described."[35] Although doctors pursue this evidence to uncover the harm done by perpetrators, their clinical language often employs a voyeuristic tone in its description of techniques used to examine and verify sexual violation of female bodies.

A disturbing example is found in a description of the most recent advances in this forensic technology. New methods of examining rape victims have sought to "enhance visualization" during examinations.[36] This more advanced technology for observing female genital structures is the videocolposcope, an improvement on the simple colposcope which is a "noninvasive magnifying instrument with an excellent built in light source."[37] The new technology incorporates a "beam splitter in their optics [which] allows the simultaneous attachment and use of video and still photography."[38] The proponents of this new technology argue that it creates benefits both for the "examiner and the child": "The examiner no longer positions their eyes in the colposcope's binoculars which place them within approximately 12 inches of the child's genitalia. A more distanced view provided by the video monitor is a more comfortable position for the examiner and allows both observation of the child's reaction to the examination and an ability to respond quickly to changes in the child's demeanor."[39] The language that describes the medical examination parallels sadistic voyeurism in that it seeks to preserve images of violence enacted on bodies. When the doctor describes his procedures, however, he takes care to dispel the impression of performing a violation, such as referring to its noninvasive approach or noting the child's ability to maintain some kind of control over the visual invasion of her body. This is not to imply that professionals are perpetrators of violence but rather to demonstrate that "trauma" is visually reenacted in the process of producing evidence for the legal process.

The doctor's account reveals how the representation of trauma is a powerful trope not only utilized by feminists in their portrayals of sexual violence but also in the reenactment of the violence for the purposes of verifying it. This trope is seen in medical methodologies, as shown above, but it is also a representational schema that influences how sexual violence is verified in trials. The acceptance of the trauma model in the public consciousness also means that in order for claims of sexual violence to be considered credible, the claimants must now show verifiable signs and symptoms of trauma. This can come about when victims produce a story that conforms to the feminist account of sadistic torture or when charges are substantiated by medical evidence of their behavior and/or injuries. Most importantly, it creates the presumption that trauma can *always* be seen by highly trained professionals. This assumption profoundly influences cultural perceptions about the credibility of women who press rape and battery charges and creates the expectation that medical science will uncover any *real* sexual violation. It also poses a dilemma for any efforts to account for and interpret representations of sexual violence, as I do in this book. In exposing voyeuristic accounts, such as that of the medical doctor quoted above and those from the trials discussed in chapter 3, there is always the risk of replaying the violence produced by the discourse itself. Although it is impossible to escape this potential, the clear intent of this book is to shine a critical light on this often unconscious motif within both feminism and the professional project.

dilemmas of representation

As described above, the representational motifs of "icons" and "trauma" limit our understanding and constrain our responses to sexual violence. In the context of a gender war, each of these motifs provides the structure to both locate violence in a social landscape and to describe events incomprehensible to ordinary family life. Yet when feminists brought sexual violence onto the public agenda, they found themselves in the predicament of representing sex within a complex system of social knowledge. Despite the remarkable volume of words spoken about and images shown of domestic violence, rape, child abuse, and the murder of women, silencing comes from the complex ways in which those who claim authority and expertise about the issue authorize what can be said about sexual violence. Michel Foucault describes this repression of sexual discourse:

> Between the state and the individual, sex became an issue, and a public issue no less; a whole web of discourses, special knowledges, analyses, and injunctions settled upon it. . . . Not any less was said about it; on the contrary. But things were said in a different way; it was different people who said them, from different points of view, and in order to obtain different results. Silence itself, the things one declines to say, or is forbidden to name, the discretion that is required between different speakers, is less the absolute limit of discourse, the other side from which it is separated by a strict boundary, than an element that functions alongside the things said, with them and in relation to them within over-all strategies.[40]

The opening up of knowledge about sex, as seen in the proliferation of discourse in popular forums and professional settings, is accompanied by impulses to silence and to forbid sexual knowledge. Now that rape and sexual battery are the subject of specialists, these discourses "manage" how we perceive the reality of violence as well as what is excluded from public discussion.

The chapters that follow consider the consequences of the representational schemas introduced by the gender war and their effect on the social construction of sexual violence by the media, within the legal system, and in professional discourse. As the next chapter explores, the high-profile trial introduced cultural narratives that squarely placed blame for the prevalence of violence on the sadistic impulses of unruly racial minorities. The epistemology of violence in such an account is grounded in the sadistic motivations of the perpetrators, motivations that typically arise from a thirst for sexual domination and intense hatred of women. As we will see, in the context of a trial, these representations have a powerful influence on how the law is mobilized to protect victims and punish perpetrators.

3

EXPRESSIVE JUSTICE

the symbolic function of the gang rape trial

The politicized [crime control policy] . . . takes two recurring forms. Either
it willfully *denies* the predicament and reasserts the old myth of the sovereign state and its plenary power to punish. Or else it abandons reasoned,
instrumental action and retreats into an expressive mode that we might,
continuing the psychoanalytic metaphor, describe as acting out—a mode
that is concerned not so much with controlling crime as with expressing the
anger and outrage that crime provokes. It is this predicament . . . that [has]
shaped crime control and criminal justice in the late modern period.
—David Garland

The cultural anxieties raised by sexual violence create an ominous
predicament for the governance of modern democratic societies. In
the face of "sexual terrorism," the state's essential challenge is to
create order and respond to demands for justice. This demand on the
state produces what David Garland terms the "sovereign" response
to crime: the state reassures an anxious public by demonstrating its
ability to protect citizens with immediate and authoritative police
power. This mythology of state omnipotence has gained credence over
the past thirty years in the United States, as the state poses itself as
always ready to wage war against crime. At the same time, the fear of
sex crime has grown, making it all the more essential for police and
judicial authorities to demonstrate their capacity to cope with sexual
violence wherever and whenever it occurs.[1]

This system of crime control leads to a bifurcated response to sustain the myth of sovereignty. The first response is, essentially, a political reaction to the increased levels of insecurity and the actual rise in crime rates. Politicians act in an "expressive mode . . . that is concerned not so much with controlling crime as with expressing the anger and outrage that crime provokes."[2] "Expressive justice" often involves drawing attention to high-profile events, like notable rape cases, that provide opportunities for prosecutors to publicize symbolic messages about the risk of victimization. The second response involves the expansion of the administrative apparatus of the criminal justice system and other bureaucracies that exercise routine forms of social control over victims and perpetrators. In the second mode, a highly complex organization of administrators, experts, and reformers works to serve the interest of victims while increasing crime control capacity.

This chapter examines how the first response, "expressive justice," has been employed to respond to sexual violence under the conditions of neoliberalism. By declaring war against sexual terrorism, police power is legitimated and the state maintains monopolistic power to control sex crimes. Under these conditions, targeting celebrated crime may enhance the legitimacy of the state while in effect doing little to improve the actual capacity of authorities to respond to the prevalent and ordinary conditions of sexual violence. When prosecutors draw attention to such cases, they stimulate the passions of mass audiences while reassuring this audience of the state's capacity to respond to the threat of dangerous sexual predators. In celebrated trials, stories about sexual violence are renarrated for the purpose of locating the threat to society and justifying a punitive response. As this chapter will illustrate, the prosecution of cases involving interracial gang rape has been a prime outlet for expressive justice.

political trials of gang rape

One of the most common and frequent ways that individuals come into contact with the legal system is through television news and newspaper reports about notorious crimes, criminal trials, and defendants. These trials are a prolific source of powerful legal symbols as well as a dramatic presentation of the most shocking aspects of crimes and their consequences.[3] Such trials provide ripe opportunities for courtroom actors to send a message about how to reconcile the social vision of a good society with justice in the individual case.[4] This view of the symbolic function of trials is in stark contrast to the interpretation of legal realists who attributed the symbolic function of the trial to the process of affirming the morality of government. To them, the criminal trial was a "great stabilizing institution" with the ability to reconcile contradictory ideas and to prevent popular hysteria.[5] The realists' vision of symbolic justice placed faith in the rectitude, certainty, and humaneness of the trial. In so doing, it failed to look beyond procedural functions to the trial's legitimating role.

Many feminist reformers shared the realists' vision and therefore assumed they could employ the symbolic trial as a means to make public the historical silence about rape. In fact, feminist reaction and response to notable trials served as a primary vehicle for a new scrutiny and examination of rape law and the legal process. It was the hope of many reformers that these trials would be instrumental in playing an educative function by disseminating the new feminist understanding of rape and displacing old myths that blame the victim.[6] Their re-enactment of the victimization process, feminist reformers believed, would create a focal point for consciousness-raising strategies.[7]

Unfortunately, since the trials employed traditional definitions of rape and framed the issues in terms of legal discourse, the reformers' strategies reinforced dominant cultural stereotypes as opposed to providing an opportunity to transform political consciousness about rape.[8] Moreover, these trials provided symbolically powerful forums in which stories about rape and the character of the victim reinforced theories about disreputable women. So, despite significant reforms in sexual assault statutes designed to protect the victim from "being put on trial," cultural mythologies about rape and rape victims invariably still frame the stories constructed by prosecutors and defense attorneys.

When symbolic trials involve interracial crimes, particularly those involving gang rapes with black defendants, they also serve to excite hostilities toward racial groups. The myths created in patriarchal and racist societies reinforce each other in ways that distort how we see the threat of rape: the cultural presupposition that rape is a violation of white women only serves to encourage silence about the more common occurrence of intraracial rape between nonstrangers. The playing out of these mythologies occurs frequently and prominently in trials that capture the public imagination about racially marked and dangerous strangers. Two of the most notable gang-rape trials within the last twenty-five years, the New Bedford trial of 1984 and the Central Park Jogger trial of 1991, garnered historic levels of media attention and launched major legal controversies about criminal justice policies concerning rape. The extensive reporting of the trials brought attention to the horrendous aspects of the crime of gang rape in such a way that the trials themselves became a source of graphic dissemination of the brutal accounts of violations against victims' bodies. Both trials show how criminal justice professionals employ tactics of expressive justice; in these cases, it was to quash the symbolic threat imposed by groups of dangerous men. These trials also demonstrate how prosecutors both directly and indirectly employ interethnic and interracial aspects of the crime into their theories of particular cases.[9]

the New Bedford case

The New Bedford gang rape led to a symbolic trial that focused the attention of the New Bedford community and the wider world on the American justice system's treatment of sexual violence and ethnic prejudice.[10] The 1984 rape trial of six Portuguese immigrant men in New Bedford, Massachusetts,[11] encouraged the public audience to imagine vicariously and draw judgments about the sequence of events in the bar called Big Dan's. The media constructed the story in a way that intensified and polarized issues for the purposes of the alternative agendas of the feminist and Portuguese communities. The newspapers reported a lurid "spectacle" in which a "gang" of Portuguese men engaged in "senseless brutality" against a lone woman pinned down on a pool table. Although violent sexual assaults occur frequently in New Bedford and other communities across the country, this case was the subject of immense publicity because it was depicted as an inconceivably brutal gang rape cheered on by pitiless bystanders. Six Portuguese immigrants were tried for aggravated sexual assault and sexual assault in a Fall River, Massachusetts, courtroom about one year after the incident at Big Dan's. Because it received massive local and international newspaper coverage, the rape became an important symbol in popular culture and a focal point for the mobilization of feminist groups. The extensive publicity surrounding the Big Dan's incident largely arose from the uniqueness of the circumstances.

In the *New Bedford Standard Times*'s characterization of the incident, the implied motives and intentions of the victim and defendants were cast into a wider perspective framed by legal authorities and community organizations. Although a considerable amount of reportage was allotted to the defendants (their arrest, court hearings, personal information, and statements by their attorneys), the language employed by the press, at least superficially, focused the spotlight on the victim. One news story, for example, described the rape as the "victim's ordeal," in which "ordeal" broadly referred to the acts of violent sexual aggression, the trial, and the publicity surrounding the trial. For the most part, references to the victim ignored her as an individual who had her own specific responses to rape. Either the victim was named by her formal legal status and demographic qualities (e.g., the "complainant," "young woman," "a 21-year-old city woman") or more elaborate discussion was carried out through references to "generic" victims of rape (e.g., anti-rape activists' statements of solidarity with the victim and special reporting features about rape crisis centers' efforts to respond to the psychological trauma of victims).

Most of the news stories were unqualified in their description of the brutality of the crime and full of sympathy for the victim and hostility toward the perpetrators. The newspapers told of a mob scene: "[according to police and witness reports] the bar was whipped into a lurid, cheering frenzy, as they watched the sexual assault." A rape-reform activist is reported to have said: "The rapists knew exactly what they were doing. It went on so long. They obviously had a chance to consider what they were undertaking. The bail is ridiculously low." Her words are one example of the panoply of law-and-order demands that gain their intensity from the symbolic invocation of enemies. The Portuguese defendants metaphorically took on the instinctive qualities and look of uncivilized people. For example, one news report quoted a Portuguese man in the neighborhood who called the accused "barbarians."

Although the references to the victim tended to be sympathetic, there were ambivalent undercurrents in her portrayal. A New Bedford reporter attributed a heavenly innocence to her through the rhetorical questioning of an investigating police officer: "Where will she go from here? She'll probably have to leave New Bedford. . . . She won't be able to handle the memories. Look at her angelic face. It's *almost* full of innocence. She'll never be innocent again." It is not just earthly innocence that is attributed to her but the innocence of an angel fallen from grace.

The portrayal of the victim and the defendants was complemented by the symbolic representations in the media and in the courtroom of the setting of the crime.[12] The tone was set by the first major local newspaper story about the rape, which included a large photograph of Big Dan's Tavern. Thus, attention was drawn to the incompatibility of the setting with the expected norms of human behavior. The fact that the incident occurred in a *public* place, in a barroom and on a pool table, is discordant with the social conception of consensual sex as a private and intimate act. The public nature of the crime has significance beyond its location; the image of a gang yelling, mocking, and humiliating the woman jars common sensibilities about personal dignity in social interactions. The early coverage employed the shock of these circumstances as a rhetorical device to establish that illegitimate sex occurred. The effect was to inhibit further speculation about the woman's responsibility for the violence. Reporting about the scene of the crime implied that "no woman" would want "that" to happen. The reports seemed to make the victim's behavior irrelevant to public judgment about the outrageousness of the crime and attributed the events to the atmosphere in a bar portrayed as a "sore spot" where only the "riffraff goes."

The negative depictions of the setting of the crime created a picture of the personalities of the actors and set the framework for popular interpretations. Public reports of this incident intensified hostilities toward the Portuguese community by emphasizing the social setting of the rape, a bar frequented primarily by men from this ethnic group. Because popular reports emphasized the setting, the terms of the political discussion were polarized between the anger of the Portuguese community about slanders against New Bedford as an indecent place and demands of feminists that women must have the freedom to associate safely in public places. For the "Take Back the Night" protesters, the setting of the crime clarified the underlying moral issues, that whatever this woman's character and circumstances, *any* woman should have the freedom of movement to enter a public bar without the fear of being gang raped. Supporters of the Portuguese defendants objected to newspaper reporting that, in their view, employed inappropriate references to the ethnicity of the defendants. Moreover, the characterizations of Big Dan's as a bad establishment in a marginal neighborhood in the city created the impression that New Bedford was the Portuguese "rape capital" of the country.

Central Park jogger

The infamy of the New Bedford case was conceivably surpassed by one of the most notorious interracial gang rape trials: the Central Park Jogger trial in 1991. The initial reports portrayed this horrendous crime as a threat to maintaining order in New York City. These news reports introduced the term "wilding" into the national imagination; this was the word reportedly used by the gang to describe their Central Park marauding, as they robbed, beat, and raped everyone in their path. Ultimately, the trial and the publicity that surrounded it became the public forum for reconciling the horror of gang violence with demands to reestablish the rule of law in the city.

In the trial, one black and two Hispanic teenage boys were charged with the sexual and physical assault of a young professional woman in Central Park. The prosecution argued that while jogging in Central Park the young woman was raped by a roving band of black and Hispanic teenagers. Because the jogger had no memory of the night of the incident when she testified at the trial, the prosecution's case relied on forensic photographs of her body and the written and videotaped confessions of the defendants. The viewing of the jogger's body and the defendants' confessions produced a spectacle in the courtroom that was reproduced by the media for a larger public audience.

The encounter with the "specter" of the "nearly dead white woman's body" presented for the purposes of the trial and then reproduced by the media became a site of "uncanny strangeness,"[13] arousing images of evil blackness and unseen dangers. In this way, the trial gained a hyperbolic significance as a cultural metaphor for racial dangers that can be barely known or contained. During the 1990s, the visual spectacle of the Central Park Jogger trial as well as other events, including the replaying of the videotape of the Rodney King beating, served as vehicles for relaying a message about the connection between race and rising crime rates and for locating, in the collective unconscious, these destructive criminal elements on an urban landscape.[14]

The public narration was orchestrated by locating all visual points of relevance on this landscape. For example, in the Central Park Jogger trial, each statement made by the police who responded to the reports of roving bands of teenage boys was tied to a geographic reference, charted for the jury on maps and aerial photographs. In this way, Central Park operated as a textual reference point that enabled precise visualizations of the scene, while also concretely locating the attack on a white woman by black and Hispanic teenage boys in a space of contested urban geography.

The park is the focus for the clash over the ownership of public space between a woman who represents the hopes of a new professional class and teenage boys who represent young lives wasted by the forces of racism and poverty. The overlays of buildings and streets outside the boundaries of the park functioned as markers for the places within and structured realistic images of the proximity and distance between social classes and races: that is, the closeness of shared recreational space evidenced by the proximity of the Schomberg Housing Project where the defendants lived and the jogger's East Side apartment. For the writer Joan Didion, who covered the trial for the *New York Review of Books,* the perceived social distance between the victim and the assailants produced a crime story that precisely conflates "victim and city" and "personal woe with public distress."[15] Racial transgression and sexual danger in the park became a context for playing out a struggle over who owns the city.

If Central Park is seen as the textual landscape, however, the contest arises over the manageability of space according to human designs, or rather the taming of the wild in a contained environment. The park gains presence in trial reports through its soil and debris, leaves, foliage, and rocks, and as a landscape, a terrain viewed as a product of conscious human design, planning, and cultivation. A connection between the "raped" jogger and the "ravaged" city is forged in the narrative through images of bodies and landscapes. In the reports from the trial, the Central Park jogger's body became part of the contested landscape that gives structure and form to an understanding of a racially divided urban geography.

the prosecutorial narration

The criminal law of rape, as it has evolved since the late eighteenth century, has measured sexual offense through a graduated scale of physical harm inflicted on bodies. The term "rape" refers to a legal definition in which violation is defined by, and only in terms of, physical acts taken on or against a female body. Thus rape law is manifestly interested in women's bodies, as the "site" of activity and as the definitional basis of men's criminal behavior.[16] For example, rape legislation and case law refer to the gender and age of the victim and make precise distinctions about the use of force and penile penetration.

When prosecutors narrate a case about rape, the female body provides the scene for the interpretation of events during the rape trial. Within this scene, a woman's body is viewed in a "disembodied" state. Bits of her body are visualized as they become relevant. In the courtroom, evidence is produced according to the medical model of examination: the court looks at the body for physical inscriptions of the criminal act and for signs of the victim's resistance to the attack. The physical assessments of the victim's injuries are entered into evidence as the observable markings of brute force. Other procedures produce body specimens that can be removed and evaluated, including fingernail scrapings, pubic hair sampling, and cultures from the vagina and mouth. The compilation of the observable markings and samples make up the whole body, in the legal meaning of its totality: in the New Bedford trial, for example, the prosecutor, after the presentation of this physical evidence, asked the medical examiner, "Is this a fair representation of her body?"

The visualization of the complainant's injuries in the courtroom extends beyond the medical examination of her body to the description of physical contact with the defendants. These descriptions evolve through a prescribed format of examination and cross-examination that is contrived by the language relevant to establishing criminal culpability. Given that the law defines violation as the act of penetration, the victim serves the prosecution by describing what happened to her with the physical explicitness necessary to confirm the act. However, her words must be vague enough to imply that she was literally passive and uninvolved in the sexual activity.

This is seen in the prosecutor's questioning of the victim in the New Bedford case. The questioning about the sexual act included the following examination of the complainant, whom I call Diana:

PROSECUTOR: Where did you go next?

DIANA: I went to the bar to put my drink down and to leave, somebody grabbed me from behind . . . I asked, "what in the hell do you think your doing?" I proceeded forward. Another grabbed at my feet and I fell, banging the side of my head on the pool table.

PROSECUTOR: How were you dragged?

DIANA: They had me from behind and were pulling, they picked up my feet, and got on top; first man had intercourse. I couldn't see from the waist down.

PROSECUTOR: Did you see his penis?

DIANA: No.

PROSECUTOR: Feel it?

DIANA: Inside of me.

PROSECUTOR: Where was your head?

DIANA: Hanging off the edge.

This model of questioning was repeated in reference to each defendant and sexual act. Each time, the prosecutor asked the complainant to specify what she saw and felt. Then, in equally precise terms, he questioned her about the placement of her head and torso. On redirect, the defense attorneys again questioned her about the movement of the defendants and the placement of her body parts. For example, one defense attorney tried to elicit from her distinctions between being "punched" in the stomach and "elbowed" while on the pool table.

This manner of talking about bodies and actions is also found in the testimony of observers in the barroom. A man named Pacheko (an eyewitness and friend of the defendants) describes the rape from the observer's perspective:

PROSECUTOR: What did you see next?

PACHEKO: I saw [Daniel] take the girl around the bar to the pool table.

PROSECUTOR: How was she taken?

PACHEKO: In his arms.

PROSECUTOR: What did he do?

PACHEKO: I wasn't noticing, well, because the other guys were going after him.

PROSECUTOR: Was she walking to the pool table?

PACHEKO: No.

PROSECUTOR: Did you see her hands?

PACHEKO: It was on Falfa's shoulder.

PROSECUTOR: What were they doing?

PACHEKO: Nothing. Later I saw the boy with blond hair, talking with her; he pushed her hand off his shoulder.

PROSECUTOR: Did you hear anything from the girl?

PACHEKO: No. She was talking to the boy from the South, but I couldn't understand what she was saying.

PROSECUTOR: How was she dressed?

PACHEKO: I saw her sitting on the pool table. Daniel was with her, along with two boys from the South. When I looked up again, I saw Daniel on top of her.

PROSECUTOR: What was Daniel doing?

PACHEKO: He? I don't know. She knows [witness smiles].

In the recounted scene, Diana is given a doll-like presence. She lies there, motionless or held still, except for the movement of her hands. The only body movements noted by witnesses are changes in her facial expression, which is at first reported as fixed in almost a masklike picture of happiness and then later suddenly transformed into a crying face. The prosecutor pressed the witnesses to describe the body movements that fit the legal definition of rape, but this ironically required them to report on movements that were unseen (notwithstanding, Pacheko makes the implicit assumption with the words "she knows" that what is not seen is pleasurable). The visual representation of rape, moreover, is not supplemented by the victim's spoken words during the attack. Her words are strangely irrelevant, as if once she was buried under the men no one expected her to speak. And in any case, the din created by the men's activity made her cries inaudible.

The medical and legal construction of events treats her body as a terrain of verifiability: first, it shows that harm has been inflicted, and second, its injuries reveal that she has offered resistance to the rape. This way of viewing the crime strips away her agency because she can report only what has been done to her body. In this way, what she has to say about the attack is only legally relevant to making the case if it also confirms what can be seen by spectators. The legal verification of rape in the courtroom diminishes her voice in contrast to the overwhelming presence of her body: she is a voiceless form or mechanical woman. Without the victim's voice, the power of interpretation belongs to the law's vision of sexual crime. The legal filter of relevancy erases her own experience from a retelling of events that focuses on men's transgression against her body.

In fact, what constitutes the retelling of the actual violence for the prosecution is virtually a vision of transgression of bodies and scene. The courtroom witnesses describe a point of transition, at which the actors in a barroom move from behaving according to *normal* rules of male-female interaction into a shattered world of violence. In the description of the relations in the barroom before the rape, the victim knows the number of bodies present (about fifteen men and one woman) and can recount their movements around the tavern. She describes the bar when she entered it as nonthreatening by agreeing, in fact, with the defense lawyer's description of the goings-on as neither "boisterous nor crazy." As might be expected when a young woman comes into an unfamiliar place, Diana draws close to the only other woman present and strikes up a conversation. The men playing pool appear to be friendly. She testifies that, at first, two of the men "treated her like a lady" and spoke to her "politely."

At the moment of transgression, voice disappears from the scene.[17] The bodily boundaries become confused. In testimony about the attack, witnesses no longer recall meaningful words; they hear only the victim's screams. The content of her cries, to whom they are directed, and who is listening or is anticipated to respond is unclear in these accounts. The male voices are described as loud, but the only audible words reported by witnesses are shouts of "do it!" After the scene becomes transgressive, the victim cannot count the number of men involved. Nor can she name or distinguish between the men attacking her. In cross-examination she states: "They all started to look alike."

A room designed to house primarily groups of men for the pleasure of drink and sport was transformed into a torture chamber for one woman. The artifacts of the room became the weapons of her torture. The pool table, ordinarily a place for men to play a competitive game, is transformed into a platform on which men competed for sexual access to the victim's body; the horseshoe-shaped bar where men requested drinks was transformed in the victim's mind to the backdrop of a queue waiting to have sex with her; the instruments of eating and drinking pleasure become weapons as knives are put in front of her face and straws are poked in the men's butts by bystanders. The everyday objects found in the barroom were transformed by the sexual energies unleashed by the violence.

The sexuality of the scene is not expressed as bodily pleasure or as a form of gratification. The experience of sexuality presented in the legal forum is visual, as if the participants are in a pornographic film in which the pleasure of the scene is projected through the experience of the onlookers. The bartender describes himself as "just looking" and wanting the men to "just finish with that." The focus of visual attention, moreover, was not the woman's body or what they were doing with her body (in fact, it was difficult to derive any information from the witnesses about the degree to which the woman was undressed during the assault). The witnesses were primarily interested in looking at the men humiliate each other. There is both a refusal to see the woman as a living creature and the overwhelming presence of her body as voiceless and buried underneath the men. She enacts this deadness when the men momentarily let her go and she remains frozen, failing to escape from the room.

The ethos in the barroom was humor: as one defense attorney summed up the event, "everyone thought it was a big joke." The joke was about embarrassing the men who *exposed* themselves in the barroom and the onlookers participated by trying to stick straws into the rapists' exposed behinds. The next day the joke continued. A witness named Cuna described how he was kidding around with one defendant and chided him about "sticking a straw up his ass," but "Danny said he didn't remember anything that happened." The prosecutors, in an attempt to establish the elements of the crime, became the unintended narrators of an account of the disordering of social relations between men and their homoerotic pleasures in viewing rape (from the backside). In the trial proceedings, the victim's body is a battlefield, around which the attackers strategically position themselves. The body is left behind, ravished, after the (erotic) war among the men is over.

The prosecutor in the Central Park Jogger trial employs a similar methodology of using the victim's body to verify the crime, but the telling is more macabre given that she was unconscious and left for dead. The first sighting of the victim was by a Hispanic man named Vanico. Vanico began his testimony by recounting his journey through Central Park on the night of April 19, 1989. He explained that he was talking and drinking beer with his friend Carlos while walking home through the park by way of 100th Street and Central Park West. He was startled by the sounds of "someone" moaning. He looked in the direction of the moans. He testified about what he saw: "I knew it was a body, I don't know if it was a man or woman." His report of the first sighting of the body became a moment for the rather unexpected release of tension. Spectators in the courtroom burst into spontaneous laughter as Vanico mimicked the sounds of her moaning ("mum, mum, mum"). He then enacted a complex gender and racial evasion: "I don't know who it was; I don't know who she is; I knew it was a body hurt, a human being; and I thought she was a man." When later asked by a defense attorney, "Did you see the race?" He answered: "No, I couldn't tell, all that mud was on top of her."

Through a series of questions designed to document the condition and placement of the discovered body, the spectators get their first glance at the jogger's nearly dead body. The manifest pleasure of the spectator arises in response to the seeming absurdity of Vanico's claim to know, without seeing: he looked and heard, but he nervously asserted that he couldn't see her as "alive," "white," or as a "woman." Vanico's expression of fear and excitement in witnessing, both at the moment of discovery and during the trial, suggest how socially dangerous the act of spectatorship is. To be caught looking involves the risk of being seen (and marked as criminal) by authorities, or being watched in the act of discovering her body by the perpetrator. A defense attorney touches on the danger of being caught looking when he asks Vanico, "Did they take body sample or tissue samples [from you]?" Yet in another sense, Vanico as a "witness" both in his certainty and in his evasions secures the belief that an act of violence, both real and imagined, has occurred.

Thus, the victim's body is sighted as part of the terrain. A paramedic who was asked to describe "what she saw" in a ravine illuminated by police car headlights said: "It was heavily wooded, yet as I approached, I saw her in a spasmodic state, moving around." She said she didn't touch the body but "did a visual examination of her wounds." Here, through the paramedic's field of vision and in its narrative reconstruction, seeing the wounds is a way of seeing the violence itself. The paramedic also reports that she didn't cut a cloth wrapped around the woman's neck even though it was obstructing her breathing because "it was a crime scene." But the paramedic noted the woman's position: "her chest was in the water and her head in an easterly direction." This visual inspection also detected "mud and blood all over her."

After the body was stabilized and transported to the hospital, the police supervisor in charge testified that he decided to "hold the scene." Since in the supervisor's mind the area was too vast and dark "to do properly," he put police officers at 102nd Street and at the bottom of the ravine. He told them, "Don't let anybody into the area." He kept the shirt that had been taken off the body and treated it as an artifact representing the mutilated body resting on the ground: "It was a blood-soaked shirt, turned inside out, a twisted shirt with a hole above the right breast."

The second step in the containment of the scene was to "note areas of blood" and then photograph them. The police officers' vision of the crime scene was, in fact, subsequently reproduced in the trial in the presentation of this series of photographs. Through them the jury is shown the marks of the jogger's blood on the terrain: "Drag marks toward the tree; significant amount of blood in the area; paths of blood, disturbed by dirt; tree roots covered in blood." The photographs depict her clothes strewn throughout the wooded area: "A shoe and instep in an area of blood; a right shoe and jogging tight 92 feet east off the lower path; and left sneaker down the ravine closer to the stream."

As if to complete the picture, the rest of the landscape is made visible on the victim's body, tagged "unknown white woman," in photographs taken as she lay unconscious in the hospital. When these photographs were later displayed as evidence, the marks of the landscape were seen and inscribed on her body. Referring to a photograph showing the backs of her legs, the forensic pathologist, testifying for the state, said: "Here is a multitude of scratches and bruises that run in different directions, consistent with roots, twigs, branches, and the ground cover of the area." On the quarter view, left frontal aspect, of her head we are shown, "a crushing, tearing injury, that is consistent with a rock," "rough enough to break the skin, and heavy enough" to cause the injury. In his testimony, this expert spoke of the jogger's body as itself a terrain, describing, for example, "abrasions that show horizontal impact left to right and right to left" and "intervening regions of uninjured skin."

The body is repeatedly made visible in the trial as a figure on the terrain. The jogger's body and clothes and blood and hair specimens are all placed in a field on which visual inspection reveals her inundation by mud and blood and her defilement by abrasions and blows. She "exists" and is recognizable only within the landscape of her injuries. She is unrecognizable elsewhere: accordingly, a friend who looks at her body in the hospital the next morning finds her unidentifiable except for a ring on her finger.

Physical contact between the teenage boys and the woman is also verified through the marks on her body and the terrain. The marks are traces, the remains left from the assailants' touching and bludgeoning of the body. These disturbances on the body preserve the reality of physical contact and sexual union. In this way, an unmarked woman, a white woman, is marked by the violence of strangers. The marks on her body, in effect, signify the violence as the penetration of foreign substance on the white woman's body. These traces are indistinguishable from the violence itself, and their significance is racialized at the level of pure materiality. In other words, the marks of the foreign, the dirt, and the forceful objects make racial transgression visible.

In contrast, the defendants' bodies, once brought into police captivity, are sampled rather than visually inspected. Their muddy clothing is shown to the jury so that its members can take notice of the "cuttings," the holes of fabric where samples have been removed and sent to the lab. Their bodies are disaggregated and analyzed by means of microscopic viewing. Thus, in an exchange about one defendant, Clarence Thomas (no relation to the Supreme Court justice), a detective was asked:

> PROSECUTOR: Did you remove anything from Clarence Thomas?
> DETECTIVE: No, he indicated he washed his hands.
> PROSECUTOR: Are you not interested in whether he washed the rest of his body?
> DETECTIVE: No, [I am] only [interested] in fingernail scrapings.

Here the detective explains how the visually marked body of the black teenage boy has evidentiary relevance only for the possibility of what could be extracted from its unclean reservoirs. The image of the defendants, in contrast to the display of the victim's body, is a kind of photographic negative to be looked at for distinguishable evidence in a blackened scene.

Blood in the Central Park Jogger trial signified the mixing of bodily fluids and, therefore, transgression. The victim's body, when it was discovered, had lost almost all of its blood, which according to the doctor's testimony made her survival a "medical miracle." But the draining of her blood also created a phantasm of racially transgressive violence, the possibility of white blood, that she could be living without her blood, full of innocence and purity, beyond life and death.

Because of the lack of witnesses, the prosecutor is forced to make a case in the confines of a story in which the woman and the defendants are never seen at the scene of the crime; both escape vision except as part of the landscape. Even the prosecutor's attempt to place the defendants in the ravine at the estimated time of the attack operates in the narrative outside the realm of seeing. Given the number of police in the area that night, it seems inexplicable that no one saw the roving band near the place where the body was discovered. But the fact that the defendants were unseen is also essential to the narrative about their actions in the darkness. The prosecutor's narrative depends upon the staging of appearance as disappearance, and thus the defendants' presence in the landscape is marked by their seeming ability to slip away into the park or to stay out of view even when the officers coordinated their locations in efforts to "head off the pack." The officers who testified could only speak of radio transmissions about roving bands of black and Hispanic teenagers in the north end of the park or report glimpses from a distance as the pack "jumped over a wall and started to separate." The prosecution's inability to place the defendants at the scene of the crime is at one level an evidentiary problem in making the case. Yet the boys' unseen presence at the site brings to the narrative an erotic dimension, in that the prosecution must overtly interject a theory about how the defendants' desires give a *reality* to their presence on the scene.

Primarily, the prosecutor is the author of a story about the crime that has the official purpose of making the case about the guilt of the defendants. Yet, as political actors, prosecutors must produce stories that do more than satisfy the love of justice. Indeed, the narrative must also satisfy the fantasies that make the sexual transgression both real and containable within the cultural imagination. The pleasure of the text does not arise from gratuitous sensationalism of the sexual aspects of the crime but rather from how the prosecution needs to advance a narrative that establishes and embellishes the sadistic motives of the boys.

In the Central Park trial, the prosecutor, Elizabeth Lederer, sought to secure the vision of racial transgression and sexual danger in the narrative. As argued above, her efforts were encumbered by the ways in which the defendants appeared to escape from the actual physical and textual landscape of the crime scene. The prosecutor "recaptures" the defendants at the scene in two ways: first, by focusing on the defendants' videotaped confessions in which they recount their own viewing of the attack; and second, by asserting that the teenage boys were motivated by the sexual pleasure of assaulting and raping the jogger. These strategies require the prosecutor to revision the rape scene by assigning motives to the boys as she replayed the movement of sexual action around the jogger's body.

In her summation, the prosecutor tells the story about the defendants marking the jogger as the chosen victim. She portrays the defendants as evil boys who, once arriving on the scene, hide behind bushes before overwhelming their victim by virtue of their size and strength. In the prosecutor's version, the defendants are given the capacity to *pick out* a white woman as she runs north on East Drive and becomes "illuminated for the defendants and others to see." Then the boys ambushed her, and she fell to the ground (leaving her first trace). More traces were made when the boys dragged her into the woods and darkness off the roadway. By evoking racial images of a lurking animal waiting to attack, the prosecutor makes the defendants assume the status of rational monsters; stalking, choosing, and seizing a particular and unknown white woman.

The pleasure of looking at the violence is replicated for the purposes of the Central Park Jogger trial not only by Lederer's account of the motivations of the defendants in her summation but also in the presentation of two videotaped confessions made by the defendants, which were replayed numerous times over the course of the month-long trial. The prosecutor used the videotapes to invite the jury to visualize fully the violence enacted on the woman's body: the beating, rape, and sodomy. In each of the videotaped confessions, the camera is focused on the boys cornered in a small room at the police station while Lederer sits across a table (out of view) asking a series of questions about their own and others' activities in the park that night.[18] The boys sat nervously. Raymond Santana slumped down in his chair and rocked back and forth. Lederer began her interview by asking him to "sit up," in the manner of a teacher speaking to an elementary school student.

Her initial questions focus on the number of boys involved and their reasons for going to the park that night. The thirteen-year-old Anton explains that he went outside to "play" before a late dinner, while the fourteen-year-old Raymond admits to joining friends to "rob bikes and other stuff" from people in the park. By asking detailed questions, Lederer systematically elicits information about the series of attacks on other people in the park: "Who saw him first?" "Did you kick him?" "How many times?" "Did you see blood?" The same questions are addressed regarding their encounter with the woman they described as a "lady" dressed in jogging clothes. The boys answer all the questions with minimum embellishment and in an emotionless monotone. Each boy describes the attack almost entirely through his report of watching other boys struggle with her, knock her down to the ground, and have sex with her. Each recounts other boys grabbing hold of her shirt and starting to "feel her up." Both Raymond and Anton claim to have "heard nothing" during the attack. When probed further, one of them reports that another defendant, Steven Lopez, covered her mouth to stop her screaming. Then he yelled, "Smash her!" and said, "Shut up, you bitch." Yet she keeps on screaming and he "just kept smashing her and hitting her with a brick." The defendant explained: "She was like shocked, she just stood there and didn't do anything."

In Anton McCray's videotape he describes himself as not actively involved but watching the other boys hitting the jogger and removing her clothing; he later admits to taking his pants down and getting on top of her "so it would look like we were having sex. I was just doing it so everyone knew I did it." Lederer asks him to be more precise, by questioning, "Your penis wasn't inside her?" He says (with obvious embarrassment): "I didn't do nothing to her, I didn't put my penis in her." Raymond Santana, who claims he left before doing anything other than "grabbing the lady's tits," is then asked specific questions about how he knew the first boy to get on top of her "had sex with her." "Did they pull her pants down?" "Were her legs open?" "Did he open his fly or pull his pants down?" "How far down were his pants?" "Did you see his penis?" "Did he have an erection?" "Did he put his penis anywhere else?" "How long was he lying on top of her?" Raymond tells her, "I didn't bother to look" and claims that he knows the first boy had sex with her because he was "doing what you are supposed to do when you have sex."

During the interview the boys are also questioned about what happened as they left Central Park that night. The police spotted them and began a chase through the park. A few of the twenty to thirty boys were caught as they left the park, while others hid in the bushes and eventually made their way home. Anton jumped over a fence and hid in a muddy ravine. When he got home, he told his mother he "was playing tag" and that was why he was so dirty and had forgotten to go to the store for her. Later that night, the boy who escaped with him said: "I'm not doin' that any more . . . we didn't really do nothing, we didn't do nothing, we shouldn't have run [from the police]."

In these videotaped interviews, the prosecutor organized her questioning about the events to obtain the information she needed to establish that a crime had been committed. In her interrogation, Lederer sought an account that demonstrated how each boy participated in the act of rape, which maximized their culpability. Lederer took the liberty of suggesting how and in what erotic terms the boys experienced the attack as pleasurable. She explained that Raymond came to the park "ready" to rob and beat people. He "was not about to stand by and not be involved with the woman." In her erotic imagining, Lederer asked those listening to visualize the scene, which lasted only ten to twenty minutes, in which each boy was waiting to take a turn. In her closing statement she suggested an explanation for the absence of bodily traces: "It is not difficult to imagine each person could not remain inside her to climax. They ejaculated before they could ever penetrate her."

The prosecutor needed to fashion a narrative that tied together the real with the realistic, by constructing the sexual desire of the event as driven by the opportunity for heterosexual performance and limiting the visual eroticism to the boys' desire to have their turn with the woman. In the prosecutor's retelling of the story the young boys are not wandering aimlessly in the park; instead they are identified as dark-skinned men deliberately seeking out a targeted white woman. This theory is further established by suggesting that the boys knew that their violence would leave telling marks of their erotic desires. Lederer refers to the confession of Yusef Salaam to demonstrate his own belief in the reality of his violence. She explains that Yusef was compelled to make his statement because he believed he would be caught when the police officers told him that they "could get finger prints off her breasts." Lederer brings us full circle in the process of nervous spectatorship. As the white, middle-class agent of the law, she made her case through her own graphic imaginings of the sexual excitement experienced by these teenage boys.

The Central Park Jogger trial was a replication of violence, a textual landscape on which marks on bodies and terrain demonstrated the presence of racial transgression, and on which seemingly apparitional visions were brought into focus by realistic reenactments of pleasure. This trial as a spectacle is a negative cultural achievement, even a triumph for the dominant fictions about crime control, in its narrative ability to locate real and imagined pleasures on the highly recognizable terrain of urban geography. The representational practices of the trial make racism seem more threatening, concrete, and embedded in the risks of daily existence. The iconic representation of the jogger as a "white" symbol clearly evokes the special threat of dark-skinned men against white women. This icon, as a representation that brings moral certainty to circumstances in which a woman has been destroyed, provides a mask for the state to "hide" behind as it employs racialized theories of sexual aggression. This spectacle, in fact, enables observers' unconscious desires and fears of racial others to find a concrete manifestation as highly observable events that give evidence to racial transgression on the street, in the park, and other public spaces in urban life.

Because the Central Park jogger was widely described as a woman driven by the regularity of her work hours, who jogged the same time every day, socialized with friends of the same class and interests, and used a park where she carefully planned jogging routes, the attack could only be an encounter with the strange, the unforeseen forces of racial violence so unimaginable that they shattered her conscious memory of that night. The play of strangeness was also highlighted in media accounts of the trial, in which violence is sold in predictable and marketable forms of shock and horror.[19] And thus, the effect of the trial was to locate the strange outside the familiar and to attempt to prove that virtual contact with the racial other is catastrophic. Racism, as a way of seeing, invades, and is protected within, unconscious sexual desire, through the projection of scenes that enlarge our capacity to keep fantasies (of ghosts, roving bands of animals, and violence as really pleasurable) alive in spectacles of the alien other.

This analysis of two sensational gang-rape trials demonstrates how such public events are vehicles for acting out expressive justice in ways that serve the state's need to portray itself as containing the horrors of unleashed sexual atrocities. Prosecutors, who are entrusted with the enforcement of the law, are also politicians both inside and outside the courtroom, and in that role they respond reactively to the public arousal caused by shocking and atypical cases. This is seen most vividly in the prosecution's telling of the crime story, in which most assuredly the punishment is made to fit the crime through the process of "imagining the acts" as motivated by evils worthy of the most punitive measures. This narration not only attributes evil to the defendants but also creates a rhetorical avenue for state agents to profess their outrage and will to counteract it. These dramatic reactions to notorious rape cases potentially have enormous significance for how rape is conceived in the context of a high-crime society. Prosecutors transform victims into innocent bystanders, young boys into evil black men, and homoerotic spectacles into the culmination of sadistic passions of dangerous strangers. This representation of sexual violence may have ultimately contributed to the failure of criminal justice authorities to seek out the real perpetrator of the crime in the Central Park case.

looking back at the Central Park jogger trial

Thirteen years after the incidents that led to the Central Park Jogger trials, "new" evidence considered by the New York courts exculpated the five defendants tried and convicted for their participation in the rape.[20] The reversal of justice for these five men raises serious doubts about the integrity of the criminal justice system and is, of course, a personal tragedy for the teenagers, who had been collectively incarcerated for more than fifty years.[21] The swift identification of these defendants, the aggressive tactics used to build a case against them, and the handing down of punitive sentences demonstrate the kind of excessiveness and arbitrariness that result from the dominance of the crime control model.[22] This miscarriage of justice has greater significance still in the questions it raises about the underlying sensibilities of the modern feminist campaigns against sexual violence. The growth of a "culture of control" makes all the more worrisome the feminist movement's insistence on aggressive sex crime prosecution and activism which promotes the view that the Central Park case was "only about the abuse of women."

In 1991, three of the defendants, Anton McCray, Yusef Salaam, and Raymond Santana, were convicted in the first trial. Two other defendants, Kharey Wise and Kevin Richardson, were tried and convicted in a separate hearing in order to avoid the presentation of evidence that would implicate codefendants. In late 2002, motions were filed to vacate the verdicts by three of the defendants' attorneys. The subsequent reversal of the convictions of these five young men gives new significance to the lack of material evidence in this case and the effects of racial imageries in implicating the defendants in their trials. This rehearing also sheds new light on the videotaped interviews of the defendants.[23] The District Attorney's office had conducted middle-of-the-night interviews in the police station with all the defendants from both trials (except Yusef Salaam) and an alleged "accomplice," Steven Lopez (who accepted a plea). Viewed retrospectively, these interviews raise concerns about the excessive police power in interrogations, the legal rights of juveniles during police interrogation, and the misuse of confessions in criminal cases that are unsupported by material evidence.[24] The prosecutor used many controversial tactics that may have violated Miranda protections, including exploiting suggestive materials (photos of the crime scene), falsely implying the existence of incriminating evidence, threats of implication through DNA analysis, and promises of better outcomes as rewards for "telling all."[25] Yet it is important to note that the videotaped sessions were conducted in a manner of almost eerie civility.

Short excerpts from the interviews (as they were used in the trial and picked up by the media) make it appear that these teenagers are giving accounts of their brutal attack of the jogger in ways that look all the more abhorrent because they minimize their own actions and fail to comprehend the gravity of her injuries. However, reviewing all the tapes, each in full and in combination with each other, creates a more complex understanding. Lederer's interview with Kharey Wise, the first defendant videotaped that night, is noteworthy in that it is much longer than the other videotaped interviews. Much of this interview is devoted to overt efforts to get him to give details that match the facts (known by the prosecutor) about the placement of the woman in a ravine and of her injuries. In all the interviews, the boys are more forthcoming about describing the series of events in the park that occurred prior to the encounter with the jogger (which included talking with friends, entering the park with a group of approximately thirty teenagers, kicking and stealing food from a three-hundred-pound "bum," intimidating a bicyclist and a male jogger, and throwing a rock at a car) than they are about the actual attack on the woman. At the point in the interviews when the teenagers are questioned about this attack, significant inconsistencies emerge about the location of the crime and which teenagers were involved.

Furthermore, the narrative style of the interviews does not accord with the conventions of a confessional statement.[26] The teenagers' replies are so telegraphic that they rarely utter more than three-word phrases, and even then only to reply to the prosecutor. While there are numerous instances where the teenagers are admitting to misbehavior and imply "guilt" about their actions, the admissions are oddly not related to the attack on the jogger but to a variety of other things, including having a can of Pepsi on the desk during the interview, disobeying their parents' curfew, and violating the confidences of friends. In retrospect, their lack of "shame" appears to be due to their knowing little about what happened to the jogger and the grisly details of the crime.

As suggested above, when these videotaped interviews were used in the trial they provided visual evidence for the prosecutorial narrative about "sexual danger and racial transgression." The telling of events is, in fact, dependent not only on available information about the crime as presented by the prosecutor but also on the intrusion of her own presumptions about sexual desire and deviance. This is shown in the numerous attempts Lederer makes to get Kharey Wise to report that the act of rape (which we now know these teenagers did not commit) was pleasurable. When asked "How do you know she was forced?" Wise has a great deal of trouble articulating a description of the jogger's acts of resistance and works from a very elementary concept of rape. He says, "She didn't want to go" and "She was like, kidnapped." When asked "What happened to her?" again, he reports flatly, "They had sex and used her." Lederer makes repeated attempts to get Wise to give a report of another teenager raping the woman. She eventually rephrases the question to "How he was moving" and he answers simply, "wild." In a subsequent interview with Kevin Richardson, Lederer improved this line of questioning to give the teenagers more help in describing the sex act, including asking "Was he thrusting against her?" and "Did he look like he was having a good time?"

Lederer probes each teenager about the details of the attack. These questions appear carefully orchestrated to encourage them to corroborate the physical evidence (presumably acquired from medical information about the condition of the jogger's body). This is most evident in the prosecutor's unsuccessful attempts to get these teenagers to give an account of the rape in a way that could explain both residues of semen left on the body (which were not found) and the injuries she suffered. This requires at least one (and probably only one) of them to have completed the sex act (technically, to have ejaculated inside her body) and in all probability to have used a large object, like a rock, to beat her face and head (to generate the amount of force required to produce skull fractures). Lederer's efforts to make the interview accounts compatible with the evidence lead her to redundant questioning of each teenager about what they hit her with, where did they hit her, and how many times, which elicited responses like "with [their] hands," "slapped across the face," and "put her hand over her mouth to shut her up," and "used a knife to cut up her legs." (All of which fails to account for the severity of her head injuries or creates factual inconsistencies given that the medical evidence did not indicate knife wounds.)

Lederer also steers the teenagers to confirm her version of their sexual arousal and performance. For example, she asks Wise if he saw others "masturbate on top of her" and Richardson if they "[felt] good about what they had done." To account for the degree and type of the jogger's injuries, Lederer attempts to elicit statements from the boys suggesting that their behavior was driven by a violent frenzy. In this regard, Lederer asked questions that alluded to their desires to "ambush" the victim. When the teenagers are prompted to describe how they "hid behind trees," "laid in wait for her," and remained "quiet" so as not to alert her to the oncoming attack, they produced answers that were nonsensical or contradictory of the implied image of a rushing pack of wild boys. This line of questioning led to peculiar exchanges about the teenagers' vocal presence at the scene. While the prosecutor's approach was designed to push them to admit to lurking "quietly" before the rampage and to suppressing the jogger's screams by using her shirt to gag her, the teenagers' accounts of their escapades in the park that night were based on their sense of power through visibility (they knew their numbers were scary even without taking any aggressive actions against bystanders), verbal harassment, and expressions of bravado (i.e., "We'll get you"). In Wise's videotaped interview, Lederer eventually loses her temper and insists: "You explain how she got so badly hurt!"

These interviews were popularly understood and presented at trial as "confessions." In retrospect, this raises the question of why these boys would admit to a horrendous crime that they did not commit. But a more detailed look at the narrative structure of these interviews reveals that none of these boys was "confessing" as that speech act is usually understood. This is the case, in part, because the prosecutor is presenting the sequence of events and eliciting their responses, but, more precisely, the teenagers seem to be complying with the prosecutor's demand to produce statements that "witness" the crime. This results in an exchange in which the defendants perceive themselves as making admissions in order to help the prosecutor implicate the other boys in the park that night. None of the five "confessions" are delivered in the form of "narratives" that describe their rape of the jogger (except for McCray, who claims to have pretended to rape her), and all descriptions of the rape are put in terms of watching others do it or asserting that something "must of happened." In this way, both the defendants and the prosecution are voyeurs of the rape—yet only the prosecutor's vision is evocative of bestial desire.

Clearly, important questions could be asked about these middle-of-the-night interviews that pertain to legal treatment of juveniles and police tactics implemented to encourage false confessions. But the more pressing issue is why the repressive prosecution of these five defendants (and the striking display of the illegitimate use of state violence) remained inscrutable to a worldwide audience. While graphic reports about the injuries sustained by the victim were instantaneously newsworthy, the state-inflicted injuries on these teenage boys received little news interest or attention. A possible explanation is that much of the force of "expressive justice" has become sanitized within the routine processing of criminal cases and appears less coercive and discriminatory in its application. In these interviews, for example, the coercive power of the state is subtly employed. The prosecutor and the police are able to "force" false confessions without using overt force or violating professional norms or regulations. The recently published New York City Police Department's Central Park Jogger Case Panel Report claims that in their investigation of police actions they found no evidence of "coercion in the questioning of the defendants" and no reason to criticize the interrogation and arrest techniques. Although this report is based upon "inside information" and relies mostly on police sources, it no doubt reflects a fairly sophisticated understanding of how police power, even under conditions of public hysteria, can effectively operate to secure evidence for convictions without resorting to overt forms of illegality.[27]

Moreover, when police power is exerted to its fullest extent it is often seen as a direct response to the brutal actions of the defendants. Metaphorically, this means that the state can hide behind the violence done to the victim. In the videotaped interviews in the Central Park Jogger case, the prosecutor, literally at one point, stands behind the brutalized body of the victim. Lederer, who in terms of gender, age, race, and professional status bears a resemblance to the jogger, places on the table between herself and Kharey Wise a picture of the victim lying in her hospital bed with her face swollen beyond recognition. After setting this scene, she reminds Wise, as he breaks into tears, about the "seriousness" of the situation. Although she is confrontational, she conducts the interviews in accordance with professional norms of politeness, thoroughness, organization, and personal restraint (in fact, her manner often appears to imitate a teacher disciplining a pupil in a classroom). Even her presence as a highly trained professional in the police station lends a kind of respectability to the interrogation process (and is the result of highly developed forms of cooperation between police districts and prosecutors). In effect, the forms of coercion that were implemented in the police station are masked under conditions of highly "civilized" forms of bureaucratic control. As the prosecution of violence against women falls increasingly under the domain of specialized sex crime units, this more civilized form of coercion becomes institutionalized and easily mobilized for both high-profile crimes, like the Central Park Jogger case and the prosecution of routine cases. Since this conduct often stays within the boundaries of the "law" it can be used aggressively to bring sex criminals to court in the name of protecting the interests of women. These developments are compatible with and reinforcing of expressive justice and allow for more "rationalized" forms of social control to serve the interests of most "deserving" victims and to target "dangerous" classes of perpetuators.

4

ADMINISTRATIVE INJUSTICE

the growth of the therapeutic state

Modern conditions made possible the emergence of a resourceful state, capable of replacing the whole network of social and economic controls by political command and administration. More importantly still, modern conditions provide substance for that command and administration. Modernity ... is an age of artificial order and grand designs ... the era of ... "gardeners" who treat society as a virgin plot of land to be expertly designed and then cultivated and doctored to keep to the designed form.—Zygmunt Bauman

As the last chapter shows, the sexual violence agenda has been incorporated into the crime control function of the state and provided a prime opportunity for "expressive justice." High-profile crimes create occasions for prosecutors to draw attention to horrendous acts of violence and the state's swift and punitive response to criminals. In these highly publicized court cases, victims and perpetrators are recast and events retold to legitimize a culture of control. This often means that stereotypical views of both victims and perpetuators are disseminated for mass publics and crime scenarios are based on simplistic stories about evil and innocence. As my analysis of the Central Park trial demonstrates, the pursuit of expressive justice has become rationalized in criminal justice administration so that the coercive policing and prosecution of suspects is exercised in the form of routine practices. In this case, the aggressive prosecution of teenage boys, who were racialized and vilified in public arenas, was accomplished without violating professional norms. This example suggests that the devices of expressive justice to some extent have joined with the administrative functions of the state.

This chapter looks at the growth of administrative control and its relation to the feminist campaign against sexual violence. Under the conditions of neoliberalism, the principal focus of the penal/welfare apparatus is on victims, in terms of both retribution in their names and the development of programming to manage their needs.[1] This is partly an outgrowth of expressive justice and its public branding of sex criminals and it has hardened the view of perpetrators as deserving of severe punishment and as being incapable of rehabilitation. The marking of these men as criminals encourages the belief that the only effective solution for dealing with perpetrators is to isolate this class of dangerous persons from the rest of society. Consequently, energies are directed to "treating" the victim rather than waiting for the unlikely rehabilitation of perpetrators.[2] This victim-focused agenda has contributed to the growth of administrative power exercised over clients who experience sexual violence. The primary objective of these services is to turn women who have experienced the traumas of violence into successful survivors. This generally involves "retraining" women to protect themselves from future violence as well as to seek help from professionals who can guide them through the process of psychological recovery. The primary means of administration is through extending responsibilities for identifying and treating the problem onto the professional classes of therapists, doctors, and lawyers.

Addressing problems of victims of sexual violence has become part of the routine screening practices of professionals as they deliver medical care, counseling, and legal assistance. This assumption of responsibility has not only transformed professional practices to be more open to the possibility of identifying and treating sexual violence but has also placed the client of a wide range of services under increased scrutiny. The problem of sexual violence is now managed by private professionals and public agents who are often required to both recognize and respond appropriately to the victims. This kind of attention to the problem of rape and domestic violence is often seen as an unqualified good, particularly when professionals have long ignored the prevalence of harm done to women by intimates. The assumption is that women are better off when professionals are able to correctly recognize their situation as battered women or rape victims and treat them accordingly. This is achieved by educating professionals to take sexual violence seriously and to understand women's problems from a feminist perspective.

Certainly improvements are made when professionals are taught and apply new forms of knowledge about sexual violence, especially in cases where this information helps them to abandon sexist notions that blame women. But the education of professionals is neither value neutral nor proscriptively feminist; it is part of complex sociological processes in which certain forms of knowledge are accepted because of their usefulness to the status of the professions and their reinforcement of internal hierarchies. The increased surveillance of clients has also become a primary means to extend state control over citizens' lives.[3] Much of the analysis in this chapter highlights how and why the new feminist knowledge about sexual violence became relevant to and incorporated within professional practice. These processes ultimately have important consequences for how clients and potential clients of these helping networks are able to exercise agency vis-à-vis professionals and under the conditions of neoliberalism.[4]

feminist organizations

Initially the violence against women movement spawned new feminist organizations designed to address the problem. During the late 1970s and 1980s rape crisis centers and battered women's shelters sprang up in the United States, Canada, and Europe. As discussed in chapter 1, often these organizations grew directly out of grassroots efforts and followed feminist ideology and principles that stress nonhierarchal arrangements and democratic decision making. As these organizations matured, they faced both internal and external pressure for more bureaucracy and professionalization, especially as they sought state funding, and thus were subjected to review and evaluation by government bureaucracies.[5] There has been active debate in the feminist community and among scholars as to whether this maturation has diminished the ability of these organizations to further explicitly feminist goals.

Gradually the issue of violence against women drew the attention of those enterprises that traditionally protected the welfare of individuals and families, including the social work bureaucracy, the medical profession, the police, and other public agencies. These services worked in conjunction with the welfare system to create a "feminized terrain" in which services are almost exclusively focused on needy women and their children.[6] On the surface this sounds as if it complements the efforts of the feminist organizations. However, one aspect of this project which is usually overlooked but warrants critical attention is the increased regulation of women by the state both inside and outside shelters. As women have become the subjects of a more expansive welfare state, social service agencies have viewed women and their needs in ways that often have discouraged them from resisting regulations and from being active participants in their own decisions.[7] According to the political theorist Nancy Fraser, the social welfare system substitutes the "juridical, administrative, and therapeutic management of need satisfaction for the politics of need interpretation."[8] The expert discourses related to the management of needs, she argues, coexist and compete with oppositional (politicized or grassroots) discourses (like the voices of the early shelter movement) that created space for more open-ended self-understandings. Thus, any effort among women to redefine their problems in their own terms often competes with or is suppressed by professional assessments of these problems. Moreover, when women express dissatisfaction with current state policies, their voices are muted by conservative political forces that stigmatize poor women and blame them for their reliance on state resources in ways that essentially recreate the old forms of social work revictimization. In this expanding territory of need management, the social worker and other professionals exercise the power to label women and to define who fits the category of "rape survivor" or "battered woman."

client advocacy

This new feminized terrain first took hold in the social work profession. In fact, the growing awareness of sexual violence as a social problem corresponded with feminist-inspired changes in social workers' practices. Although violence against women, especially domestic violence, had often been seen as a persistent and age-old problem, women lacked options for getting help within conventional support systems because of the failure of the old social work bureaucracy to legitimize women's complaints and the inability of women to claim their rights within the traditional confines of marriage.[9] Even some of the early battered women's shelters still employed the old social work style of family service and consequently modeled themselves after and sought funding in conjunction with alcoholic treatment programs.[10] Yet the further development of the shelter and rape crisis model influenced reforms in the social work profession. An integral part of this reform agenda was to correct a social work orientation that was unsympathetic to women, favorable to the interests of men and fathers, and devoted to the preservation of the family unit.[11] From the perspective of reformist social workers, their mission was to transform the practices of the legal and mental health system that only served to revictimize abused women who sought help.

Through these reforms the social work academy also attempted to solidify its authority by gaining influence and promoting its professionalization. Two strategies were employed: first, the recruitment of a new professional corps trained in academic schools of social work, mostly young and male, to replace older working-class women; and second, the reconstruction of the social work discipline as a composite of the functionalist approaches of psychology, sociology, and other human sciences.[12] The new social work perspective challenged the "masochist" hypothesis, which had influenced traditional professional practices. The traditional social worker believed that women brought violence onto themselves because it gratified internalized needs for punishment. The reformers hoped to replace harmful "victim-blaming" attitudes with new professional approaches that identified the violence as symptomatic of complex social, structural, and individual conditions that create stress on normal families.[13]

These reforms introduced a new social work ideology. It placed the professional clearly in the role of "doing good" for the client by rejecting theories that implicitly criticized, placed blame, or revictimized the woman. Having rejected the regressive attitudes of the masochism hypothesis, social workers designated themselves as advocates for the best interests of their clients: the new ideology manifestly asserted that the job of the social worker was to counteract the stigmatic effects of victimization, support the woman, and work to prevent intimate violence. Social workers acquired a mandate to eradicate intimate violence through the treatment of victims rather than focusing on solutions that would require changing the behavior of perpetrators. This new class of professionals had to balance this alliance with victims with their obligation as professionals to remain neutral and distanced toward their clients.

Undeniably, modern social workers have redefined their stance toward sexual violence in many ways that improve attitudes toward victims. Contemporary social work practices, for example, encourage battered women to understand how they are victims of a "cycle of violence" and to take responsibility for their own recovery.[14] However, professionals ultimately exercise the power to make characterizations about the signs and symptoms of trauma, to educate women about the true nature of their victimization and to define successful recovery. The new social work ideology is also strongly influenced by the medical model: the professional treats the problems of a client or patient who fits the category or diagnosis. Thus, professional judgments about battered women or rape survivors follow from already defined expectations about their problems, needs, and pattern of recovery. The choice of treatment strategies, such as how to best encourage "client transformation," remains a controversial issue as can be seen in the professional literature on this subject. These discussions are informed by large-scale research studies that raise uncertainties about how to define the problem and provide prevalence data. Increasingly, the study of domestic violence and rape (often by intimates) has been grouped into a single categorization of "intimate partner violence" (IPV).[15] There is also an expansive literature by practitioners outlining the "best practices" and attempting to influence other professionals to update their methods and become more aware of the scope of the problem. Interestingly, in spite of the lively discussions and debates that surround the question of gathering data and treatment, fundamental questions about professionals' exercise of power over their clients and how these scientific and medical approaches create preconceptions about violence against women are rarely addressed.

In addition, as social workers transformed their understanding of the problem, they recast women's experiences with violence in therapeutic and administrative language. The domination of professional language turns the effects of violence on individual lives, family, and the community into treatable symptoms that are best managed by professionals. Implicit in these treatment strategies are expert interpretations of the causes of male violence. This normative vision influences how women's needs are defined and consequently public understanding of the issue. These assumptions about the nature of the social problem, which are often based on unstated premises about gender dynamics and the causes of violence, have become, over time, the commonsense wisdom about the psychology of victims.

These developments have evolved into current practices in which rape victims and battered women have assumed a place as a special population of clients of medical practitioners, therapists, and social scientific researchers. Professionals assert their role in addressing violence against women by owning special knowledge about the identification and treatment of distinct forms of abuse, including wife battering, child abuse, marital rape, acquaintance rape, and sexual harassment. Cadres of researchers and practitioners now perform what has become a necessary function within the social service delivery systems of the modern welfare state. This chapter examines the discourse in specialized medical and social work journals that advocates increased awareness and new approaches for the treatment of abused women in an attempt to expand specialized knowledge into this domain. Among other things, this literature provides advice about training professionals who can potentially identify and respond to battered women and rape victims when they encounter them in critical situations—in shelters, emergency rooms, and doctors' offices. The writers are often specialists in the field and their intended audience is generalists who might overlook opportunities for intervention and treatment. Although the intent of these professionals (who are part of a progressive mission to improve the treatment of rape victims and battered women and eradicate harmful practices) should not be misconstrued, it is important to recognize how this expert language has characterized women and defined their problem.

public health surveillance

When violence against women gained recognition as a social problem it also gained a place on the national public health agenda. Both the medical and social work professions are part of and serve public health bureaucracies. These bureaucracies, in fact, depend upon these professionals to monitor and report on threats to health and welfare in order to adequately assess and address the needs of the population. Public health approaches to preventing violence against women focus on gathering data, identifying vulnerable groups, developing intervention strategies, and measuring the effectiveness of these interventions. These approaches have influenced how professionals see the problem and, even more importantly, their role in addressing it.

This public health mission has been carried out through identifying female victims of intimate violence and channeling them into appropriate services. For example, the shelter house is deemed an essential part of a netting system that brings women in crisis into the domain of therapeutic programs.[16] To carry on with this work, professionals must provide adequate surveillance of battered women after their initial contact with shelters and hospital emergency rooms because it is infeasible to conduct "structured treatment programs" without a high probability of completion.[17] Clients who enter safe houses are considered to be at an opportune moment for clinical intervention;[18] these women are viewed as ripe for psychological intervention and lifestyle change during such a "state of disequilibrium."[19] One study, applying the cycle-of-violence theory, defines an "open-window" phase (after a severely violent incident and before the next honeymoon period) in which women will demonstrate help-seeking and reality behaviors.[20] Another study characterizes batterer intervention programs as a particularly unique "contact point" with battered women.[21] A similar surveillance strategy is applied to rape victims, who may seek help from social workers and medical professionals but not report their rape experience as the source of their problem. Frontline professionals are reminded and advised to uncover the "countless number of *hidden* victims of sexual assault."[22]

Currently, as part of the process of making battered women's shelters more professional, a mandate exists for changing the primary methods by which shelters work—requiring them to move away from encouraging women's transformation through consciousness raising to a more service-oriented model that involves administrating clients' needs. This process usually begins with assessing each woman's needs (such as parenting skills, education, housing, and psychiatric assistance) and then setting individual objectives for clients. To measure success rates, centers must document client progress by outlining specific objectives so that the "client knows what she needs to accomplish."[23] When "meaningfully stated behavioral objectives" are in place, the professionals can measure the overall success of treatment strategies within the center, and the client is given a clear message about the "terminal behavior or skills she will need to demonstrate success."[24] In the journals of social medicine, battered women are evaluated in terms of their "susceptibility to treatment."[25] Similarly, rape victims are judged in terms of their "readiness" to address their experience with trauma.[26] Giving battered women the attention and support they need requires assessment of their attitudes toward psychosocial support and their incentives to complete or default on a therapeutic program. The implementation of these approaches to measuring success and assessing receptivity to treatment has put shelters that fail to keep up to date in formulating their programmatic goals under scrutiny. When old-style feminist shelters profess only a general statement of purpose (such as providing space for women of need in the community and directing them to the survival resources they need outside the shelter home), professionals raise questions about how these shelters can be evaluated if they offer only unspecified expectations of the transformation of clients' psychological profiles. Moreover, evaluators complain that not only is it impossible to document success rates of these shelters but they may end up releasing women back into society without adequate tracking mechanisms.

The social work model of effective service delivery also requires both rape crisis centers and battered women's programs to establish themselves within a network of social service bureaucracies. A program is judged successful when it "take[s] the initiative to ally itself with an established and respected [social service agency]."[27] These connections are seen as part of the process of professionalizing the service personnel and eliminating the high reliance on volunteers or "paraprofessionals," who, although "cost effective," are "not a substitute for professional counseling."[28] In fact, social workers maintain that their expertise is indispensable to the feminist shelter movement. As a social work pioneer in the battered women's field claims, "Researchers came forth to validate the data gathered by the shelter movement."[29] The professionals also believe they have to offer the expertise and personnel needed to bring shelters to their full potential. From this perspective, concerns are often raised about whether shelters staffed by paraprofessionals can provide anything more than affective support.[30] One member of the social work academy offers the urgent prediction that in times of "shrinking government spending . . . unless established social service and traditional mental health agencies incorporate spouse abuse components into their programs, one can predict that the treatment of spouse abuse will disappear."[31]

The challenge is sometimes framed as a question about whether paraprofessional or volunteer staff possess the expertise required to treat other women with "extensive and severe trauma" and the argument is made that only a therapist can "help them achieve understanding of their past."[32] The case against the use of paraprofessionals has been presented in numerous social work studies. For example, in one case study a volunteer worker draws on personal examples of surviving violent relationships to comfort a shelter resident who had a series of emotional outbursts. The social worker commenting on this case contends that such reassurance from the volunteer was inappropriate given differences in individual levels of psychological health; according to the social worker this volunteer had "no knowledge of the basics of clinical intervention."[33] Another reason given for phasing out untrained volunteers is the growing use and success of "couples counseling" which presents an extremely delicate therapist/client relationship and requires a "skilled therapist . . . to facilitate the couple's homeostasis."[34]

Over time, this call for increased contact with professional rather than laypersons has been fueled by the incorporation of the science of "risk assessment" into the treatment of battered women. As the social service sector has developed, providers have been confronted with increased demands for service and the necessity to screen complex cases. As the primary proponent of this science explains: "The increased use of these systems has necessitated some sort of *triaging* of cases. . . . The systems are starting to articulate the need for validated tools to use to divide cases into those needing immediate services."[35] In this regard, shelters are urged to use these formalized assessment instruments not only to predict the level of dangerousness of the women's situation but also, given mandatory court policies, to help the legal system sort out the most serious cases.

These new practices are not entirely at odds with the original orientation of the shelter movement because they ultimately encourage women to become independent and return to jobs, relationships, and the community. Yet the growing professionalism of shelter practices renders the forms of collective self-help at the core of feminist shelter philosophy useless, if not harmful, to a woman's readjustment to a normal life. Since the current focus is on each individual woman gaining the capacities to get on with her own life, there is now little opportunity in shelter life to understand problems in a collective manner. The greatest risk of adopting these goals is that it diminishes the likelihood that shelters will be the focal point of systematic challenges to institutions (such as family courts and welfare agencies) that can actually make a battered woman's struggle for independence more difficult. Even though some veteran shelter workers are former victims, these women are overwhelmed with helping clients meet their immediate goals and have limited opportunities to use long-term experience dealing with courts and social services systems to advocate for large-scale change.

The netting and treatment of women into programs where professionals are mandated to promote high success rates can be dramatically contrasted with a less optimistic perspective on treatment programs for batterers. In many regards, the professional methodologies are similar. Programs are run by personnel with professional degrees, designed as short-term interventions, and rely on similar individual behavioral and conjoint therapy treatment modalities. Yet the most recent comprehensive evaluation of multiple studies of effectiveness rates of men's programs shows that the effect of treatment is very limited.[36] In addition, batterers have high dropout rates or often fail to comply with even court-mandated treatment. Since psychologically based programs rely on clients to participate voluntarily and to demonstrate willingness to change, the clients in men's programs are often unreceptive to treatment methodologies. This very low success rate and the inability to improve it using current methodologies discourages the development of programs designed for men. Treatment programs for rapists and other sex offenders follow from paradigmatic understandings of deviant behavior and criminality. Psychological studies of factors relating to motivations and recidivism focus on poor socialization, hostility toward women, and sexual pathologies.[37] Sex offenders are a highly heterogeneous treatment population, however, making it difficult for professionals to make reliable risk assessments or apply appropriate methodologies. As a result of these complexities, high recidivism, and the overall tendency to criminalize, men who batter or rape are not the primary target of public health initiatives.

diagnosis: seeing domestic violence

The role of physicians is similar in some ways to programs like rape crisis centers and shelters because physicians begin the process of "netting in" women for professional treatment. Once women are identified as victims of intimate partner violence, physicians make referrals to mental health services and battered women's shelters. The medical profession's growing interest in the problem of physical and psychological abuse against women is chronicled in the exchange of ideas about the importance of intimate violence in specialized medical journals. The authors of these articles usually offer advice about how and when knowledge about violence in the family is called for and expedient to the practice of medicine. There is an acute interest in the problems that sexual violence introduces to diagnosis and treatment, and these challenges are written about extensively; hundreds of articles have been published over the past twenty-five years.[38] Most articles are written from the perspective of social work and nursing and focus on improving service delivery to this specialized group of patients. Others are written from the vantage point of practice specialties, such as ophthalmology, dentistry, emergency medicine, pediatrics, epidemiology, and forensic medicine. This writing offers sometimes remarkable evidence about the bearing sexual violence has on diagnosis and medical practice in general.

One factor contributing to the developing recognition of sexual abuse by the medical profession is the increased number and status of women in the medical field, many of whom are publishing and speaking about their experiences treating battered women. Yet although these articles are written by women or men who represent a progressive wing of the profession, their rigid application of the medical model to this issue narrows their vision of the problem. Their efforts to call attention to sexual violence ultimately allows them to advance an understanding that subsumes complex and irrational life experiences into symptoms that can be addressed through a rational model of diagnosis and treatment. Medical professionals, for good reasons, portray battered women's problems as potentially treatable under current practice methodologies, but unfortunately this filters out a messy picture about these women's troubles and their connection to non-medical issues.[39]

In medical journals, authors use the case study method. This often involves reporting highly unusual cases and offering new insights and possibilities about diagnosis and treatment. This method is applied to illustrate the relevance of intimate violence and to convince physicians to pay attention to the physical signs of sexual abuse and woman battery and to consider these symptoms of vital importance in a complete patient history. This fact is often the crux of an argument for intervention that does not challenge the traditional confines of the doctor/patient relationship: accurate diagnosis and treatment plans cannot be made without knowledge of the underlying causes of illness or injury.

In one case study, a forty-one-year-old woman, divorced and living with a young son, was evaluated and questions arose about the relationship between a possible stroke, prior cocaine use, and domestic violence. The reporting doctor commented that "knowledge of domestic violence is important for rational diagnosis and treatment of the patient and may help explain the otherwise mysterious symptoms often reported in the doctor's office."[40] In the treatment of this patient, the emergency room physician had ruled out a variety of causes for the stroke and then became suspicious that an unreported traumatic event had produced an embolus in the brain. The doctor's hypothesis about abuse was confirmed when the patient's mother arrived in the hospital the next day and reportedly explained that several months earlier her daughter's ex-husband had attempted to strangle her. The author of the case study emphasizes not only the importance of obtaining the knowledge of the abuse history to make the proper diagnosis but also the high prevalence and morbidity rate of the "disease" of domestic violence. For effective intervention, therefore, it is argued that doctors must routinely ask patients specific questions about violence in the home and phrase them in a way that will encourage frank discussion. A careful examination of the doctor's language, however, reveals that the strategy of the case report is to refer to symptoms that could potentially remain "mysterious" and outside the domain of scientific medicine and to incorporate them into a rational process of culling information about patient history. For example, this doctor reports about a series of soft neurological signs observed in a patient that are difficult to add up to a diagnosis unless one or more incidences of physical abuse are also recorded. This case study assures physicians that attention to women's experiences of violence is part of good diagnostic procedure.

For similar reasons, the full impact of the violence may not be revealed without a complete account of the history of physical trauma. For example, a woman treated by a neuro-ophthalmologist has symptoms of a unilateral headache and ptosis (drooping upper eyelid).[41] Although she does not initially report trauma, she later reveals a pattern of physical abuse by a boyfriend, including an attempted strangulation before the onset of symptoms. The doctor diagnoses a likely carotid dissection (a brain injury) and suspects there is a relationship between the trauma and her medical condition. The case study concludes by emphasizing the need for appropriate suspicion about domestic violence to analyze such a case adequately.

etiology: battering as an illness

Another branch of medical literature about battered women attempts to show the correlations between injury types and partner abuse. Again, the precise purpose of these studies is to improve the technical assessment of the patient in diagnostic and treatment protocols. Unlike the case of trauma injury discussed above, in which battering becomes relevant to a proper diagnosis, in this literature, "battering" is recognized as a distinct illness. Both injury patterns and symptoms can be used to identify domestic violence as the underlying cause of a medical problem. The injury pattern is dramatically predictive: battered women are more likely to be injured in the head, neck, face, throat, chest, and abdomen.[42] A study of women's injuries as reported in emergency department records finds that women with injuries resulting from assault were thirteen times more likely than those with unintentional injuries to have injuries to the head.[43] Certain injuries have strong positive predictive values for woman battering. For example, if a woman arrives at an emergency room with a rupture of the tympanic membrane or a rectal/perineal injury, there is close to a 100 percent chance that the injuries occurred through domestic violence. There is almost as high a probability that facial abrasions and contusions in women are the result of battering.[44]

Another way physicians are urged to properly assess the evidence of domestic violence is to be alert to a pattern that indicates a "battering syndrome," marked by particular symptoms and/or multiple symptoms that are likely correlated with domestic violence. Besides acute physical trauma, domestic violence is associated with many physical and psychological sequelae including multiple somatic symptoms, chronic pain, gastrointestinal disorders, anxiety, depression and other psychological disorders.[45] For example, a history of childhood and adult sexual trauma is even significantly associated with "elevated dental fear."[46]

The strong correlation between certain types of injuries and partner abuse is shown in the treatment of orbital fractures. If a woman seeks medical assistance from an ophthalmologist for an orbital eye fracture there is a significant probability that she is a victim of domestic violence. One study found that orbital fracture was the result of sexual assault in one-third of the female patients presenting with this injury (the rest were the result of automobile accidents), but no male patients reported this cause. When physicians press for information about domestic violence, they are often able to get more accurate information about the nature of the trauma to the face. For example, the study finds that for orbital eye fractures, 86 percent were caused by a punch in the face and the others by bottles, beer cans, and other household items used as projectiles.[47]

The connection between a history of abuse and gastrointestinal disorders also shows an etiological link. A major study of the relation between previous abuse and gastrointestinal disorders found that 60 percent of patients had a history of abuse.[48] While there was no significant difference in abuse incidence between illnesses labeled as structural and functional, those women with functional disorders fared worst as to pain scores, daily functioning, and psychological distress.[49] The study concludes that diagnosis of the gastrointestinal illness alone is insufficient for clinical treatment because psychosocial contributions to these illnesses, including a history of abuse, must also be considered. These clinical studies hypothesize "psychophysiologic and psychodynamic effects" as factors in the illness, but they also suggest that the illness might be explained by enhanced visceral sensitivity: "prolonged visceral stimulation from injury or inflammation evokes the activity of previously unresponsive silent nociceptors that, along with other sensory afferents, amplify peripheral input to the central nervous system to produce persistent pain even after peripheral afferent activity decreases."[50] Hence, traumatic stimulation of the vagina and anus in childhood could lead to increased pain sensitivity in the abdominal and pelvic region later in life. This raises the possibility that abuse not only has general consequences that cause patients with gastrointestinal problems to fare worse but it may have specific disease-inducing effects. Again, a clear message is given to gastroenterologists that if they fail to investigate the history of past and present sexual abuse adequately they cannot provide an effective treatment response. This literature also prescribes that the doctors' vigilance should be increased if the patients "use health care frequently, have concurrent psychiatric disorders, or do not improve on standard therapy."[51]

Yet another study attempted to determine whether domestic violence is more frequent among patients with neurological disorders, hypothesizing that the social, psychological, and physical disabilities associated with these disorders are more vulnerable to domestic violence.[52] The study did not find this to be the case. In fact, a woman with a neurological disability may be at a lower risk for violence because her obvious physical impairment may be a deterrent for some perpetrators. But what the results did suggest is that domestic violence may be an important etiological factor for neurological disorder, such as structural brain disorders. Looking at this population carefully for the prevalence of domestic violence, however, ended up revealing that abuse is most often seen as a precipitating factor in neurological conditions (i.e., domestic violence is often the cause of the neurological deficient, rather than the neurological condition creating an opportunity for abuse).

Abuse and battering during pregnancy also leads to poorer pregnancy outcomes (i.e., fewer healthy babies).[53] Woman battering is characterized in this way as a health problem for the unborn: "abuse during pregnancy is a serious perinatal health problem that is receiving increased attention in both research and practice."[54] The prevalence of abuse perpetrated against pregnant women is often noted, and its causes are the subject of speculation. Abuse before pregnancy is a strong risk factor for abuse during pregnancy, and while pregnancy may be the occasion for a moratorium on abuse, it may also be a dynamic factor in precipitating the battering. Battered women present with behaviors and conditions that doctors find have a negative impact on fetal health, including smoking, extensive use of antidepressants and other prescription drugs, illegal substance abuse, epilepsy, asthma, and use of social work services.[55] Battered women have more frequent miscarriages and low-birth-weight babies than other women. More affluent battered women are likely to delay entry into prenatal care if they are experiencing physical violence in the home (while poor and younger women who fail to seek early prenatal care may be influenced by other factors).[56]

This information is presented in the medical literature for its value in improving accuracy in diagnosis and for improving public health services to targeted populations of potential battered women. These etiological studies provide shocking evidence about the seriousness of injuries that result from men battering women. Aside from their professional purposes, these studies show the regularity with which physicians are confronted with obvious signs of horrific brutality and the ways in which injury patterns tell vivid stories about women who are thrown, kicked, hit, sexually molested, and impaled with weapons.

More generally, the review of the medical literature shows that physicians are successful in establishing clear guidelines for their duty to intervene in cases of sexual violence, though possibly at the cost of ignoring these women's immense needs for health and safety. Because the primary responsibility of the professional is to provide a proper assessment of patients' medical condition, the *good* doctor needs to focus only on information that is relevant for the diagnosis. Yet the good doctor is defined narrowly as someone who can see beyond his or her image of the ideal patient (who would be a good reporter of her condition) and realize that getting at a correct diagnosis and treatment plan requires an objective reading of the symptoms.

Good doctoring, according to the current standards, also requires fitting domestic violence and its treatment squarely within the paradigm of disease.[57] This means that the reality of the violence, first, must be detected as symptoms. Once translated into the symptoms of the battering condition, the effects of domestic violence are no longer seen as some "mysterious" affliction eluding proper understanding by health care professionals but as valuable information about how physicians can effectively address this health problem and prevent its recurrence. Ironically, these medical journals provide evidence about patterns of injury which document a wide-scale, gender-specific form of assault on women's bodies, but such evidence is only relevant in the literature as a tool for the physician in the diagnosis and treatment of an illness. In fact, their inquiry into the origins of disease, because it often requires doctors to look closely at the history of violence experienced by the patient and the specificity of injury related to battering, may actually give physicians unusual insights about the effects of battering on women's bodies. For example, the unseen effects of violence are made noticeable in the newly developing diagnostic efforts of gastroenterologists who link trauma in certain regions of the body with long developing structural abnormalities and neurologists who find unrelated brain conditions arising after strangulation attempts (even when there are no longer marks on the body providing evidence of the attacks). But in this process of turning the marks of violence into symptoms of a disease, a comfortable distance is established between the good doctor, an advocate for his abused patient, and the realm of irrational intimate conflict which is the source of devastating injuries to women's bodies.

universal screening

In these case studies as in others, physicians speak their customary language of illness and cure. Domestic violence and sexual traumas are "diseases" that must be managed as a threat to public health. According to the physicians who are bringing this illness to the attention of the profession, the incidence of sexual violence has reached epidemic proportions; they argue that the endemic nature of the problem requires a response similar to the methods and approaches of managing other health-related epidemics. Public health statistics are cited to document the enormity of the problem: one in six couples have experienced one or more episodes of partner violence in the previous year and victim-related costs are estimated at $67 million a year.[58] The assistant director for the United States Public Health Service describes the problem in terms of crisis management: "Public health methods of study and data collection are being applied to the problems of violence similar to those we apply to other epidemics. And we are developing an extensive body of knowledge—both on the causes of violent behavior and the risk factors for victimization."[59]

As discussed earlier, battered women's shelters and emergency rooms are seen as crucial sites for the identification and tracking of new clients. In official government documents that assess the problem of violence against women, the ongoing collection of information about women is termed "public health surveillance."[60] The collection of epidemiological data about domestic violence invites a strategy for controlling the disease and consequently puts medical professionals in the role of surveilling *all* women as potential victims. The regulation of domestic violence as a disease requires professionals to know more about its incidence rates and to keep informed about its prevalence. This need to monitor all clients is backed by statistical evidence of high rates.[61] Evidence also shows that when women (as opposed to men) experience partner violence they are more likely to sustain injuries that require medical attention.[62] There are clear demographic patterns (which dispute the feminist position that domestic violence can happen to any woman): the highest domestic violence rates occur in highly concentrated urban areas with low-income populations.[63] The rate of violence against women increases during and after pregnancy,[64] and black and Hispanic pregnant women have an even higher risk factor.[65] Perpetrators are not more likely than other men to suffer from personality disorders, mental illness, or frontal lobe deficits.[66] Women are more likely to be abused as adults if they experienced childhood sexual or physical abuse.[67] And, as with rape incidents, there is seasonal variation in domestic violence, with increased prevalence during the hottest summer months.[68] Similar demographic patterns are noticed in rape-prevalence studies. For example, a recent study demonstrates the Hmong girls suffer a high probability of severe rape (committed by extrafamilial perpetrators).[69] While these studies provide valuable information about the nature and extent of domestic violence in American society, they also provide a framework from which physicians are encouraged to evaluate their women patients as potential victims and to characterize certain life choices, race and ethnicity, and other medical conditions as risk factors for domestic violence.[70]

In response to this epidemic and the epidemiological data, which pinpoint a variety of obvious and nonobvious risk factors, doctors now advocate universal screening of female patients for domestic violence and rape in all settings of primary contact between doctor and female patients, including office visits with primary care physicians, emergency room visits for trauma and other reasons, and in practice specialties in which certain conditions correlate with intimate abuse. While the obvious intention of those who advocate screening is to address both physicians' denial of abuse (when confronted with actually obvious signs) and to alert others to more subtle clues, these procedures may in fact further distance the physician from the patient's experience of violence, allowing for a perfunctory inventory of risk factors.

This distancing is seen in the physician's use of screening tools. One physician has developed a protocol he calls WAST (Woman Abuse Screening Tool) and its companion scale "Abuse Risk Inventory."[71] The WAST survey consists of eight questions with multiple-choice answers and has been shown to be statistically reliable and valid (i.e., it could effectively discriminate between abused and nonabused women in the experimental sample). These devices, which may contribute to more impersonal interactions, are offered as a way for physicians to overcome their reluctance to raise an uncomfortable topic of discussion. Another function of the tools is to help doctors refrain from making any comments that impart a negative attitude toward battered women. Physicians are counseled, likewise, to examine their own prejudices about battered women and to avoid insensitive remarks (for example, "What keeps you with a person like that?" or, "What could you have done to prevent the violence?").[72] These devices, therefore, enable doctors to maintain and project the same neutral stance with these patients as they would with any other patient suffering from an illness. This neutrality has mixed consequences. Optimistically, it prevents unsympathetic doctors from treating women in a judgmental fashion, but it also places possibly unrealistic expectations on doctors to fully appreciate the complexity of the problem and the extent of the women's needs.

For this reason, advocates also make the case that physicians need to take responsibility for the primary care of battered women beyond treating the injuries, to arrange for close follow-up and appropriate referrals. To the extent that these patients require special care, primary care physicians are advised to use additional protocols, such as one with the acronym RADAR (Remember to ask, Ask directly, Document medical findings, and Review options).[73] Similar protocols exist for treating rape victims that require physicians not only to complete a rape kit but to follow up with venereal disease and pregnancy counseling. This case for special responsibility for the needs of battered women and rape victims rests upon well-established principles about the role of physicians not only to diagnose and treat illness but also to prevent it. Moreover, numerous reports refer to the problem of repetition of the injury and describe domestic violence as leading to a unique condition of injury recidivism. This factor broadens the duty of care: "if physicians fail to acknowledge this violent mode of injury they unintentionally may be perpetuating the abuse and recurrence of harm to the victim."[74]

As physicians' screening efforts have developed, interest in identifying cases has extended to treating children and the unborn children of battered women. The call is given to pediatric emergency room physicians to identify battering in their patients' mothers, which then signals the need to intervene to help the "secondary victims of domestic violence."[75] Studies have suggested that identifying battered mothers may be the single most important avenue for identifying child abuse. It is primarily seen as another screening device, because mothers may not seek medical attention for themselves but will bring their children to the doctor. But it is also an effort to protect children as the primary patient. The argument is made that "30% to 59% of mothers of children reported for child abuse also are battered. In homes where domestic violence occurs, the children are at increased risk of physical abuse or neglect."[76] Children who witness battering of their mothers are "at risk for psychosocial sequelae including developmental delays and posttraumatic stress disorder."[77] Obviously, using battered mothers as a screening device for child abuse raises questions about the control exercised by the medical profession over women's lives.[78] Since doctors are mandatory reporters of child abuse, technically any admission of violence in the home puts the woman at risk of scrutiny by state agencies.

Fulfilling this responsibility of care, therefore, may require physicians to take an unusual interest in this violence, but physician advocates for battered women argue that it is indeed appropriate for the physician to take this interest as part of proper treatment. This interest in violence evokes uncertainty about appropriate boundaries between doctor and patient, leading advocates to call for raising the standards of care for battered women to reassure physicians that asking questions about the causes of injury is simply part of routine medical practices. For example, the literature appeals to the functional role of doctors in investigating the cause of an illness, stressing that effective treatment requires them to reach out to discuss issues that are sensitive and personal for both doctor and patient. A doctor states outright: "It is appropriate for an ophthalmologist to assist their patients [in finding support for domestic violence] . . . by offering to refer them to help agencies."[79] Another doctor states, "It is also important not only to treat ocular injuries, but to investigate the real source of their health problems—abusive domestic situations."[80]

Improvements in physicians' ability to recognize battering as a cause of illness and diagnose it as a disease are considered an inevitable consequence of the ordinary course of pursuing good investigative practices. The appeals to increased physician awareness are couched so as to alleviate professionals' nervousness about overinvolvement in the personal aspects of their patient's lives. But this does not come without a hyperarticulation of the rationality of looking at violence. The shift toward greater awareness of women battering, with concomitant heightened responsibility of physicians, is supported precisely because it promotes a reinforcement of careful methods of diagnosis and treatment, and implicitly because professionals may actually increase the risk of women's exposure to violence if they fail to contain the rampant spread of this disease.

These arguments for more medical intervention are clearly driven by forward-thinking professionals who believe that physicians can no longer be blind to the prevalence of domestic violence. However, the incorporation of domestic violence into the domain of medical problems funnels attention and resources onto treatable victims rather than encouraging the investments of public health resources elsewhere. These developments further entrench women in systems that manage their needs.

the treatment narrative

The new social work methodology relies on a certain definition of the battered woman's problem: that a woman's situation is derivative of her psychological incapacities that caused the crisis in the first place, specifically, the woman's inability to make choices that would end her physical abuse. Hence, women need to be trained to make better choices. The therapeutic model is applied to move women beyond these psychological barriers to good decision making and to allow them to participate in a normal, nonviolent family.

Social work practitioners stress the importance of treating battered women as members of violent families.[81] During the early years of therapeutic intervention, the favored treatment strategies emphasized the reintegration of family units and fell within the so-called family therapy modality.[82] According to this professional logic it simply makes good economic sense to treat everyone at once and to bring the rest of the family into the social service network.[83]

The couple or conjoint therapy model is based on the therapeutic assumption that marriages are managed in equilibrium. Violence is the result of disruptions in that equilibrium, which occur when one individual (presumably the wife) moves to what professionals call a higher differentiation of self. This theory holds that it is primarily the wife who introduces stresses on the relationship, through the imposition of children and childcare responsibilities or by her demands for employment and recognition outside the family. The husband, in response to the introduction of these new stresses, is sometimes unable to communicate his frustrations or possible counterclaims on family resources. Some men, presumably because they function and communicate intellectually at levels best suited for the economic world outside the family, are often functionally incapable of emotionally expressing their grievances, and thus violence becomes the outlet for their frustrations.[84]

In the conjoint therapy model, acts of physical violence are recast as communication disorders. The scientific project that verifies and refines this model is called the "comprehensive assessment of the psychological adjustment of wife abusers and their spouses."[85] These studies attempt to establish the causal connections between violent marriages and social skills or impaired communication styles. The results indicate that abusive males have "more speech disturbances . . . and used less praise/appreciation [references] than satisfactorily married husbands."[86] The data on abused women, in contrast, indicate strong similarities between the relationship skills of "abused wives and their nonabused counterparts."[87] Rather than concluding that these results tell us something about the aberrations of violent men, the interpreters of this research emphasize the need to understand marital relationships as "interdependent . . . on multiple factors" that "influence commission of these violent acts."[88]

The therapist may use the dysfunctional communication strategies that already exist within the family to coercively create compliance with the conjoint strategy. Social workers justify imposing conjoint therapy because of its advantages for legitimating therapeutic intervention; couples therapy promotes trust in the therapist for both partners by ensuring there are "no secrets" (from a "third party" husband).[89] Moreover, social workers suggest that the frequency with which battered women return to live with their spouses and the dangers encountered by wives returning to the family make couple's therapy the more realistic option.

In a model case study written by one advocate of couples therapy, the abused wife was advised over the phone during her initial contact with the social worker to convince her husband to come to therapy.[90] When the woman suggested that she would have difficulty persuading her husband to speak with a therapist, she was told to "find a way to get him in." After further resistance to the social worker's insistence to get her husband to commit to therapy, she was told simply to look at her options, one of which was to "come in alone but the violence wouldn't stop." The social worker justified the imposition of responsibility on the wife by linking this choice (to come into therapy with or without her partner) to her wish to stay married. Yet the exchange is possibly more revealing about how the social worker's conjoint therapy methodology is dependent on the image of the woman as the instigator of marital disequilibrium. The therapist needs to maintain her alliance with the woman and her commitment to the goal of promoting a nonviolent family. But this rests on her ability to convince the battered woman that her best interests are served by the conjoint model both inside and outside the therapist's office.

In literature that studies the intrapersonal correlates of domestic violence, the language of therapy reconstructs the feminine personality. As previously stated, the new professional discourse of social work positions itself against the masochist hypothesis of self-blame. Though the new professional discourse of social work rejects this victim-blaming perspective, the social scientific research that defines intrapersonal correlates ends up reinforcing the image of women as pathological in a gender-neutral fashion.[91] One author maintains: "Although investigations still rely on pathological indexes, women's symptoms are viewed as sequelae of abuse, rather than concomitants or precursors of abuse. These studies indicate, for example, that women who have been battered tend to suffer from depression, anxiety, alcohol abuse, and have elevated MMPI profiles."[92] In this professional's mind the "sequelae of abuse" approach allows these qualities to be viewed analytically and abstractly. The desirability of new language rests on two assumptions: first, that these qualities are not gender specific, and that victims of extreme violence would manifest these pathologies whatever their gender. Second, assigning these attributes to women is not stigmatic when the professional appropriately employs these profiles for the purposes of predicting, diagnosing, and treating domestic violence. Modern professionals understand that these psychological manifestations of sexual abuse are not symptoms of inherently weak personality structures but are often survival mechanisms for the victim. However, their treatment approaches presume that these pathologies take hold because these women maintain unrealistic fears and overvalue male power. Any effort to reconcile these contradictory views involves affirming the therapist's view of reasonable responses to violence and disengaging from a woman's perspective on social reality.

Moreover, when these psychological theories are applied in clinical settings, the social worker's understanding that every woman's situation is different is likely to mean only that there are differences in relationship skills and levels of emotional stability.[93] The social worker's language has a universalizing quality, in which women are taken out of their gender, class, and racial situation and their problems are discussed as if all persons are equally vulnerable.

The myth of the masochistic woman is generated anew in its genderless formation. The language of therapy reconstructs women so that a "de-gendered" submissiveness is part of a complex of psychological attributes. For example, the psychological disorder of "parentification" has replaced outward sexist claims that women are too dependent on their role as mothers.[94] Parentification is a condition of battered women that results from their overinvolvement with the needs of others, to such an extent that they disregard their own needs. In this psychological theory the battered woman's dysfunctions arise from her own exaggerated sense of obligations to others, in particular the needs of her children or husband, and paralyze her from taking action that may not conform to her notion of "doing the right thing." This potentially sensitive account of why women remain in abusive relationships has the drawback of projecting society's undervaluation of motherhood as the psychological problem of individual women.[95] The conditions that create women's vulnerability to men's power are reduced to psychosomatic reactions. The concept of parentification is incompatible with the early shelter movement's belief that the battered woman's "status as a mother provides the starting point for building a new identity."[96] This label has potentially negative consequences if social workers' evaluations end up being used as legal evidence about the woman's ability to care for or protect her child from her spouse's abuse. Assigning the new terminology to individual women can potentially become a mechanism to take children away from battered women.

Some social workers favor interpersonal pathologies as explanatory variables for domestic violence. These researchers pose the questions of which family types are potentially at risk for wife abuse. They find that the types at risk include couples with rigid sex role attitudes; pairings of traditional husbands with nontraditional wives; relationships in which the male partner has an undifferentiated personality and lower masculinity; and families with a history of acceptance of violence or where there is low self-esteem in either partner.[97] This risk analysis is applied in the development of treatment and prediction models in a way that reaffirms the rigidity of sexual roles. For example, this theory has been employed to warn against therapists suggesting patriarchal explanations of family violence to their clients, because if such suggestion instigates a push for greater equality within the family, it may, in the short run, exacerbate tension and promote more family violence.[98]

Yet another facet of the interpersonal pathologies approach is that it views women as a threat to men's position within intimate relationships. For example, a woman's hyperdevelopment of verbal skills is seen as the precipitating factor in marital disequilibrium. According to this theory, men's aggression is a response to their wives' verbal abuse; however, this hostility is driven by the gender imbalance in verbal skills (women have higher verbal IQ scores than men).[99] Theories that emphasize the importance of the more advanced verbal skills of women also put the responsibility on women to change the relationship dynamics because they are more emotionally skilled: these studies show the female psyche is more differentiated and capable of transformation than the male psychological configuration.[100] (The author of one study even asserts that the women are often the more attractive party and thus can easily reenter nonviolent marital relationships.) Moreover, social programs designed to improve battered wives' relationships and problem-solving skills are suggested as "more cost efficient than secondary interventions (that focus on the batterer)."[101]

Consequently, the assumption of the malleability of "gendered relationship attributes" allows the social worker to suggest that women should take advantage of normal feminine coping mechanisms to readjust the dynamics of the violent home. The social worker's strategy to maintain family equilibrium is based upon a false and contradictory construction of the woman who employs her feminine self to cope within the constraints of rigid sex roles in a marriage while she is therapeutically managed as a gender-neutral person who fulfills the male expectations of normal family life. In the therapeutic rendering of the healthy female personality, therefore, the successful woman plays it both ways, by conforming to the gender-neutral expectations about good partnerships in healthy families while fulfilling her gender specific role as a caretaker of a man and children.

Both theory and practice create well-defined boundaries between good professional practice and engagement with the reality and threat of violence. The social work paradigm espouses a view in which professional distance is commensurate with "doing good" for the client. These practices justify state intervention in women's lives but limit the professional's ability to fully address the needs of battered women. The professional literature provides advice about how to deal with the overwhelming impulse to become overinvolved in helping clients deal with traumatic situations. For example, one study observed that social workers are often pulled between the poles of taking on strategies of compassion or control. The impulse for a compassionate approach is considered problematic because the professional's excessive identification with the plight of clients may lull him or her into the impression that forming an emotional bond is actually helping the client.[102] Although the model of compassion counteracts the indifference of the old social work approach, this literature promotes the more "effective" control models which recommend "aggressive use of intervention to limit, and if necessary, to punish domestic violence."[103] The preference for control strategies legitimizes the trend for social workers to mediate their powers through state agencies—placing the protection of the battered woman within a complex system of government bureaucracies rather than defending their client against the state's neglect and indifference.[104] The social work bureaucracy assumes a regulatory role over the social welfare apparatus, including the police, schools, and child protective services. This function, in turn, solidifies the power of the social work profession and establishes its crucial position in the training of police officers and other professionals who deal with abused women.[105]

The proximity of violence is most evident to professionals when they confront the risks they themselves run by placing themselves in contact with clients and their batterers. The therapist, for example, may consider this risk as manageable within the norms of professional practice. According to one mental health provider, "The danger that the professional faces for her/himself parallels that of the battered woman; they both have equally little control over the batterer's violence. The professional has the opportunity to make use of a full range of options to maximize her/his safety, thus providing a positive model for the battered women."[106] But this statement only trivializes the battered woman's experience of violence by comparing it to professionals' exposure to risk. It also has a self-congratulatory tone and makes an exaggerated claim about the professional's ability to choose better options. Professional training, even when it has involved responding to other emergencies, may not necessarily prepare one for handling situations of domestic violence. Although some physicians, for example, are reluctant to intervene on the behalf of patients experiencing domestic violence out of concern for their own personal safety or that of their office staff, others are sure that potentially volatile situations, like the arrival of an angry batterer in their office, can be avoided if they adhere to strict patient confidentiality.

The language of professionals also serves as a barrier to their envisioning the reality of violence. Social scientific methodology creates indicators that stifle the potential for reimagining violence. In part this is accomplished by research that classifies family violence by using scales and precise definitions of battering. Social scientists employ narrowly constructed definitions of battered women that rule out insignificant physical acts of aggression, emotional abuse, and quasi-legitimate forms of physical discipline. In definitions of family violence, the abuse is not seen as expressive of irrationality; it is the symptom of a dysfunction in the equilibrium of the family and a cause of physical injury.

In rigorous social science research on battered women the construction of the reality of family life may be presented in ways that do not reflect the vagaries of human interactions:[107] the dynamics of family life can even be studied by a computer program, SIMFAM, which simulates a crisis between real persons. And in social science models the definition of domestic violence is limited to "an act carried out with the intention, or perceived intention of causing physical pain or injury to another person."[108] This definition is designed to include only violence that has a high potential for causing an injury. It facilitates quantified measurement of harm imposed on others yet avoids the unquantifiable qualities of violence that permeate the relationships under study. By studying the correlates of violence, the researcher may create a cause-and-effect scenario that bears no relevance to how violence expresses anger, pain, and desires to control. For example, research that attempts to account for the high prevalence of spouse beating during pregnancy has suggested that the violence was occasioned by a woman's propensity to irritability during pregnancy and that in some cases it was abuse directed at the unborn child. Thus violence against battered women is essentially prenatal child abuse and may serve as a predictor of future abuse of children in these families. This account dismisses the expressive reality of men's complex emotions of hate and jealousy toward pregnant women; the significance of the violence against pregnant women is reduced to its use as a predictor of further violence. The scientific language thus fulfills a self-contained system of meaning, in which the value of measuring violence is measured by its value to predict more violence. Recent studies challenge what is called the "asymmetry assumption," that violence in domestic relationships is more likely perpetrated by males than females. These studies show that women are as likely, or even more likely, than men to engage in violence in relationships.[109]

forensic evidence

When cases involving violence against women enter the courts, the powers of therapeutic and legal discourses are linked in the endeavor to produce evidence. This often has the effect of solidifying an expert definition of the problem but discouraging commonsense perspectives. For example, the introduction of Battered Women's Syndrome to criminal defense strategies has created a public forum for professional knowledge about abused women. These trials create spectacles that reinforce the dominant stereotypes of victimized women. In the courtroom, the applicability of battered women's syndrome is solely dependent on expert opinion because, as a medical diagnosis, it is "beyond the ken of the average laymen."[110] In this way, expert testimony is given authority as knowledge "generally accepted in the psychological community," in place of commonsense wisdom.[111] But the claims of psychological experts often conflict with a battered woman's own defense of her actions. In some cases, experts may even suggest that a battered woman's self-understanding is actually evidence of pathology associated with the syndrome. For example, a woman who sees herself as coping well may be characterized by an expert as suffering from what social workers call "minimization."

Although these psychological tools are sometimes useful in obtaining a restraining order against a batterer, the notion of a battered women's syndrome has primarily been useful to defense attorneys in trials of women accused of murdering a violent partner. The recognition of the syndrome has fueled public attention to the unusual cases of women killing violent spouses.[112] Consequently, the reliance on expert testimony ends up furthering the assumption that abused women are fearful, desperate, and driven to murder. The use of the syndrome defense is sometimes a strategically advantageous choice made by defense attorneys, but it is employed at the cost of creating a special category of insanity for battered women. In fact, the indicators of battered women's syndrome on the prevailing tool, the DSM (*Diagnostic and Statistical Manual of Mental Disorders*) diagnostic criteria for post–traumatic stress disorders,[113] are the same as the symptoms of schizophrenia and borderline personality disorders.[114]

A parallel phenomenon has occurred in relation to rape victims' experience of trauma. A highly medicalized view of trauma has influenced both treatment methodologies and the interpretation of victims' stories in prosecutors' offices and at trial. Trauma theory has been successfully used to explain and account for women's behavior in the aftermath of rape, including self-blame and delay in reporting the crime and seeking medical attention. When new practitioners are trained, they are told to evaluate victims according to rape trauma syndrome because it "allows for professionals in the field, as well as the legal system to have a baseline of normal behaviors, as well as some not so normal behaviors that rape survivors experience."[115] Yet as practitioners have applied this theory, those most sensitive to women's experience have realized that "the trauma response paradigm and the diagnostic classification of posttraumatic stress disorder (PTSD), when used as a lens for viewing sexual violence, may restrict our understanding of survivors' experiences."[116] The model creates a fundamental assumption that a rape or sexual battery is an isolated traumatic event that provokes shattering feelings of fear and horror. This assumption may not apply for a variety of reasons that relate to the social context of the events, including the pervasiveness of other sources of harm, prior acceptance of a life of victimization, and specific ethno-cultural coping mechanisms. When women fail to conform to the expectation that they will experience sexual violence as trauma, their reactions are often seen as either especially dysfunctional or evidence that they were not sexually violated.

The importance of gathering forensic evidence has an extremely powerful effect on the treatment of rape victims by first medical responders. In most cases, rape kit exams are performed by emergency room doctors and nurses, although a growing number of emergency room practitioners are being specially trained to collect evidence from rape victims. The Department of Justice has funded hundreds of SANE programs (Sexual Assault Nurse Examiner) around the country that are often the core component of a coordinated community response. SANE programs are designed to meet two goals—to reduce the psychological trauma of the medical examination and to improve the collection of forensic evidence. These programs are proposed as a major improvement in victim services largely because they place trained staff in emergency rooms who make sexual assault victims their priority and who are proficient at evidentiary exams and collection procedures.[117] The SANE program, however, should be distinguished from victim advocacy.[118] Rather, SANE practitioners provide a medical-legal response; their role as caretaker commences after emergency room personnel (doctors and nurses) have stabilized the patient or determined medical care is not required. Their work is closely allied with law enforcement personnel, so they often collaborate with victim advocates, but they see themselves as interacting with "victims and their families in an objective and neutral manner that promotes informed decisions regarding evidence collection and available treatment options."[119]

These practitioners set the stage for increased professionalism in the treatment of victims in emergency rooms and provide administrative improvements to the recurrent problem of revictimization by professionals: they are skilled but compassionate collectors of evidence who provide the new standard of rape victims' care. Through coordinated efforts with other "service providers" including victim advocates, SANE initiatives are designed to standardize procedures, improve surveillance, and redefine victim-focused interventions. Although studies see progress in the treatment of victims and a dramatic improvement in the reliability of evidence, these programs further remove advocacy and instantiate the pretext of neutral practitioner working in the service of law enforcement objectives. More critically, these programs elevate the role of evidence collection in service delivery, in fact, making sure that it is the primary objective and outcome of victim response. For example, the collection of evidence is dictated by the instructions in commercially made kits that are provided by law enforcement officials to emergency room doctors and nurses (who may be unfamiliar with how to best collect the evidence). Completing this exam may require standardized procedures, such as plucking pubic hairs from victims (for the analysis of the live roots), regardless of their relevance to the case (for example in acquaintance rape, where the identity of the perpetrator is not in question) and despite the questionable value of this evidence for building a case.[120] These protocols set up guidelines for the gathering of evidence but then fail to ensure that the victim is cared for in regard to emergency contraception and sexually transmitted diseases. Even though the risk of pregnancy after sexual assault is significant (4.7 percent), the national protocol does not provide an option of immediate treatment for pregnancy prevention (as directed by national policy).[121] Screening for sexually transmitted diseases is not routinely performed because "a positive test can and has been used against victims in court cases."[122]

As described in chapter 2, with the modern recognition of sexual assault, a new forensic science developed which was devoted to examining the marks of violence on children's and women's bodies. This led to techniques designed to improve viewing the inside of women's bodies and to their routine application in sexual assault examinations. Over time, these techniques have improved, but the photocolposcopy examination used to document visual evidence of physical trauma to the genitals is still clinical protocol. Despite the routine use of this exam, studies show a paradoxical effect of focusing on this kind of physical evidence. They find that evidence of genital injury is quite rare, especially in the absence of physical injury to other parts of the body.[123] The rate of prosecution and conviction increases, however, when genital injuries are documented by these examinations.[124] Studies that attempt to determine the correlates of genital injury find that physical injury is by far the most significant predictor, but skin color and time elapsed between the assault and the examination are also factors.[125] The studies that specifically look at the evidence collected from adolescent victims find that sexual assault does not routinely allow for the documentation of hymenal tears even in the examination of virgins.[126] This lack of physical evidence is further compounded by the prevalence of rape by family members among adolescent girls and the increased likelihood of delays in reporting.

The routine production of this kind of evidence based on the visualization of genital injury creates expectations about the power of medical-legal knowledge and the verifiability of rape. In fact, the authors of these studies acknowledge that commonplace assumptions about "real" rape victims having medically documented injuries is not warranted by the statistical data on the likelihood that these injuries will be detectable by the best technological means available. False expectations about the ability of medical-legal procedures to verify rape on women's bodies may be counterproductive to the overall goal of dismantling mythologies about the unreliability of rape victims. As one study aptly concludes: "Although scientific conclusions drawn from forensic technologies such as the [rape kit] . . . are largely accepted as objective, technical measures of the 'truth' of a sexual assault, the kit may carry a legitimacy and a symbolic value that exceeds the capabilities of science to objectively determine the 'facts' of a case."[127]

conclusion

Professionals inescapably confront violence when they take on the social problem of rape and domestic abuse, and encountering this violence is the raison d'etre of their endeavors.[128] While professionals frequently acknowledge the precariousness of their involvement with abused women, the language of experts decidedly supports a disengaged stance toward the victim and her injuries. This remoteness may cause professionals who consider themselves sensitive to these issues to have limited awareness about the depth and intensity of clients' difficulties in coping with their experiences and their reactions to the system designed to help them. For example, one study of client/ professional perceptions demonstrated that despite better training and improved sensibilities toward clients, professionals did not recognize the impact they had on women and the high level of stress women experienced as a result of system contact.[129] Moreover, the ascribed role of professionals, especially their gender-neutral orientation, often prevents them from appreciating the full significance of the violence in the context of women's lives.

These professional practices are indicative of a victim-centered public health approach. This is due in part to the abandonment of the rehabilitation model, so that the primary means of risk reduction is channeling offenders into the prison system. Yet risk is also managed from a public health perspective by placing responsibility on women to either become experts themselves in prevention strategies or, if already victimized, to recognize the necessity for professional help. This is promoted through the surveillance practices of professionals as well as familiar public education campaigns about domestic violence and rape that are directed toward all women as potential victims (rather than all men as potential abusers).

In this context, ordinary understandings of women's problems are displaced by expert discourse on victims and therapeutic definitions of women's needs. This does not occur without some dissent within the feminist community. Some feminists on the frontline acknowledge the costs of professionalization but see a tradeoff in better funding for programs and their ability to provide their clients with a broader range of services.[130] Dedicated feminist social workers have vehemently supported feminist counseling, such as rape crisis intervention that involves long-term group work that explicitly addresses the effects of patriarchy. Even these projects, however, are constrained by requirements to demonstrate that programs show "measurable and observable goals that are achievable."[131] Although feminist programs still exist and thrive in some communities, it is important to recognize that most women who experience violence and seek help will receive it from mainstream service providers who have adopted these new professionalized practices. In fact, the explicit goal of public health officials is to apply these practices expansively and universally in most clinical settings. This has enormous consequences for the vast range of clients who have contact with social and medical services—they are routinely subject not only to the authority of experts but to compulsory reporting to public health officials, unwanted lab tests, and mandatory child abuse reporting. Now with enormous predictability, women's experiences with violence quickly result in their introduction into a maze of patron/client relationships. Under systems of expanded surveillance, when women seek any kind of professional help they can be identified and treated as victims even without seeking out a specialized program or initiating legal action against a perpetrator. As the next chapter will show, this phenomenon often puts women in debilitating situations as clients of the social welfare system.

5

VICTIM INSURGENCY

the state as a dangerous stranger

I told her, "How dare you!" I says, "You know, I come [to this shelter] and, you're supposed to be here helping me. And you're making me feel worse than my husband. Cause you're a stranger, you know."—Donna (pseudonym for a woman in a housing program for battered women)

Thus far, this book has explored how the campaign against sexual violence has evolved under the conditions of neoliberalism and how it has led to an expansion in crime control strategies and a feminized terrain of victim services. One effect of both of these changes has been to authorize legal, medical, and therapeutic interpretations of victims' experiences and needs. Despite feminist-inspired reforms, many of which were explicitly designed to empower "victims" to exercise more "choice" or protect against retraumatization, the voices and desires of women are often muted by the more dominant discourse of the state. By drawing from victims' testimony in the Central Park and New Bedford trials and interviews with women in shelters, this chapter shows how women experience their interactions with the state and strive to surmount their socially constructed roles as "victims."

Rape victims and battered women who seek help inevitably become "dependent subjects" of the state. Their status is similar to, or in conjunction with, other categories of dependency, such as welfare mother, juvenile delinquent, unwed mother, substance abuser, and the homeless. These dependencies are the primary means by which the modern welfare state asserts its authority over potentially unruly women. Moreover, these women often have no choice but to be dependent on the state to escape the violence encountered in their private lives. In efforts to redress violation or as refugees from domestic violence, these "victims" enter into a perilous involvement with the penal/welfare state. Thrust into new relationships within the public sphere, women often find that they experience brutalities that mimic the violence they hoped to leave behind.

When women turn to the state for welfare, social services, support and/or redress, they encounter the dilemma of avoiding either the "Scylla of private patriarchy" or the "Charybdis of public patriarchy."[1] In both the public and private spheres, forging autonomy and equality requires "dependent subjects" to go up against the masculine norms of the family and state. These women are always at risk of trading one form of dependency for another; by seeking protection outside the family they are risking the imposition of new forms of control by a multiplicity of laws and agents of the state.

The state exercises this power by creating the structural conditions in which women are dependent or require protection for both their material and psychological needs. Yet the language justifying this protection often masks the state's role in creating this category of dependent subjects. The feminist theorists Nancy Fraser and Linda Gordon analyze the semantics of dependency from a historical perspective and show how the concept has been transformed to signal a negative feminine pathology. Dependency has been psychologized in the latter half of the twentieth century; in particular, it has been employed to suggest immaturity among single women on welfare. Dependency has also been racially marked, in that, historically, white women have been portrayed as excessively dependent, whereas black women have typically been charged with excessive independence. More recently, the image of the black welfare mother has been increasingly pathologized; black women who were once seen as unruly yet powerful matriarchs of the family are now portrayed as passive unmarried teenage mothers perpetually on welfare. Gordon and Fraser conclude that the semantics of dependency elides the social/economic developments that reinforce domination: "with economic dependency now a synonym for poverty, and with moral/psychological dependency now a personality disorder, talk of dependency as a social relation of subordination has become increasingly rare."[2] The rhetorical attribution of dependency masks the structural conditions which produce unequal power arrangements and perpetuate gender domination.

This chapter examines how dependencies on the state function in the context of women's lives and explores how women, in their everyday practices, reinvent their relationships with authorities. Activists, and women themselves, recognize how experiences of sexual violence lead to dependent relationships with the state, and likewise they recognize the necessity of resisting. Yet such resistance must be forged in the context of disrupted lives. These encounters with more powerful state actors occur in the context of personal disorganization and the breakdown of intimate relationships. Women are often hindered in these efforts because they do not fit the ideal model of worker, caregiver, or dependent. And these women may not possess the kind of social or personal capital that would allow them to take full advantage of greater fairness or gender equity in social policy. This means that women do not necessarily benefit from policies that would "even the playing field." In fact, greater formal equality may even aggravate the condition of those whose situations may prevent them from functioning well in both the private and the public sphere. This is why well-meaning social policy or reforms often fail and even worsen dependencies. More realistic solutions must begin with the recognition of how violence and other aspects of women's situations have created a complex web of social disadvantage.

the victim's trial

In the rare situation that a rape case comes to trial, victims usually must testify for the prosecution as "witnesses" of their own attack. Despite formal legal restrictions adopted in most jurisdictions in the United States designed to protect rape victims on the stand, these women are still "put on trial." This is of course to some degree unavoidable given the rights of defendants to raise questions about the credibility of any form of evidence that leads to their incrimination, including the reports of the victim. The legal narrative in the high-profile rape trial is driven by the prosecutors' theory of the crime and by the fact that prosecutors have incentives to characterize violent episodes as driven by the sexual brutality of dangerous persons. This at the very minimum requires victims to cooperate with the prosecution and to strive to describe the rape in ways which conform to the prosecutor's narrative about the attack. Yet more complicated situations often arise for victims because either their own reactions may lead to inconsistent retelling of what happened to them or, more critically, they are resistant to theories of the crime, which may in effect make them invisible.

In the Central Park Jogger trial, the role played by the victim was typical in many respects: her status as a victim was based on assumptions about her innocence and denials of pleasure. But her victim status was distinctive given her lost memory of all events during the evening of her attack. This, ironically, turned her into an unassailable woman because her amnesia made it impossible to accuse her of lying about her willful participation in the sexual act—while for those who saw the trial as an affront to the racial and ethnic communities in New York City, her amnesia made the victim's story suspect and allowed critics to claim she was an example of a white woman crying rape and then hiding behind the contrivances of patriarchy.

In the trial, samples of the victim's blood, taken from all parts of the terrain of the attack—rocks, leaves, twigs, soil, clothes, and pavement—were on display. This mixing of blood and landscape was reproduced in the courtroom by photographs and physical specimens (held in the prosecutor's latex-gloved hands) as a visual reenactment of how the body was moved across the scene. Yet her blood was never found on the defendants' clothes or any other sample removed from their persons.

Thus, the defendants seemed to carry away nothing of her. Forensic tests failed to definitively link the bodily traces of the defendants with the victim, except for traces of mud on their clothing that could have come from any location within the park. For those who sought to contest the reality constructed in the trial, in particular supporters of the defendants who voiced their disbelief in the courthouse hallways, this missing link fueled their sense of the jogger as a ghost, a white person's paranoid fantasy, an apparition on the urban landscape.

When the moment came for the woman known as the Central Park jogger to enter the physical space of the courtroom, she appeared somehow "out of frame." A defense attorney stated in his summation, "We all applaud the efforts of the female jogger and her recovery, yet her presence [here, in the courtroom] raises more questions than if she had not been called [to the witness stand] at all." The vision of her as whole and alive was dissonant with the visual dismemberment and landscaping of her body that had taken place in the courtroom before her arrival. When she arrived on the scene, it was necessary for the prosecutor to rhetorically reconstitute the jogger as a whole being. This was brought about by using her short time on the stand as an opportunity to reconfigure her body. In a series of questions, she asks the jogger as witness, in essence, to lay claim to parts of her body, as follows:

> PROSECUTOR: Did you see number 33 in evidence?
> WITNESS: Yes.
> PROSECUTOR: Do you recognize it?
> WITNESS: This is the shirt I used to wear.
> PROSECUTOR: Prior to April 19, 1989, what color was it?
> WITNESS: It was white.
> PROSECUTOR: Were there holes there?
> WITNESS: No.
> PROSECUTOR: Will you examine these tights?
> WITNESS: I recognize those as the tights I go running in.
> PROSECUTOR: Do you recognize People's exhibit 13a and 6?
> WITNESS: Those are my running shoes.
> PROSECUTOR: Do you recognize People's 115 and 117?
> WITNESS: Those look like my socks.

After this exchange, the defense attorneys chose not to cross-examine. The decision not to engage in an aggressive cross-examination, which typifies defense attorneys' strategy in rape trials, enhanced her appearance as a ghost, or a "supra object" that can counter deadly violence.

The jogger's brief presence in the courtroom gave her no opportunity to convey her story and permitted skeptics to see her as a prop used by the prosecution. In the hallways, supporters of the defendants could be heard expressing their disbelief that she was the "real" Central Park jogger. They supposed she was an actress, too sophisticated and educated to enable us to see the truth about her, and that despite her proper appearance, she was probably a whore.

These spectators did not recognize how the jogger's very live presence in the courtroom was testimony to her heroic efforts to recover from her multiple injuries. Although she did not tell that story in a legal setting, the jogger, Trisha Meili, later revealed her identity and told her story in a book, *I Am the Central Park Jogger*. During the trial, however, she was reduced to a stand-in for the victimized body in Central Park.

The consummate victim performance took place in the New Bedford trial. In the victim's testimony in the courtroom, for example, she attempted to give voice to another interpretation of events inside the barroom and courtroom. One predominant question explored in the New Bedford trial was the "innocence" of the victim. Both the prosecution and the defense produced theories to account for her motivations for going to the bar and the appropriateness of her behavior. As defense attorney Lindahl questioned: "At first your only intention was to buy cigarettes . . . at some point you decided to stay. . . . *That's the decision* you regret most about that night?" Defense attorney Edward Harrington posed the question: "If you're living with a man, what are you doing running around the streets getting raped?" This frame of reference inevitably flows from the definition of rape that forces the prosecution to show nonconsent to prove that a sexual assault has been committed. The state of mind of the victim is the window to the *mens rea* that establishes the culpability of the defendant. This requires the woman's behavior and implied state of mind to confirm that she acted like a rape victim. In the courtroom, Diana became the object of a theory about nonconsent that opened up speculation not only about her behavior during the day of the rape but also about the moral choices she had made throughout her lifetime.

The best defense in a rape trial, therefore, is often the indictment of the victim. That is why the defense attorneys attempted to incriminate Diana by posing a series of questions intended to raise doubts about the sincerity of her charge of rape: Was she desperate to have sex that night? So desperate that she would agree to sex in a public place? Was her behavior irresponsible or inviting? Was she too drunk to know what was happening?

The testimony of witnesses who actually heard and saw Diana that night, along with her own testimony, gives accounts of her motives, words, and actions. Defense attorneys challenged the inconsistencies in this evidence. For example, Diana's recollections immediately after the rape differed from her testimony at the trial. The defense tracked down inconsistencies in the voluminous record, including Diana's recollections, written police reports, and reports of witnessed confrontations in the bar and police station. As the story unfolded in the courtroom, the social mechanisms that privilege certain forms of communication predetermined the value of the facts brought into the body of evidence. Here, this meant that the simple and direct recollection of the facts Diana gave in court would stand against the enormous collection of documents recording the events of the crime and her life.

As she testified in a calm monotone, she tried to present herself in society's image of an innocent victim rather than reveal her weakness and anger. Adopting the pose of the innocent victim required her to show that her actions conformed to what is expected of a person of good character: consistency, sobriety, and responsibility. While the defense attorney's questions constrained her ability to explain her actions, her responses were also limited by the prosecution, which was concerned that her testimony would contradict the police officers' official version and the testimony of witnesses who were in the tavern during the rape. The defense attempted to question her credibility by pointing out inconsistencies in the accounts she gave to the police; even her private conferences with a rape counselor were introduced into evidence. Faced with such constraints, her strategy was not to reveal the *whole* story but to construct a narrative that she felt would best establish her innocence. In a firm voice she recounted what she believed to be the truth about her victimization.

Given the focus on her innocence, the task was to convince the court of her capability to be cognizant of and explain all that had happened to her. This meant she had to qualify her own emotional distress to preserve the credibility of her statements. When subjected to an extensive cross-examination that disputed the version of the facts she gave immediately after the rape, she defended her ability to perceive and report events in a state of mind that was (in her words) "near" hysterical and "slightly" confused.

The major challenge to her credibility rested on the record of her "exaggerations" in the police report written the night of the attack. In subsequent police reports she retracted the claim that there were fifteen men involved, including six who had sexual intercourse with her, by saying that she had "lost count." She also modified the statement that "the men had knives" to "one man held a knife in front of her face" (then again, she "admits" he did not *say* anything threatening to her). Continually questioned by the defense attorneys about these inconsistencies, she responded that she "doesn't know" how to account for them.

Ultimately none of her explanations captured the shock or trauma she had experienced. Instead she offered admissions that she was tired and slightly confused. She said that "the events are clearer now than then"; and about the first police report, "I don't remember anything I said"; "I was tired, I didn't want to talk to anybody and I wanted to be left alone." Defense attorney Lindahl's effort to get her to justify her statement to the police produced this moment in the trial:

LINDAHL: Did you tell [Officer Sacramento] twelve or fifteen men were involved?

DIANA: Every man there was involved.

LINDAHL: Did you say six men had sexual intercourse with you? When in fact two men had intercourse?

DIANA: Yes.

LINDAHL: Is this your testimony to the jury today? If you said twelve or fifteen; if you said twelve or fifteen; if you said sixteen or more; if you said—

DIANA: I believe everybody that was there was guilty!

LINDAHL: Objection!

[At this point the jury was asked to disregard the witness's statement.]

Diana makes her point through spontaneous outbursts. She challenges the narrowness of legal thinking by emphatically asserting that everyone was guilty and characterizing her "exaggerations" as a product of the horror she experienced that night. Lindahl's next question was, "Maybe you were so upset you exaggerated." Diana's response was "no." Her straightforward denial is her best effort at resisting the attorney's move to characterize her as unreliable. Diana also shows Lindahl that she is willing to defend her own view of moral responsibility, which justified her rage against all the men in the tavern.

The defense attorneys not only used Diana's self-incriminating statements to undermine her story about the course of events; they also developed these statements into theories about consent. They did so by comparing the victim's character with the moral position of other women who were principal actors in the retelling of the story. These comparisons are poignantly brought forth in the testimony of the women who were with Diana during the day she was raped. The first witness called by the defense was Rosetta, who testified about their activities during the afternoon before Diana went to Big Dan's. Rosetta was asked a series of questions about their consumption of drinks at the Knotty Pine, an Italian restaurant and bar, where they stopped to get soup for their boyfriends. Defense attorney Harrington appeared disappointed with her testimony, as if he expected her to provide a more definitive answer to whether or not Diana consumed alcoholic beverages that afternoon before arriving at Big Dan's. However, the defense could establish that Diana had asked Rosetta if she would like to go out with her for a drink. The defense attorney initiated the following exchange on cross-examination:

> WAXLER: [Diana] wanted more to drink?
>
> ROSETTA: Yes.
>
> WAXLER: What did you say?
>
> ROSETTA: I told her she should just go home.
>
> WAXLER: Did she respond?
>
> ROSETTA: No.
>
> WAXLER: Did she say anything further?
>
> ROSETTA: No.

The purpose of the exchange was to attempt to establish that Diana intended to go out drinking when she left home at dusk. Rosetta insinuated that she disapproved of Diana's desire to get out of the house and, in so doing, implied that Diana's own restlessness was responsible for her being raped at Big Dan's. Her testimony also enabled the defense to draw a contrast between Rosetta, who had recently married and decided wisely to stay home, and Diana, who lived illegitimately with the father of her two children and fatefully decided to go out that night.

Another incriminating voice came from the other woman who had been in Big Dan's. Marie was introduced to the court as a reliable person with professional credentials: she was employed as a nurse and was much older than Diana (probably in her forties). (She is called the "fat lady" in the testimony because the men in the bar did not know her name.) She went out that night to get something to eat, but when she discovered that the restaurant across the street was closed, she decided to see if she could get a sandwich at Big Dan's. Marie was a regular in the bar, and in fact she knew several men quite well. Previously, she had helped the defendant Victor Rapozo find a job. Marie gave the following description of Diana's actions in the tavern:

> HARRINGTON: What did you see her do?
>
> MARIE: She went to the bar to get a drink.
>
> HARRINGTON: Were you seated at the table?
>
> MARIE: Yes.
>
> HARRINGTON: Did she come to the table?
>
> MARIE: Next thing she did is, [she] came over and asked if [she] could sit down.

HARRINGTON: Then?

MARIE: I said "You can sit down, but I am leaving shortly."

HARRINGTON: What observations did you make about the young lady?

MARIE: She was bubbly; she was bouncing around the chair; she never stood still, her pupils were very large and her eyes were glassy.

Marie added that during their ten-minute conversation Diana had told her that "she didn't have sex for several months, I think nine months," and that her "boyfriend or ex-husband [suggested that she] should get out and meet people because she is a lonely person."

A third confrontation with the morality of other women came from Diana's closest relative and substitute parent, her grandmother. This confrontation was recorded for the official record because it was overheard by the police officer accompanying her to the hospital and by the nurse. Her grandmother, when she first saw Diana in the hospital, called her a drunk, accused her of shaming the family, and asked her why she was not at home with her children. At trial Diana was reluctant to talk about her grandmother's denouncements, and at one point insisted they were irrelevant:

LINDAHL: Do you remember the conversation with your grandmother?

DIANA: I don't want my grandmother brought into this.

LINDAHL: The reason you didn't remember is because you didn't want to talk about your grandmother?

DIANA: Yes, it is.

LINDAHL: It was true you didn't remember?

DIANA: It wasn't a lie. I don't think it should have been brought up.

LINDAHL: Isn't it true, whenever you don't want anything brought up, you say I don't remember?

Diana obviously cared deeply about her grandmother's opinion of her. She justified her grandmother's reaction by asserting that her grandmother must have been so upset that she did not realize her words were harmful. Diana tried to protect both herself and her image of her grandmother's affection by depicting her loved one as venting frustration about the calamity to her grandfather rather than delivering insults to her. The reenactment in the trial of her grandmother's assault on her character not only revealed the powerful forces of condemnation at work in her private life but also brought these painful experiences into the realm of public judgment.

Using the morality of other women to incriminate Diana exemplifies how the social conception of rape finds authority in women's duty to protect themselves. The defendants, however, relied on more overt challenges based on their ordinary treatment of women. As defendant Cordeiro told the court in his testimony on his own behalf, he was surprised to hear the next morning that the police were looking for him because there had been a rape in Big Dan's Tavern. He said, "A rape? Nobody raped anybody." When asked in the trial if he knew what rape was, Cordeiro responded, "It is when you tear off their clothes." In Cordeiro's account of that night, he left Big Dan's for a short while. When he came back, he saw Diana on the pool table with defendant Joe Viera on top of her. He watched defendant Rapozo put his penis in her mouth. Then he did the same thing, while Diana was "smiling and laughing at them." Cordeiro was relatively unconcerned about talking to the police the next morning because all he believed he had to do was to "tell the truth . . . *the truth never hurts.*" His confidence turned out to be misplaced, but his lack of concern is revealing about the state of mind of a rapist. There was initially no reason for him to doubt his own opinion about what the woman wanted to have happen to her that night.

Defendant Daniel Silva's story was less frank and based upon more complicated assumptions about how Diana had communicated her desire to be raped. Silva claimed that he had met Diana a few months earlier and had a short conversation with her in a café named Pals Four. By his account, Diana approached him at Big Dan's and asked if he had any drugs. According to Silva she asked, "Do you want to play, fool around?" He responded "yes," and claimed that Diana "looked very happy." He explained to her that he could not take her home, however, because he lived with his mother. As they continued to fool around with each other, the other thing that concerned Silva was that he "thought she was holding me too tight; like a hysterical woman; like she wanted something." Daniel Silva portrayed the situation in Big Dan's as an ordinary "pickup" in a bar, at least until the other men started participating in the attack.

Sometimes the effort to make sense of Diana's motives and actions in terms of her background and past experiences suited the purposes of both the prosecution and the defense, while at other times the details of her situation were ignored. The defense characterized her life as filled with hardships but suggested that she responded to those conditions in immoral and desperate ways. Information that could have made her a sympathetic character was turned against her. She was depicted as unloved and forsaken by those who should have cared about her and as the type of person who somehow deserved her attack. The defense wanted to know: Where was her boyfriend Michael during the night of the attack? Why didn't he call the police when she didn't come home? Did they fight before she left the house? Why didn't the police officer see Michael when Diana was brought back to her home? The consequence of this line of questioning was that Diana's intimate life and her emotional fragility became relevant to a legal argument about consent. Moreover, that undermined her credibility as a woman whose value was determined exclusively by the judgment of men. It was somehow indicative of her culpability that the rape did not upset (or violate the interests of) the man she lived with, and that she got into trouble while seeking escape from her domestic responsibilities.

Since Diana had received public assistance in the past, the defense attorneys had access to information that could only be obtained from government records. Her Medicaid records contained a report of a hospital visit in 1981 for medical treatment after a rape, though she denied having made a previous report and argued with the defense attorneys about the verifiability of her Medicaid number. But this dispute over factual evidence contributed to the aura of guilt around her: "Do you check over your yearly public assistance reports?" asked one defense attorney. "Do you give out your Medicaid number 'willy-nilly' to other persons?"

The prosecution, in contrast, tried to evoke a sympathetic understanding of Diana's life by focusing on her role as a mother. In his opening statement the district attorney noted that she had given her child medication before she put her to bed. In direct examination of Diana, the district attorney allowed her to mention that while at Big Dan's she had shown Marie pictures of her children. The prosecution orchestrated this look into her personal life, but there were other, more unexpected moments in the trial when she revealed herself. When questioned further about her grandmother, she became so upset that the judge had to intervene. She also refused to use her grandmother's name in the courtroom and was granted permission by the judge to use a pseudonym. Diana's determination to protect her grandmother revealed the same courage that had allowed her to bring the charge of rape in the first place and possibly subject both herself and her family to public embarrassment and harassment. At these moments, when she struggled to protect her dignity and privacy, she presented herself as a worthy "victim," and she broke out of the monotonic response pattern to assert her feelings of violation. This also gave her the opportunity to assert the moral authority of her position and to implicitly offer alternative theories of responsibility and blame.

Although the convictions of four of the defendants might be seen as symbolic vindication of the victim's innocence, even the overwhelming power of stories about multiple acts of violence in the presence of witnesses did not spare Diana from being put in the vulnerable position of a woman as an accuser. When the case was presented initially, it appeared that the public nature of the violent act served to affirm the victim's "innocence" while vilifying the Portuguese defendants and their conduct in the community. As the facts became public, however, the unnamed complainant was portrayed as a confused young woman of unreliable character. The public persona of the victim was transformed in a reconstructed account that scrutinized her behavior in the tavern and compared it negatively to "reasonable" standards of women's propriety. Within the legal forum, her fearful assertion of violation was obscured by questioning that implied personal irresponsibility in protecting herself from male aggression while raising suspicion about her sexual motivations as a woman: she was forced to defend the propriety of her actions and held suspect as a promiscuous and capricious woman.

The victim's victory, hence, is minimized by the systematic ways in which her telling of events and assignments of responsibility were overshadowed by the prosecutors' efforts to construct a theory of the crime that firmly established the motives and guilt of the men on trial. Tragic circumstances made it impossible for her to reestablish a life for herself (soon after the trial she moved to Florida and was killed in an automobile accident). However, her ability to assign blame and to protect against aspersions about her family (such as the reputation of her grandmother) is a testimonial to a woman's ability to hold her place in the midst of the prosecution's almost all-encompassing thirst for punitive justice.

The treatment of victims in high-profile cases is not an aberration but is reproduced in routine sexual assault cases.[3] The techniques used to denigrate the victims in the New Bedford and Central Park cases are systematically applied in almost all rape cases that come to trial. From the very beginning of the process, either in the emergency room or police station, the victim's account is treated with suspicion by law enforcement officials. If they have a feeling that something is wrong with the account they may submit the victim to a lie detector test.[4] Overall, prosecutors tend to treat victims poorly because the complicities of the assault and their lives are seen as a deterrent to building a good case, while defense attorneys see their best strategy for winning as one of "trashing the victim."[5] For most situations, the involvement with the law will not proceed beyond the initial interview, and even in cases that go to trial the woman will have little opportunity to tell her story or influence how the prosecution will present the case. As a result, victims rarely are able to exercise real choices vis-à-vis the justice system. This also means that processing their experiences usually occurs in the context of short-term therapy available in rape crisis centers (for the fortunate) or in mental health facilities. In this therapeutic environment women are treated as victims of "trauma"; as described in the preceding chapter, this model may not enable them to best articulate their situation or seek support.

speaking with battered women

The following sections of this chapter explore the relationship between women and the state by drawing upon intensive interviews with six women who were participants in a transitional housing program for battered women. All these women stayed in shelters and then applied and were selected for the follow-up housing program. This program offers comprehensive services: weekly support groups, temporary housing (in private apartments), counseling, and assistance with job and child care referrals. In addition, the analysis presented also draws upon observations of meetings of a short-lived local grassroots organization of battered women. This spontaneously formed group included women who were interested in political organizing and increasing public awareness about the problems facing battered women. Since some of these women have concerns about their safety, the names of all of them have been changed and any information that might identify them or their place of residence has been eliminated.[6]

These women were not asked directly to give accounts of being battered. Instead, our conversations were focused on their interactions with social service agencies. This series of questions seemed to evoke the most relevant issues in their lives at that moment. Their stories bear a striking resemblance to Diana's above, in that the expression of injustice is centered on indignities perpetrated by the system rather than the individual men who battered them. Indeed, the stories that they had to tell were more often about what the police or DSS had done to them than about their abusers. During several interviews the women's children were present, usually coming in and out of the room. Unexpectedly, their interruptions turned into important contributions.

patriarchy reborn

All the battered women described their relationship with the state by telling stories about difficult events that occurred as they struggled to gain control over their lives after leaving an abusive partner. For most of them these events were harrowing experiences that represented their failure to receive help when they most desperately needed it. These were experiences of initiation into a forced intimacy with the state, often mixed with a betrayal of their expectations to be treated as deserving and worthy of protection. Their storytelling provides accounts of events that disturbed their sense of the boundaries between private and public life and that formed the basis of their personal narratives about the origins of their status as battered women.

When Alice left her abusive husband for good, she escaped from her home without her possessions. Her husband also took her son, but she used legal action to get him back in a few days. Both occasions lead to involvements with the police:

> ALICE: First . . . he had possession of my son for three days so I had to attempt to get him back. [I did that through] the shelter with a domestic violence officer to retrieve my son. Um, that was, that was great. . . . But the officer that helped me to remove my belongings, made me feel very uncomfortable. Um, I was rushing. Trying to get as much as I could, as fast as I could. And she told me, she stopped me and, told me to speak with my abuser. And, that I was acting childish and that she would file a report against me for my behavior. Um, she was convincing my abuser, um, or trying to convince me to move back home with him and try to work things out. And that I was overreacting . . . [He was] trying to get information about the shelter and, how to find me. Um, at this point I left. I got out of there as fast as I could.
> KB: Do you remember the things you said back to her?
> ALICE: I started to cry. My son was the only thing on my mind . . . So tears fell down my face and I agreed with her and slowed down instead of running in and out of the apartment filling my car. And,

she wouldn't let me take any toys. She said that I would be returning. So I was only allowed to get clothing.

[Child starts swinging an object around the room]

ALICE: Craig, that will break apart and hit someone. I will throw it away. Please put it down. Thank you. Other than that . . . I had to flee the state and come to [another state]. I wasn't able to file a report against the officer. I didn't get her name or number.

The child acted out during the interview at the point at which the mother illuminated the shock of her interaction with the female police officer. The police officer, presumably from lack of sympathy for her situation, prevented her from taking the toys that would complete her separation from her old life with the batterer to her new life as an independent woman. Alice was horrified that the officer called her "childish" when she expected her to use her authority to protect her against the imminent threat to her well-being and safety imposed by her spouse. As she recalled this scene, she deeply regretted that her need to flee the state prevented her from reporting the officer. Yet the act of "reporting" the official (particularly after the officer used the threat of "reporting" her) would have satisfied her desire to retaliate against the behavior of the police and the ways in which it made her feel helpless and infantile.

Another scene involving the police centered on their failure to respond despite the pleas of a battered woman. Joyce lived in a small town and was often subjected to police harassment. She hung out with the local Hispanic gangs (she is white) and "because I would associate with them on the street, [the police] thought I was just like them. They used to hassle me and stop my car." (She doesn't present herself as innocent: right off the bat she told me that she has been a troublemaker.) She feels this explains why the police were not helpful when she reported being battered by her boyfriend:

> They would categorize me with them. And I was being beaten by my boyfriend at that time and they would come and, they just like, blew it off. They just blew it off. They didn't really care. I had to contact the people [at the shelter] . . . when I kicked my ex out of my house, the police weren't watching and helping me out like they should have been doing.

The lack of responsiveness by the police is made more vivid by Joyce's accounts of their doing nothing while being "nearby" and sometimes *watching* the violence:

JOYCE: There was the one time Jacob ended up trying to choke me. And I almost died there. You know I was passed out, knocked out, you know it took them, I was already awake by the time the cops knocked on my door. He was gone. Cops finally knocked on my door . . . I mean, the police station is only five blocks down from my house.

KB: Yeah.

JOYCE: It wasn't like I was living out in the boondocks and the police station was downtown. And they always sat across from my house. Watching inside my house!

KB: They're standing outside while you're being beaten?

JOYCE: They used to just. They'd park right next to my bank and they'd peer right into my apartment. And, they'd just sit there, you know? They'd see me, you know, they'd see me. And, they see him throw things at me or whatever. Cause I walk out there and they'd be like, hey, how'd you like that plate? I'd be like, asshole. You know? I'd just keep walking . . . I do what I had to do and go back, they didn't care. You know? They didn't care.

Joyce has acute political sensibilities—she realized that her association with local gangs disqualified her from police protection. At the same time, she strongly believed that it was the responsibility of the police to stop her boyfriend's violence. Her recollection of scenes in which the boyfriend was beating her reveals her shock and dismay at the officers who watched and did nothing ("They didn't care"). Hence, the dynamics of the situation rested on the failure of the father/protector figure to come to her aid just when the violence was *exposed* to public viewing. Her introduction to her public life as a battered woman was marked by her new "state" protector watching her being abused and then shaming her as she came out into the street.

A third scene involving the police was written into a fictional account by Patricia.[7] In this account, the woman gets a particularly severe beating by her spouse. She flees and walks to the local police station. She presents herself to the officer in charge. She has a bruised face and an obviously broken arm (because it was twisted the wrong direction). The first question the police officer asks is, "Did you touch him?" She said yes, that she pushed him away, not yet realizing the officer's intent in posing the question. The police officer then tells her that he can't do anything because there was provocation. Patricia expresses her outrage that her injuries do not speak for themselves and about the authority figure's malicious use of a "technicality." In this scene, Patricia is being initiated into a Kafka-like relationship with the law; she learns that when she approaches the law it draws her into a place where justice is elusive. The scene is a shattering experience for her because it defies her sense that her injuries are self-evident. The event marks the beginning of her struggle to have her perceptions of the reality of the abuse recognized by impersonal authorities.

A similar event occurred when Vicki appeared before a judge seeking a restraining order. The event took on the form of a ritual of abuse—a reenactment of the loss of dignity that comes from being battered by someone you love:

> Well, I remember one time a judge said to me, as I am standing there with black eyes, a broken nose, I mean the whole bit, I mean it's obvious I was beat up, you know it was very obvious, and Larry's standing right next to me cause they called you up to the side. [The judge says] what's going on here—what's going on here? And I explained the whole situation, how he battered me, I didn't know why, he came in drinking you know blah, blah, blah, blah . . . And then he turned to Larry and said, "Why did you do this?" and Larry all Mr. Prim and Proper in court says, "Well, I don't know, I just don't know" and then the judge turned to me and said, "Is it really, really this serious that you need a restraining order?" And then I said, like this, "I don't know—you tell me?"

Remarkably, another woman's formative moment connecting with the public welfare system was like being visited by a guardian angel. The interventions by the state arose out of violent circumstances, but in this case it was the violent act Donna, a black woman in her thirties, committed after experiencing overwhelming stress as an abused wife:

> DONNA: I just needed to find out who was going to take care of my kids. I was going to do it. It was just, that's how crazy he made me . . . And, um, one day this parent aid, I had requested a parent aid and, she came in and we just had this huge fight and I was like, just like, she knocked on the door and I was like . . . help me! And it was like, she looked at me and it was like, okay. She didn't know. She didn't have any idea . . . what was going on. And she started calling all these shelters . . . And that's how, you know, I started.
>
> KB: This person, the parent aid, she was someone who was like, right there at the right time, when you really—

DONNA: Exactly.

KB: And where did she come from?

DONNA: Um, I was involved in a—I assaulted this girl. And because, and because of it, they, DSS, they put that I neglected—the girl said that it was my daughter and I, so they put neglect. And uh, so they didn't visit me. They didn't really think that it carried any weight. The complaint. But I was arrested . . . and the police had to report it. But I asked for a parent aid. And, well services, and it was I tell you, it was the best thing that ever happened because she walked in and it was, I just let her take me. She says come with me and we'll go make all these phone calls and it was just like . . . I was calling and I was telling these people on the other end, these people that I didn't even know existed, what my husband used to do to me on a regular basis, you know. And they're like, oh my God! And it was like, you know it was like [they understood] and I haven't even told them the bad part!

She remembered the scene as though it were a supernatural affair. The parent aid, an agent of mercy, arrived at just the right moment to save her from another horrible fight with her spouse. She instantly trusted the woman to lead her in the right direction, and she submitted to her heavenly authority by letting "her take me." Ironically, this new path for Donna was born in the violence of her assault against another woman and the subsequent disciplinary intervention by DSS. Her immediate request for a parent aid seems to have saved her from more radical action by the agency and gave rise to events that opened her life to a public world that she didn't know existed. Despite this one example of the fortuitous arrival of a helpful person, initiating these events is just the beginning of an association with the state in which women ultimately make great gains but not without the fear of more traumatic losses.

parenting with the state

The tactic of accusing the victim of being a perpetrator of violence is often the defining motif of the interaction between battered women and state authorities. Women's fears about false accusations are most acute in divorce proceedings and in their relations with children's welfare authorities. All these women worried about losing their children to either their batterer or the state.

Although before the custody hearing Alice acutely feared losing her son, her experience in court did not prove her worst expectations. She said her husband was represented by a "friend of his sister's" who didn't spend much time on the case. He came into court hoping to win by "just using his authority." She was impressed by the way her lawyer and the judge treated her:

> At one point in the beginning they had him up first. My abuser, and the judge looked at me and rolled his eyes. Which relieved all my stress immediately . . . After that, um, when he gave us, a fifteen-minute break, when I was emotionally distraught up on the stand, he, he only made me speak of one incident. And he already made his rulings. Um, so I, I was told I would have to recall twenty-seven incidents considering I was in a relationship for nine, ten, years. I just spoke of the last incident prior to leaving. . . that was all he needed to hear. The judge said Miss March, you can go home. And it seemed almost personal. And the stenographer, the officer, even a woman that was witnessing, all congratulated me after court. And wished me well and blessed me. It was a true, uh, personal experience.

Afterward she uncertainly asked her lawyer if she had won (and he laughed). Despite the successful outcome she described her day in court as the "most fearful experience of my life." And she expects that nothing in her life will be as difficult as that day and dealing with the "possibility of losing custody of her child."

The threat of removing children from the home and Department of Social Service supervision is more immediate for some other battered women. Jill explains that she doesn't like the way DSS treats her because they "make issues." During the interview I played with her four-year-old daughter who was in and out of the room. At one point she interrupted us:

> JILL: Well, the police I only called them once. One time, the only time, in the three years that it was happening. The abuse between their father.
> KB: Uh huh.
> JILL: They were very nice.
> CHILD: Fuck you.
> JILL: No, you don't talk like that.
> CHILD: Yes I am.
> JILL: No. No. She got that from him. I've been trying to break her out of that.

Jill reports that DSS worked with her by issuing threats that just ended up making her more upset. They told her that since her child had witnessed the abuse they had "grounds to take her away" and that if she didn't remain in the shelter and away from the father they would take her away "then and there." Later in the interview she described more fully her problem with DSS:

> Why, I know they're supposed to help people, but if you don't have the resources to leave, that shouldn't be grounds to say I'm going to take your kid away because you stayed with him for so long. So, I know she's slow in a lot of things and she says that word. And other things and she doesn't say it too bad. There's only one word left that she says all the time now instead of the other ones. So, it's not as bad, but the hitting has slowed down but the attitude is still there from all the anger that she has.

Jill articulates a genuine problem she encounters in trying to communicate to DSS—they, unlike her, can't look at the situation in terms of her daughter's progress. When DSS intrudes, they wield the threats and prerogatives of a parent. But they are, in Jill's view, poor "co-parents" because they bring to the situation only fear and a bad attitude rather than constructive options for helping her daughter deal with her anger.

Joyce's child was taken from her by DSS. She believes that one police officer who peered into her apartment during the abuse "fought hard to get my son taken away." She described the circumstances that led up to DSS taking custody of her child:

> My abuser was in my house and he ended up going to jail . . . He was sitting in jail saying that he had tied my son up. Which I still believe to this day, he never did. He was just so peeved at me cause I called the cops. He said that he tied up my son and I seen him do it. And that I was there. And then two hours later, DSS people, it was on a Sunday, around Christmas time. And two DSS workers came up that I didn't even know. They just walked up in my house with two cops. Told me to throw some clothes . . . Asked no questions. And they just grabbed my son and left. They could have been strangers.

Part of the reason for her shock at the arrival of DSS workers that she "didn't even know" was that she had a long-term relationship with a DSS social worker who had proved to her that she was a "good woman" and "worked hard." In fact, DSS actions violated her sense of how things worked, even given the get-tough rules of street life. The authorities should be able to tell the difference between criminals and victims. For Joyce, the state was acting like a bad father. And she used her own father in her effort to "fight my butt off to get my son back." She detailed her strategy:

> I went to court. Went with my father. Me and my father went to court and we just kept on stressing how can you believe somebody that, that is into crack and heroin, that was sitting in a jail cell. How can you believe a man that's sitting behind bars over me? They just came and took him and left. And my father says no, you don't do that to my daughter. You don't do that to my grandson. She is a victim.

Joyce overtly enlisted her father as a mouthpiece to make the claim that both she and her child were legitimate. They made bold claims about who should and shouldn't be believed and who deserved the sympathy of the state. Their case was based on the assertion that the state had mistakenly intervened in this grandfather's family, and that his paternal rights over his daughter and grandson superseded the interests of the state.

Battered women's dependence on social services also creates situations in which the state usurps the mother's discipline of her children. These women constantly face circumstances in which they are trying to take care of their children while conducting business with bureaucrats, social workers, teachers, and counselors. Vicki reports an experience of violation of her daughter, Karen, in a welfare office:

> VICKI: Karen ran from her little cubicle office and in the process of me going to retrieve her, Rebecca had just left her cubicle to go get some paperwork that she neglected to have ready, I don't know why because she's supposed to. And she instead . . . and I was only a couple of steps behind Karen and I was reaching for her, and Karen got to Rebecca Smith before I did. And instead of her just stopping her by grabbing her by the hand, she stopped, picked her up by the collar of her shirt—right off the floor.
>
> KAREN: And I was just a baby.
>
> VICKI: You weren't a baby; she was about three.
>
> KAREN: Well mommy I was a baby.
>
> VICKI: See she remembers it too. And it was very traumatic, and I wrote all kinds of letters to her supervisor and then of course welfare started just doing anything I basically wanted them to do. Covering their own selves. So that was like, you know her supervisor started

writing . . . (Interruption) No honey, honey please, Karen, I am gonna count to three . . . thank you. Stop! Don't act up. Thank you.

KAREN: You know what mommy?

VICKI: What Karen?

KAREN: And my Daddy just picked me up by the shirt.

VICKI: Daddy's never picked you up by the shirt, Karen.

KAREN: Mommy?

VICKI: Her father never physically abused her, never.

KAREN: Mommy?

VICKI: Always let me finish talking.

KAREN: When he was beating you up . . .

This was a very complicated three-way exchange that gave evidence of the different agendas of the mother and young daughter. The mother offered a clear-cut example of welfare abuse, her story condemning the inappropriate behavior of a caseworker toward her daughter. For Vicki, this abuse is all in the family. She is a repeat player in the welfare office and she spoke in familiar terms about the caseworker and her supervisor. Her point was that this kind of abuse happens, and that women who are smart use it to their advantage. Vicki's little girl started acting out as she heard the story and then chimed in, at first to acknowledge her role as the victim. But then Karen used the opportunity (with the cunning only a six-year-old can muster) to provoke her mother's defensive reactions. The mother maintained her sense of control within her abusive "public family" by making clear-cut distinctions about who is evil, violent, or incompetent. She knows who the bad guys are, and she was relentless in trying to get them in trouble. She also guarded against any doubts being cast about her own innocence. She told me immediately afterward that her child has never been physically abused by the father: "See, *now* I feel like I have to justify this." Both mother and daughter fought to defend their place as worthy victims in a difficult family situation.

Beyond the impending presence of seemingly arbitrary police power to remove children from homes, agents of the state may actively stigmatize dependent mothers. Donna had an extremely disturbing interaction with the school counselor when she enrolled her daughter in school:

DONNA: I went to the school. She had missed a few days. It was quite a few days. Moving around, trying to leave him, she had been to like four different schools. Five different schools that year alone.

KB: Uh huh. Yeah.

DONNA: I had this guidance counselor, Mr. Heffner, at the . . . middle school. And he, I went with an advocate from [the program] and he wouldn't even look at me. He would talk to her.

KB: Uh huh.

DONNA: And he left me feeling like a total piece of shit. You know? He just wouldn't acknowledge me . . . But anyway, um, I went with her and he just would not even look at me. And the one thing he did look at me and say, "I assume you're on welfare?" He told me.

KB: He said that?

DONNA: Yeah. And I was just like, I was speechless. I didn't say anything. I was like, confused, did he, was he, mean intentionally? I just, I was really confused.

KB: Right.

DONNA: I've just left the shelter. So I was really all screwed up, you know.

KB: Uh huh.

DONNA: Really raw out to the, to the hurts.

KB: Yeah.

DONNA: . . . He also told my daughter . . . he told me, he goes, uh, "Is she going to start school, is she going to start school today?" . . . I said "Yeah because I think she's missed enough."

KB: Uh huh.

DONNA: And he looked at her and he goes, "Jesus you look horrible. Look at your lips." He told my daughter. Because her lips were chapped . . . And she had a little cold. You know what I mean? It was nothing.

KB: Yeah.

DONNA: And he goes, "Well, if it would be me, my child's health would come first. But I guess it's up to you if you want her to start."

KB: Your daughter heard him say these things?

DONNA: Yeah . . . In front of my daughter. Oh yeah, and um, it was, it was just a most horrible experience.

Donna went prepared to the meeting with the school counselor. She brought an advocate because she was concerned that she would be put under suspicion for having enrolled her daughter in so many schools. But she also felt insecure because there was a history of her abusive partner "embarrassing her" by getting into "huge arguments with the teachers." Mr. Heffner turned out to be as skillful an abuser as her former partner, however. He could exact his humiliation of Donna by showing her daughter that he could label her mother as someone "on welfare" and as an irresponsible parent who would send a sick child to school.

Parenting with the state puts battered women in an extremely vulnerable position. Women who have left the abusive fathers of their children often continue to feel imprisoned by the fear of having their children taken away even after they formally gain the legal right to retain custody. They perceive that the law still holds an absolute right to claim parental control over their children. Moreover, the ever-present threat of losing control to an abusive partner is transferred to their relationship with the state. And as these women's narratives unfortunately show, the agents of state power perpetuate all-too-familiar patterns of coercive authority. Women who think they have gained some degree of intimacy and trust with officials end up being shocked, disturbed, and violated by arbitrarily exercised state action.

my life hereafter

These women have seen it all. None of them harbors illusions about the peacefulness of domesticity. They can't, because they carry around their experience of abuse in their bodies: scars, broken bones, and terrifying memories. Despite the enormity of what they have left behind, each woman constructs a narrative about how she will choose to live her life in the hereafter.

With their eyes wide open to both the violence of their former lives and their bonds with the state, battered women strategically found spaces within these forces to make new identities. For some women this entailed an effort to reclaim a private life, expressed by attesting to ethics of personal and social responsibility. Alice proudly predicted: "Nothing right now at this point is keeping me from [her goal of having her own home]. Either way, I plan to apply for subsidized apartments. But that will not stop me [even] if I do not get accepted. I've been a hard worker and I've always kept up to four jobs if I had to, to pay my rent . . . I'm definitely ambitious and, I won't give up." Patricia is clear about having goals for herself: "I want a nice paying job. I want, you know, the little American dream type thing. I would love that, but that's far-fetched right now. I'll get there slowly. Eventually I'll get there." Jill's struggle to get back on her feet required her "to be more independent. So, I wouldn't be reliable on him, like being afraid of going outside just to go to the store for something . . . I started going outside a lot more and just doing things on my own instead of asking for someone to come with me." She likes this new independence because "I can make my own rules up as I go along . . . And not having to worry about, well, I've got to answer to this person. Now I am my own boss." Jill frequently mentioned during the interview that she just "doesn't like authority." She feels that her lifetime problem with authority was accentuated by the shelter experience, and she seeks solutions that get her out of authority's way.

At one level, these are dreams about obtaining the material acquisitions of middle-class life. The most powerful symbol of making this transition is "getting off" welfare. These women want all the accoutrements of the American dream—home ownership, car ownership, good-paying jobs, excellent childcare and schools (although nobody mentions a man in this picture). These goals also evoke the need to see themselves symbolically as good providers for their children. For example, Patricia confided to me that she would feel that she was finally recovered when she has clean children's pajamas for every day of the week.

At another level, these desires speak to the ways these women covet legitimacy. Reaching out for traditional indicators of success becomes the means by which women can attempt to reestablish boundaries between the public and private spheres. While seeking shelter to flee from domestic abuse is a deeply transformative experience, some women's survival strategies require them to rely on traditional notions of personal responsibility. For this reason, battered women often can easily accept the shelter worker's lessons about what went wrong— that they stayed in abusive relationships because they believed that the battering was their fault. The shelter workers teach the women about the cycle of violence theory. Alice described the process: "[The police] immediately got me [into the shelter] . . . Then I saw the therapist, and, um, spoke with her and, you know, it's not my fault. And, [she] explained to me about the pattern and, they educated me about the violence. And . . . why I didn't leave." Alice and others found this new way of thinking helpful; in fact, they saw it as advice that saved their lives. Significantly, the shelter's explanation for their problems encourages them to refocus their energies on parts of their lives they can take responsibility for: the care of their children, economic viability, and developing support systems among similarly situated women.

This recovery strategy, however, keeps in place and reinforces the assumption that safety is secured in the private sphere. Alice describes why her housing makes her feel safe:

> ALICE: So, again, it wasn't safe to go to my parent's house. That's where I always ran. That's where I [he] always got to bring me back . . . [The program] did an assessment and accepted my application . . . It was the best thing! And I mean, before I saw it, I didn't know anything about it. Or where it was.
>
> CHILD: Yummy licorice.
>
> ALICE: But, I was like, please, give it to me. And I'm thinking it's going to be crummy and slummy and really gross, and, and it was the total opposite. It was furnished with beautiful furniture. Plenty of furniture.
>
> KB: And a security building.
>
> ALICE: Security building!
>
> KB: Yeah.
>
> ALICE: Uh, I have five locks on my door. Um, they call me, you know, twice a week to check up. Are you okay? How's it going? How's your day? Um, it's so comforting and reassuring. And we are so comfortable here . . . And [my child] felt secure and safe, finally. And it wasn't other people. It was just me and you . . . And he's got his own room and all his belongings were left. He had nothing when we came here.

Her gratefulness to the transitional housing program largely comes from her appreciation of the ways in which they helped her to establish the comfort and security associated with a good home.

Focusing on personal responsibility also sets clear limits on how professionals should treat battered women. Alice, for example, repeatedly evaluated whether the authorities she came in contact with acted "professionally." For her that means that although they may have taken a personal interest in her difficulties, they respected her privacy. The problem with this impulse, however, is that it can justify battered women's efforts to hide the abuse. Take, for example, Jill's methods of avoidance with her doctor:

> KB: Your regular doctors, did they help you?
>
> JILL: No, I never went [if I needed a physical], if I had like, black and blues on me or something, I wouldn't. I would like cancel my appointment. Just say I'm sick or my daughter's sick and we can't make it. Can we reschedule like for next week?

KB: Uh-huh.

JILL: And they would always reschedule for me.

The insistence on professionalism is an effective device to keep at bay interference by authorities who have little capacity to understand the woman's situation. But the demand for privacy may end up encouraging women to retreat (both figuratively and literally) into homes with multiple locks on the door.

Of the women I interviewed, Alice and Jill were the most deeply invested in setting boundaries and wishing for safety in a private world. Another approach, which holds similar aspirations, is to engage in a war against the public domain. Vicki made the outright claim: "You become a battered woman and then to get assistance or any help from any social service agency, never mind the court, you get battered by them too, you get battered by a society and a system." She even described the battering by the system in physical terms: "It's very emotional and it is very traumatic because it's like, I feel like I am just being beat in the head, beat in the head, beat in the head over and over and over again." Vicki explained why she thinks that some women have a harder time with agencies than others:

> But as far as social service agencies and all that stuff. They're just—well you need our help so you have to kiss our ass. That's how I feel and I refuse to. So, and I think that's why I have a harder time with agencies, [than] some women do because some women are willing because they feel like, well, I've been doing it this long with my abusers, so why not just, and not cause any waves because that's what they have been programmed to do. Well, maybe if I don't cause any waves then he won't beat me up, and now it's like if I don't cause any waves, then maybe I won't get emotionally battered by the system.

Vicki's life is in an ongoing state of war. She describes herself as constantly "fighting" with the transitional assistance department, police, social workers, and the people upstairs. Even when she comes in off the battlefield to be treated for her injuries, the combat continues with the emergency room doctors:

> KB: What do you mean by treating you coldly?
>
> VICKI: Like emergency room Dr. Hack . . . "Yup, got some contusions, there, bleeding, ummm, a laceration." And he's like ripping my eye and it hurts even worse. You know, he's like totally, totally, unfeeling. He's like, "Did he rape you?"

KB: He said it like that?

VICKI: Yeah. And I said "No, but don't you think this is bad enough?" He said, "Well, you could take that picture [the police took] to remind you of it and maybe next time you won't go back to him."

KB: What did you say back to him, when he said that?

VICKI: I said to him, I said "You know what? I don't think it is any of your damn business," I said, "whether I go back to him or not because you get paid every time I come in here." And he said, "I have other patients to see."

This was not her worst experience with doctors. A visit to an emergency room in another state turned her body literally into a battleground. She said she knew she had to go to the emergency room because it was "one of the worst times." During the visit they "took X-rays, they looked in my eyes and they looked in my mouth" and then sent her away. Her teeth were still numb; she had a broken nose and seven broken ribs "that will never heal right." When she later visited her regular doctor in her home state, "she gave me a rib wrap type thing, but it didn't help. Because they already started healing wrong, and again the only way I can have those hopefully healed right is to have them rebroken and reset, but that is no guarantee."

Vicki knows what she is fighting for: privacy. She cries that she "can't do absolutely anything in complete privacy." In her transitional housing, they can "hear every single word we are saying" and her upstairs neighbor told her, "jokingly," "I could hear you pee." Her sense of the only way to end the war, and to get privacy, is to sever her dependence on the state by "completely getting off welfare."

Joyce is as embattled with the state as Vicki, but in her view sometimes the combative approach works. She provided an example:

DSS. I can't say all bad about the DSS. I can't because of my [particular social worker]. And, she is a pain in my butt. She really is. But she's the type of woman that should be in DSS. I'm very lucky to have her. I mean she's a bitch, excuse me, but I don't know how else to put it. She's a royal queen, mean, I mean you really got to stay on your toes. You know. She'll throw your butt in court. She's thrown my butt in court like three times just because of not doing what I was supposed to do . . . But, you know, [she'll also] leave you alone. Like right now, I'm doing so good, she doesn't even call me. Nothing.

Joyce believes herself to be savvy about the system and she thrives when she can "unmask" the intentions of the state. She responds well to the contentious style of the social worker because she feels her approach keeps everyone on their toes and promotes clarity about what the state is forcing her to do.

Joyce's tactics of defending her turf are her best means of securing control over her life and staving off encroachment by the public sphere. Another tactic is to make the battle public. This was the strategy taken by a group of women who wanted to create an activist campaign in the interests of battered women. In their first organizational meetings they sought to build a coalition that would publicize the issues facing battered women. As battered women themselves, they were more than prepared to speak out about the ongoing issues they confronted in everyday life, including welfare cuts, long waiting lists in supervised visitation centers, and judges who do not recognize the difficulties of co-parenting with a batterer. In their sessions they brainstormed about the practical and the outrageous—from finding a grant writer to making posters of the ten most wanted batterers. Their version of public action (which is similar to the methods used by coalitions of the homeless and welfare rights activists), for the most part, was about avoiding the existing power structure. For example, they knew that they couldn't be closely associated with the shelters in the area because the professionals would worry about bad publicity affecting their funding. More might be gained, however, if abused women chose to acknowledge the inevitability of the breaking down of boundaries between the private and public spheres. This recognition might end women's flight from dangerous control and lead them to staking a claim for a "life beyond misfortune."

Donna's experiences provide some insight into how battered women might move in this direction. She first learned about abuse from a brother seventeen years older than she, who used to "beat the hell" out of her. She was never deterred from talking back to her brother and telling him he was "so unfair." Her mother insisted that she "caused it all" because she wouldn't "shut up." Before she left her husband, she was deeply afraid of seeking help from social services. The husband played on her vulnerabilities by telling horror stories about homeless shelters: "He used to tell me all the time, go ahead, go to a shelter. Watch your kids get raped and know that it's your fault."

She has experienced a miraculous transformation since leaving her batterer, which comes in part from her enormous will to turn her life around. Beyond her personal strengths, she has managed to create victories out of potentially disastrous associations with social services. She tells a phenomenal story about how she got a very desirable apartment through a subsidized housing program. She "didn't even want to apply" for housing because her criminal record would likely put her at a disadvantage. When she went into the housing office the receptionist told her that the housing was "first come, first served" and handed her an application. Donna just "looked at the application." Then she decided to make her next move:

> I saw she went into her office, and I knocked on the door. And she, she told me to come in and I says, "Look, can I talk to you? You know?" And she looked at me. She's like sure. You know? I says, "Really, I want to be honest with you. I'm not going to fill out this application if I'm not going to get a place, you know? This is the story. You know, I think I am a priority," I said "because," I says, "I just came out of a domestic violence situation. I'm going to be truthful. I have a horrible credit history. Horrible, um, I have an eviction on my record. Not for nonpayment but because of noise, and stuff like that. Fights. And, um, I just got convicted of assault and battery and everybody is closing their doors on me! You know? I'm like at my wits end! I don't know what to do. And now you're telling me, well, fill it out. Knock yourself out but you're shutting the door on me." And she looked at me and she, she smiled. She goes, "Sit down." She goes, "Do you have any letters of reference?" I says, "Look, I have a lot of them. I have a lot of them!" Because I did. I had letters from everywhere I've been . . . She, says, "Look, I'm going to talk to management." . . . "Um, I just need a chance." And she looked at me and she, she says, "If I give you this apartment, would he come after you?" "No, God forbid. I told them, he's already got another woman, you know?" She said, "All right. Fill out the application." So I kind of got a really good feeling about that . . . So I take the application home. I kept it for a few days. I never filled it out. I never bothered to fill it out.

The next thing that happened was that the woman from the office sent someone to the battered women's program to get a message to Donna. The message asked her to go to the office with the application and assured her that they would help her "jump through the hoops." The person said the only remaining issue was the "conviction," but that they could go to "bat for her" if she agreed to "see somebody once a week." She only had one more problem, the building wouldn't take cats. "Getting rid of [her] cat" was a "big thing" because her kids had been through enough. But when she dropped off the security deposit at the manager's office she noticed pictures of cats and dogs all over the wall. This led her to say, "Wow, it must be really good, to be able to, you know, have your animals. I'm going to have to get rid of, I have a cat." The manager gave in and told her to keep the cat inside and she would "look the other way." Donna went home and excitedly told her son, "We can keep Snowflake." She concluded: "I got to say it worked out pretty well. I don't know what to say. I have my cat!" When prompted to say more about why she was successful, she attributed it to her honesty and just "luck." More than that, Donna's story illustrates a certain capacity to work with the system. The apparent stroke of good fortune was the product of Donna's choice to let them know "what she deserved" and her ability to show the "powers that be" that she would take full advantage of the opportunities given to her. She savored the "accomplishment" of getting "her own place" much more "because my husband used to tell me that you'd be nothing if it wasn't for me." Donna also used the public system like an astute consumer of private resources. She knew that a Section A housing certificate wasn't worth much unless she figured out how to make it into a ticket to decent and affordable housing.

More insight can be gained about Donna's abilities to negotiate between the vagaries of public and private systems from her dispute with a shelter worker. While in the shelter previously she had an altercation with a worker on the night shift who "wrote her up" for breaking the rules when she brought her son a glass of milk past the official bedtime. Earlier in the day her son was acting out, and she put him in the corner of the room:

And she told me, "Can't you control him?" She tells me. This woman. And I looked at her, I says, "I just gave him a timeout, you know." She says, "This is not acceptable." She says, "He can't act like this in here." And I was like, I know that compared to the other kids, my son was like, okay. I just guess she had it really in for me. I don' know what it was. So I just turned around and I was like, I say "Look, I just gave him a timeout." She says, "Give him a timeout upstairs." And I says, no, I said, "No other kids get timesouts upstairs." She said I should "go upstairs and give him a timeout or I'm going to write you up." I said, "You know what? Fuck you! Write me up!" And that was it. And I just started crying. I say, "You know what? I'm going back. I'm going back. Why am I going to deal with this? I could be home. I could have my things. I could be happy and I don't have to deal with this, you know?" An um, she wrote me up. Uh, they called me downstairs. I just told her everything. And I just, I went off on her. I told her, I told her, "How dare you!" I says, "You know, I come and, and you're supposed to be here helping me. And you're making me feel like, worse than my husband! Cause you're a stranger, you know." I told her everything I felt. And, uh, she told me to go into the office and talk with her. And I told her no. I told her I don't want to, cause I didn't trust her. I says, "I want witnesses." I says, "I'd rather go back to the abuser than to take this abuse from you." And I went upstairs. So she called the director of the shelter . . . She told the director of the shelter that I threatened her. Which was total . . . Like the director asks everybody there and I just, I says "Look, I don't want any trouble. All I want to do is, I, I don't want to get thrown out of the shelter." . . . So, they talked to me and they talked like, the head of, I don't know whatever he is, or she is. And they decided to get rid of her. And I just couldn't believe it. I felt, they said that we could mediate. And I said no.

Donna took a situation that she poignantly described as more abusive than being with her batterer and turned it into an event that made her feel "validated for the first time in years." This happened because she staked a claim about how she deserved to be treated when she was seeking help from others. Donna was unwilling, and she made it known, to take any censure and belittlement from someone she perceived as an illegitimate authority figure. She powerfully expressed this sense of justice by making it clear that when workers in the shelter acted unfairly they were not any better than her abusive husband. This logic challenged the implied privilege of legitimacy attributed to a public institution and its functionaries and insisted upon this legitimacy being granted to the purported beneficiary. This way of thinking, moreover, came from Donna's willingness to transcend any illusions about the good life in either the private or public sphere. Frankly, for Donna the shelter was a place of safety only to the extent that it would treat her right.

Also, the miracle of Donna's success was irreducibly connected to her experience of having lost everything she valued in domestic life. This moment of suffering over her loss created a certain kind of clarity about what was required for a decent life. It was precisely Donna's ability to see that the shelter worker's arbitrary exercise of power was no different from her batterer's, in form or effect, in its contribution to human suffering that helped her to recognize that neither treatment was an inevitable consequence of daily living. Donna avoided the hope of becoming the powerful one and knew that any system of domination brutalizes both the victim and the oppressor. The secret of her "defiance" is found in her hope for an alternative world (from living with a batterer or regimented by shelter life) that does not produce reciprocal brutalization.

When Donna talked about her relationships with professionals she described herself as frustrated by what she perceived as false boundaries. She understood that "there are really a lot of good reasons" for professional distance, but she felt uncomfortable about hiding the fact that she was close friends with some of the people who work with her, especially her complicity in the professional's efforts to keep their relationship "secret." She described her reactions: "They have chosen to keep [me] in their lives, you know, because, I don't know why, exactly, but, you know, *it's sad. That feels like a dirty love affair.* You know? It feels like, you know, it's horrible. I feel like the hidden secret. I wish it could be different." Her language described her deep attachment (which is reciprocated) to some of the professionals who helped her along the way. In her imaginings of a better system, she would be allowed to relate to these people who cared about her without "these boundaries." Ultimately, her willingness to plunge into a "love affair" with professionals, even a *"dirty little* one," marks the beginning of her new life.

insurgent voices

The victim at trial undergoes very public forms of scrutiny while the resident of battered women's shelters encounters more routine forms of denigration. The infrequent ability of victims to exercise real choices depends in some cases on serendipity, being assigned a sympathetic counselor, or the disappearance of a once unrelenting perpetrator. In other cases the women use their acute sense of how the system works to create an aperture for resistance. Yet in all situations women are not "fooled" by the rhetoric of the helping professions; they understand their contact with the system as part of their process of victimization. They are also acutely aware that in order to make gains within that system it is mandatory that they assume the role of a victim and follow the designated path to recovery.

There are many common themes that describe both rape victims and battered women's experience within, and insurgence reaction to, the penal/welfare system. The first is the ubiquity of victim status. Even a remarkably privileged victim, like the Central Park Jogger, is transmuted into a public fiction that fulfills prosecutorial imperatives. The battered women interviewed, whatever their class status before they escaped from their homes, now experience their lives as "regulated subjects." Becoming a "battered woman" means the elimination of choices in all areas of life—where to live, whether to seek employment, how to discipline children, and whom to associate with. It also means being subject to official regulations of welfare, housing policies, and courts and experiencing the intense informal authority of counselors, program managers, and staffs of social service agencies.

Second, there is no escaping the invidious comparisons with the "ideal" victim, whether that ideal is based upon an iconic representation of an innocent woman or the now commonplace medical-therapeutic wisdom about trauma and recovery. Victims are not only judged according to prevailing gender stereotypes; the factors that determine whether they are credible and deserving include the severity of their injuries, the evidence of harm, their exercise of reasonable caution, and their readiness to become successful survivors. Since very few fit the criteria when they enter the system, women learn how to become "good victims." For example, battered women "recover" by learning about their "dysfunctions," and the appropriate language to describe them, from social workers (such as "battered women's syndrome" or the "cycle of violence").

And third, both battered women and rape victims face perilous encounters with the penal/welfare system as an ancillary condition of their protection. The most notable source of fear and retribution concerns their life as mothers. In these interviews, every mother experienced the constant threat of having her children taken away by either the child's father or the state. When real fathers make themselves absent in children's lives, the state, as the symbolic father, quickly seizes his place in the family. As the state expands its domain over private lives, it asserts power through protecting child welfare, often in ways that directly challenge the authority of mothers. This is seen repeatedly in child welfare officials' involvement in the lives of women living in shelters. In addition, many battered women experience complex child custody and visitation disputes with their former partners and batterers. In these situations, the recognition of battering, and in particular the battered women's syndrome, has often worked against women. The psychological and emotional effect on women of sexual abuse or battering can be used as evidence of their unfitness as mothers. Since modern divorce law is frequently based on no-fault principles that make the violence irrelevant and apply rules of formal equality, battered women face particular difficulties in establishing their rights as custodial parents when challenged by fathers with more resources to invest in litigation.

Finally, the opportunities for meaningful choice and autonomy remain elusive for "victims."[8] Even though the professionalized services encountered by rape and domestic violence victims reward clients who make "good" decisions and demonstrate movement toward their goals, the programs themselves do not encourage the kind of autonomy and personal freedom women exercise in ordinary life. In order to be considered for services, women who live in shelters must agree to mandatory provisions and be subject to discipline for infractions, such as failing to conform to acceptable parenting practices, continuing to communicate with batterers, and noncompliance with numerous rules and regulations. Analogously, in rape prosecutions victims must be "cooperative" with law enforcement authorities and avoid any actions that might cause public scrutiny (such as being a welfare recipient, accessing emergency medical care, and seeking personal profit). Moreover, when women are acquiescent, it occurs in a context of hierarchal power relations between professionals and clients, such as when battered women demonstrate their coping abilities by avoiding conflict with difficult staff or accepting an inevitable period of dependency (while espousing the desire for independence). This performance of compliance does not prepare women for combating gender hierarchies or confronting injustices in society at large. In this way, clients of the welfare state learn to improve their short-term survival strategies rather than enlarge their life expectations. This is particularly unfortunate because many women soon return to communities where the conditions of poverty and lack of adequate government services will encumber their freedom in ways not so different from the environment of the shelter.

6

UNIVERSALIZING GENDER JUSTICE

at home and abroad

When terror would seem to be all around us, terror equated with the threat of physical violence, it is all the more imperative to articulate what it is that makes violence violent. On a certain level, it is obvious: when there is bodily injury or destruction, there is violence; but beyond that, there is the abstract and less overtly corporeal violence of a state or a multinational class that dominates those who are less powerful. This, too, is violence, but a violence less predicated on the immediately physical. . . . The point is not to show that one system [of organizing violence] is better or worse, but that they are different mechanisms of organizing power—each relying on violence of a particular sort.—Eleanor Kaufman

The most recent wave of activism focused on violence against women has attempted to use the human rights paradigm in both national and international contexts. The human rights approach follows from post–World War II efforts to use international law to curb abuses against humanity. By definition, human rights are universal ethical standards that affirm the equality and dignity of all individuals. These rights can be applied either supranationally or to groups and individuals within states. Human rights activism has addressed large-scale horrific violence, such as genocide, and has been utilized to extend civil protections and promote economic justice for politically disadvantaged groups.

Over the past thirty years, international networks of feminists have employed the human rights framework as a means to advocate for women. By framing women's right to be protected from male violence in both the home and on the streets in terms of universal human rights, leaders of this movement hope to broaden the terms of the debate within developed Western countries and extend protections to women around the globe.

In the context of violence against women, the human rights paradigm views all forms of violence against women's bodies (e.g., rape, battering, homicide, stalking, torture, and genital mutilation) as a violation of a person's fundamental rights to freedom of movement, personal dignity, and economic sustainability. These violations are primarily understood as the result of the failure of the state to protect women as a class and to promote their equal status in society. Hence, human rights principles applied to women are essentially equality doctrines that link their mistreatment to social, political, or economic status yet also tie this status to affirmative measures taken by states to promote women's interests.

This theory of women's human rights is codified in the Convention of the Elimination of All Forms of Discrimination against Women (CEDAW),[1] which was adopted by the United Nations General Assembly in 1979. This convention requires states to commit themselves to efforts to end discrimination against women and to take all appropriate measures to ensure that women enjoy human rights and fundamental freedoms. The convention commits states to incorporate this principle of equality into their legal systems, both through the abolition of discriminatory laws and the enforcement of measures to protect women from exploitation.

While CEDAW is a broad-based effort to protect women's rights in all domains of life, it addresses gender-based violence as a form of discrimination. The specific provisions focusing on violence toward women were not included in the original convention but were added under General Recommendation 19 of the revised convention in 1992. This recommendation explains that the prohibition of gender-based discrimination includes violence and requires all ratifying states to take all the necessary measures to eliminate violence. This includes legal sanctions, civil remedies, preventative measures (such as public information and education campaigns), and protective measures (such as support services for victims).[2] It establishes that discrimination is at the root of social forces that perpetuate gender-based violence. As a rights-based approach to reducing violence against women, it assumes that endemic violence against women arises from the failure to protect minimal standards of human dignity in societies.

Most discussions of CEDAW are focused on basic questions about its effectiveness as a form of international regulation. Compliance with CEDAW is formally monitored by the United Nations through the submission of national reports, but the successful enforcement of this transnational normative order is mainly dependent on internal pressure from national NGOS and indirect pressure from the international human rights community. While recognizing the limitations of enforcing international conventions, it is still important to analyze the ways in which this human rights discourse represents a view of modernization and sets in place methodologies for protecting women against violence, such as a therapeutic/psychological understanding of the problem.

This move toward a human rights paradigm to address violence against women has important implications for the issues addressed in this book, particularly in relation to the ways it potentially contributes to the growing criminalization of sexual violence that, in turn, expands the policing functions of the modern state. The human rights approach is in many ways a continuation of Western feminist activism on the issue, but it also suggests new ways of affirming women's right to be free from violence. The human rights paradigm has become a vehicle for disseminating the feminist movement against sexual violence, as it has developed in the neoliberal political conditions in the United States, into a non-Western, global context. It additionally becomes apparent that an opportunity has been created for that model to be subjected to international scrutiny.

This kind of international scrutiny is limited, however, because the United States, despite its active role in drafting the text and signing it, has never ratified the agreement due to conservative opposition in the Senate Foreign Relations Committee. Clearly accentuated by the United States' failure to ratify CEDAW, attention to violence against women as a human rights issue has placed the U.S. record in a critical light and has spurred the formation of domestic human rights groups who demand reforms related to the treatment of women by courts.

In the United States, violence against women is seen as a crime control issue that is largely left to state and local authorities. The first effort to formulate a "national" policy to address violence against women and to see it as a consequence of gender discrimination culminated in the passage of the 1994 Violence against Women Act (VAWA).[3] Although this act is not a substitute for participation in an international human rights convention, in its original formulation it constructed sexual violence as an equality issue and provided for civil rights remedies for victims of gender-based violent crimes.

Looking at both the original logic behind the VAWA as well as its erosion by the courts provides a vehicle to evaluate the difficulties of seeing violence as a consequence of discrimination and nationalizing a policy focused on protecting women in the American context. The problems associated with implementing a human rights approach run deeper than political opposition in the Senate against CEDAW. They reflect the limitations within efforts, like the VAWA, to provide a federal framework for developing standards and enforcing rights. (In the context of this chapter, comparisons are made between the political and legal logics of VAWA and CEDAW, although each act has different jurisdictions, status as a legal instrument, and enforcement mechanisms.)

The failure to implement national standards or apply an antidiscrimination policy that attends to sexual violence in the United States raises concerns about the capacity of a human rights approach to offer new and meaningful strategies to counteract sexual violence internationally. In this chapter, human rights discourse is treated as a highly differentiable form of both theory and practice that can extend the power of the state and potentially increase reliance on illegitimate forms of state violence in the name of protecting women. Although this analysis emphasizes the limitations of the human rights approach and its continuities with Western feminists' activism against sexual violence, it also identifies aspects of the human rights paradigm that capture new possibilities for the vitality of political life. Ideally, human rights strategies should seek to empower women through forms of political action that support victims' individual sovereignty, rather than reliance on state powers of surveillance and punishment.

criminalizing gender violence

When the issue of violence against women is posed as an "international problem," the immediate response of human rights activists is typically a call for the criminalization of gender violence. The pull of this solution is primarily based on the notion that this problem persists because violence against women, as opposed to other forms of interpersonal or state-sponsored violence, is not taken seriously. Following this logic, the primary objective of reform is to improve women's access to the courts and other legal mechanisms to redress violence. This is seen as a positive transformation in which sexual violence is no longer viewed and treated as a domestic, private, and predictably trivial issue but instead as a matter of public significance. In fact, domestic and other forms of interpersonal violence are seen as one of the most important barriers that prevent women from taking their rightful places within the public sphere. Consequently, human rights conventions attempt to improve conditions for women by putting pressure on states to promote serious and effective enforcement of criminal laws against interpersonal violence.

This criminalization framework targets either custom or customary legal practices that justify authoritarian gender roles or women's passivity in the face of oppression.[4] In the human rights paradigm, universal norms, such as equality and self-determination, trump customary practices that impede women's advancement in the public sphere. In such enforcement practices, progress toward compliance with international conventions is measured by the implementation of often national-level directives that rule against local (and often religious) practices.[5] Although the enforcement mechanisms are weak (usually backed by naming and shaming noncompliant countries or linked sometimes to monetary incentives), the human rights model in its global manifestation is a pseudo-criminalized system of surveillance and sanctions. At its most extreme, however, human rights policy can be used to justify military intervention. One example is the new American doctrine called "the Responsibility to Protect" that justifies intervening in a foreign state's domestic affairs in order to address human rights violations.[6] Thus, it becomes imperative to ask in both a local and global context—how do policies designed to "protect" women serve to reproduce violence?

The push to criminalize sexual violence is accompanied by other political initiatives that are directed toward regulating sexual practices in local and global markets. The most notable measures focus on the trafficking of women and the distribution of pornography, both of which are the subject of emerging "wars on crime" similar to the targeting of drug traffickers. There is also a precarious connection between new programs that target domestic violence and state interest in regulating the family, marriage, reproduction, and sexuality more generally. Although CEDAW explicitly links women's rights to reproductive freedom, these feminist moral imperatives, in practice, are subject to forms of national coalition building that give voice to policies that limit women's access to abortion or seek to regulate homosexuality. Internationally, any progress toward the criminalization of domestic violence needs to be evaluated in the context of how modernizing states are assuming new political apparatus to monitor the family and women's reproduction. For example, the recent implementation of a new domestic violence policy in Trinidad was accompanied by the criminalization of homosexuality and by a more conventional legal enactment of marriage.[7]

In a world confronting an escalation in state-sponsored violence, it is important to question the national and global implications of investing states with more power to regulate and punish acts of sexual violence. Hannah Arendt, in *On Violence,* laments the glorification of violence as a means to increase the instrumental power of governments and dissident movements. By reminding us that violence is merely instrumental and incapable of shoring up truly legitimate state power, she keenly argues against the attraction of violence even as a means for just ends. Moreover, the highly rationalized violence and its technocratic imposition found in the criminal control state have the potential to deprive ordinary people of political freedom and their capacity to act. This deprivation of political freedom ultimately attracts more violence. Arendt's analysis of politics moves beyond a simple repulsion of all forms of violence and theories of absolute nonviolence and considers how the resort to violent strategies, by states, groups, and citizens, often constitutes the absence of power rather than political might. This recognition helps to explain why the attraction to violence as an instrumental strategy is often caused by the "severe frustration of the faculty of action in the modern world."[8]

In the context of criminalizing sexual violence, state violence rarely appears to be retaliatory in nature given that it is implemented through highly rationalized systems of justice. For the most part, in modern Western states like the United States, the punitive forces of the state are fully integrated into bureaucratic and therapeutic institutions that regulate the lives of perpetrators and victims of violence. Yet, as the case studies of gang rape trials in this book have shown, when the specter of the racialized stranger emerges, even within a highly bureaucratized legal system, the ritualized fear of sexual contamination may set the stage for dramatic legal and cultural events. In these situations, the legitimacy of state action comes into question as actors, such as the police and prosecutors, use coercive power and apply racial stereotyping.

In light of Arendt's analysis of the nexus of violence and power, this phenomenon might be seen as a reflection of how the state's overinvestment in punitive responses to crime fails not only to shore up its legitimacy as the protector of women but makes the state look like a sexual oppressor itself. It is not surprising that when agents of the modern state engage in illegal forms of torture to abuse prisoners of war, for example, their actions often take the form of highly brutalized sexuality. The real legitimacy of the state to act in the name of victims is rarely directly addressed because the sovereignty of the state to punish crimes against persons is assumed as a necessary aspect of the political contract in theory and practice. As Arendt makes clear, even in terms of the protection of the peacefulness of domestic life, the use of state violence puts the state in jeopardy of losing political power.[9] Although states punish criminals virtually in "self-defense" of the social contract, these sanctions apply violence as a last resort and, politically speaking, require the consensus of the majority. So that when states act as "protectors," they must shore up the legitimacy of their actions within the polity.

Criminal justice approaches may seem like the only alternative when domestic violence protections are stepped up in new national contexts. The more highly rationalized forms of state control, like domestic violence shelters and treatment programs, often are not "exportable" because in many countries it may be unrealistic for women to divorce and establish separate households. The political theorist Uma Narayan argues that in India, for example, the movement against domestic violence has taken on very different forms from those in the United States, where much energy had been focused on establishing shelters.[10] She disputes the suggestion that this means that Indian feminists are less "developed" in their approaches and attributes this difference to "the virtual absence in India of state-provided welfare . . . [that] render[s] it very difficult for feminists to generate structures that would enable Indian women to leave the family contexts where they are victims of violence."[11]

Given the difficulties of applying the American model in other settings, it is all the more important to look at how translating human rights "standards" across cultures may lead to the overreliance on criminal justice strategies that increase surveillance and sanctioning of local institutional practices or individual men. Compliance with international conventions, in effect, provides states with mechanisms of international sovereignty that buttress their authority over local custom and practices deemed harmful to women in the name of "protection." This becomes especially problematic in situations where cultural or religious minorities are pitted against national authorities.

In general, UN enforcement of CEDAW treats each country equally regardless of local differences, especially to the extent that the claim of cultural difference is seen as a justification for repressive practices. The anthropologist Sally Merry shows how government officials representing their country in CEDAW compliance hearings use culture as a static concept in order to provide explanations for their lack of progress.[12] Sometimes culture is seen as a positive good, as in Egypt, where, despite more conservative national policies, many women took advantage of rural laws granting women the unilateral right to divorce.[13] The theory of gender inequality in CEDAW and accompanying treaties, however, can also become a focal point for opposition within Muslim countries. While officially countries are allowed "reservations" that permit reasons for noncompliance that are linked to respecting cultural practices, CEDAW was premised on the notion that traditional gender roles are an obstacle to the achievement of women's equality. This has created a counterreaction in Muslim countries where resistance to international human rights law has coalesced around women's rights. In Muslim countries, more conservative family policy may create an entirely different relation between local and state power. In these situations the state may formally agree to international human rights conventions but allow local patronage networks and religious, ethnic, and regional cleavages to bolster patriarchal family arrangements.[14] This problem is accentuated because in "countries where religious law is communalized, the state vests religious leaders and institutions with autonomy over family law as a means of consolidating power or promoting stability in a religiously pluralist society."[15] For example, the ability of Arab women living in Israel to exercise their rights is impeded by the nature of their citizenship within a Jewish state. Rather than appeal to a hostile state in order to affirm their rights, they must assert their needs in a context of communalism. Arab Israeli women's rights activists formulate strategies that bypass an appeal to the state for interventions against men within the community. These examples demonstrate how the enforcement of human rights conventions is often incompatible with conditions of pluralism between and within states.

As case studies about the actual implementation of CEDAW reveal, human rights policies are imposed in conditions influenced by both nationalist interests and local pluralism.[16] This means that the implementing states must negotiate their power to impose these standards vis-à-vis the international community and minority populations or interests. Thus, the legitimation of human rights policy is highly dependent on mechanisms, often coercive, employed by the state to shore up its legitimacy.

the violence against women act

As previously noted, the United States has failed to ratify CEDAW and essentially escapes the kind of scrutiny applied to Muslim countries by the international community. Nevertheless, internal political interests have made some headway toward legally mandating federally based equality standards. In 1994, after lengthy hearings and extensive lobbying, Congress passed the Violence against Women Act (VAWA). This was the first attempt to formulate a national policy addressing violence against women and to address the prevalence of rape, domestic violence, stalking, and other crimes. The VAWA was touted as an important measure to promote consistent crime control across states, improve funding and enforcement, and allow for court remedies for state inaction that constituted a form of discriminatory treatment. As was the case with previous federal legislative actions expanding civil rights, Congress passed the statute under the Commerce Clause and the Enforcement Clause of the Fourteenth Amendment. On the basis of the notion that violence against women has an impact on interstate commerce and that such private acts are economic in nature, Congress provided federal remedies for gender-motivated acts of violence.

The VAWA also confirmed a particular understanding of violence against women as a "social problem" that followed from the long history of feminist activism focused on this issue.[17] In particular, this act affirms the view that rape and domestic battery are not private, sexual matters but acts of violence of significant public consequence. Judith Resnik, a professor of law, explains the logic behind the VAWA: "Linking violence against women to sex and domestic life illustrates more than a problem of rhetoric; it demonstrates the ongoing effects of laws that have treated women unequally. For centuries, state laws wove notions of sex and domesticity into a fabric of toleration of violence against women. And now that federal law is trying to protect women from the residue of that discrimination."[18] Resnik reiterates the message of early movement activists by asserting that the "VAWA is not about sex" and that treating such violence as sex often "softens the brutality" and "offers the perpetrator the justification of lust."[19] The VAWA also reframes the issue as a matter of federalism. This rubric contrasts the domain of the "state" as private and domestic and permissive of "traditional" forms of mistreating women with the promise of a cosmopolitan assertion of rights-based identities in a federal system.[20] While echoing the human rights paradigm's preemption of traditional culture, the proponents of the VAWA establish women's protection from violence as a preeminent concern of the national agenda, in terms of both the expansion of basic civil liberties and the ongoing war on crime.

The VAWA victory was extremely short lived: in 2000 the Supreme Court struck down the civil rights provisions of this act as unconstitutional. In *United States v. Morrison* the Court invalidated federal remedies on the grounds that Congress exceeded its power in legislating equality rights.[21] The decision relied upon a narrow conception of federalism that gave priority to state sovereignty over the substantive purpose of congressional legislation promoting equality.[22] The *Morrison* decision also contradicts the factual conclusions reached in the congressional hearings on the act, which in anticipation of such a challenge considered testimony from women about how rape and domestic battering affected job performance and restricted their employment opportunities.[23]

Although *Morrison* is a blow to efforts to fashion anti-discrimination remedies for women and to civil rights enforcement powers more generally, the framing of violence against women as a "federal" problem is somewhat analogous to the model of enforcement created through human rights conventions. In this case, the defense of sexual violence as "violence" rather than "sex" establishes the harm as primarily linked to the impact of this violence on women's ability to perform in the public sphere. One implication of this is the rigid reinforcement of the public sphere as the domain of important activity for women and another is an implicit denial that under modern conditions of commodification "sex" is the object of commerce and state regulation. In a sense, sex is a commodity that transcends the private and public spheres in both its production and distribution.[24] Since a major purpose of the VAWA is to provide women protection from the types of violence for which there are inconsistent legal remedies across states, an important example being marital rape, the model of federalism puts misplaced insistence on recognizing violence through its impact on women's role in the public sphere. The logic seems counterintuitive when these provisions aspire to fashion legal remedies that reach into the deeply private context in which violence occurs.

The conception of sexual violence as a "public" problem in the VAWA is, of course, partly the artificial result of the necessity to fashion a compelling constitutional argument. But it also emerges from the inherent logic of federalism, a logic that finds parallels in the paradigm of human rights enforcement. Both systems of governance invest in the federal body the normative authority to set universal standards for the treatment of citizens. Such guarantees within a federalist system are indeed necessary for citizens to enjoy their political and economic rights within the public sphere. Yet the practice of citizenship is far more complicated, especially in situations involving harm in our most intimate relationships. The recognition of freedom from sexual violence as an expressly public right does not sufficiently capture how the risk to human dignity is linked to women's choices for privacy or autonomy or the ways that surviving violence may require negotiating a relationship with the state.

Specifically in the American context, breaking through the traditional notions of how privacy has prevented legal intervention may have the reverse effect of creating a situation where women lose control over their private domain because of mandatory arrest laws and no-drop policies that take away from women their power to decide whether to pursue criminal justice intervention. Renee Romens, a legal scholar from the Netherlands, suggests that in the American experience the shift of wife abuse from the private to the public domain has reinforced the underlying binary of the public and private.[25] This has led to the implementation of policies that have eroded women's choices in the private sphere, and the "fact that law, notably criminal law, has been used as a major vehicle to materialize this public responsibility only exacerbates this dynamic."[26] In contrast, Romens argues that the shifting of the definition of the "battered women" to a public identity has been less problematic in Western European countries because "there is more of a balance between the legal and the social category and the social policy strategies that the battered women's movements have pursued in trying to devise supportive policies. In

Western Europe the issue of battering has been a much more effective domain of socio-political struggle than in the U.S."[27] From this perspective, efforts to define violence against women as a national issue in the United States does less to liberate women from local custom, and more to create the circumstances for state intrusion into private lives.

Moreover, the actual application of the civil rights remedy under the VAWA requires victims to assert agencies in ways that conform to traditional private and public roles for women. The legal scholar Caroline Picart examines how in specific cases of litigants seeking remedies under the VAWA women are rhetorically configured as victims.[28] She suggests that the significance of using federal means to punish purely private acts created the burden to show that the redress was not "out of proportion" with the crime committed.[29] In order to establish themselves as "victims" women were forced to reinforce the dichotomy between the private versus the public in a stark, unproblematic way. For example, in a case of marital rape, the plaintiff Christina Bergeron had to negotiate the contrasting image of her "status as a former wife with a now 'angry' woman seeking legal redress for what was framed as an alleged attempted rape."[30] The court decision "is haunted by the same specter of male fears of false accusation; and its attempt to strongly delineate between the vengeful woman (agent) and terrified woman (victim)."[31]

The implementation of a civil rights remedy is further complicated by the necessity under the provisions to show gender animus. In order to establish a prima facie case it must be shown with the "preponderance of the evidence" that the plaintiff is a victim of a "crime of violence" and that the defendant perpetrator was "motivated to commit the crime based on the victim's gender."[32] The legislative history establishes that there is, not even in cases of rape, the *presumption* that the crime is motivated by gender bias.[33] This means that in order to apply this law, specific proof of gender bias needs to accompany the claim of sexual assault. For example, in *Ziegler v. Ziegler* the specific acts to show gender animus were "rape, gender-specific epithets, acts that perpetuated the stereotype of submissive roles for the plaintiff within marriage, severe physical attacks, particularly during pregnancy, and violence without provocation, when the plaintiff attempts to assert her independence."[34] The requirement to prove animus places the litigant under a burden to define violence as harm, to prove that violence represents the underlying hostility toward, or the subordination of, women. This burden is similar to that of anti-pornography feminists seeking to describe pornography as violence.

In a more general sense, this legal requirement forces an extremely narrow understanding of the motivations and causes of sexual violence. A clear analogy can be made to the situation of genocide in which international law has prescribed that even in such ultimate forms of violence, animus may not be a factor. In fact, genocide without animus is endemic to the modern condition. The philosopher David Luban, in his study of crimes against humanity, cites numerous examples where genocide may not occur with animus. Perpetrators may target a civilian population for reasons having nothing to do with animus—"for example, because targeting the population is the simplest way to eradicate the resistance fighters living within it, or because the population occupies strategically or economically important territory that the oppressor wishes to seize."[35]

Despite the striking down of the federal provision, individual states have enacted similar versions of the statute and have sought to apply the same criteria of animus. The predominant standard is called the "totality of circumstances approach." This approach to claims by state VAWA plaintiffs creates hierarchies of rapes, "with some acts of rape seen as 'worse' than others and thus deserving of redress, and other rapes emerging as lacking sufficiently probative indicia of gender bias. Paradigmatic 'stranger rape' VAWA claims might well succeed, but cases involving inter-spousal, same-sex, or 'provocation' rapes could well fail."[36] This creates the potential for civil rights litigation to have the opposite effect than intended by the drafters of the VAWA—the courts might well give more legitimacy to rapes in a "public" setting and fail to recognize the harm of rape in private contexts. This may cause the VAWA to be interpreted in a nonuniform fashion, and decisions will reflect the biases and social views of individual courts. The end result is that "these decisions reflected and further entrenched already existing myths of rape and gender status."[37]

The invalidation of the civil rights provision leaves intact the rest of the VAWA that primarily sets up provisions for funding crime prevention programs. Yet again, a feminist victory for a national policy for the protection of women has been transformed into a means to expand the crime control apparatus of the state. Major priorities for federal funding under the VAWA are to improve police investigation techniques and to gather forensic evidence.[38] When battered women's shelters receive VAWA funding, it is often a very small part of their overall budget.[39] This means that shelters continue to rely greatly on volunteers and soft money.

One study of the effects of VAWA on direct services for battered women finds that shelter personnel are extremely skeptical about the potential of federal policies to address the root causes of the problem.[40] On the other hand, as a direct result of VAWA funding, law enforcement agencies have promoted major new initiatives, called Coordinated Community Responses (CCR). The CCRS are usually led by local prosecutors who launch "coordinated" training and development efforts with police, emergency room examiners, and social service workers. The primary focus of CCRS is to produce more accurate and relevant information from victim examinations and to improve the training of examiners as expert witnesses. However, these CCRS are being funded at the expense of other programs that could have a more direct effect on victims' lives. For example, in one community CCRS have expanded while the only local domestic violence shelter has been closed.[41]

One of the best outcomes of the VAWA has been in the area of protecting the rights of immigrant women. One example is the recent expansion of the recognition of "extreme cruelty" by the Ninth Circuit to describe the pattern of spousal abuse experienced by a woman seeking immigration status independent from her husband.[42] Yet again, however, these important gains in the rights of immigrant women are accompanied by a major crime control effort centered on the trafficking of persons. The VAWA was packaged along with the Trafficking Victims Protection Act, intended to combat trafficking as a modern form of slavery.[43]

While trafficking of women is an increasing worldwide problem, it is important to consider it as part of a complex international phenomenon closely related to international sex markets, labor markets, and illegal immigration. The increase in trafficking is also clearly related to the excessive policing of borders and the consequent profits in organizing criminal means of transporting persons across borders. While trafficking in persons is an increasing worldwide problem, it has also been the focus of sensationalized media coverage. As Jacqueline Berman argues, "Governmental anti-organized crime initiatives have produced a new set of discursive practices that conflate violent crime against women with complex forms of post-communist gendered migration. These discourses . . . portray all international, often illegal, migration and labor as acts of violated gender and raced innocence and of international organized crime."[44] From Berman's perspective, when governments, especially those of the United States and Western European countries, focus on sex trafficking as a form of organized crime, they are drawing attention away from the underlying causes of the problem that arise largely from migration and the policing of borders. This framing of the issue creates the impression that criminalization of all activities related to trafficking is the most logical and effective means of addressing the problem.[45] It results in policies oriented toward "victims" of organized crime rather than efforts to address the underlying conditions of migration and globalization that create vulnerable populations. Moreover, the global criminalization of trafficking provides an opportunity for the United States to implement its foreign policy objectives through elements of its human rights agenda. This policing role assumed by the United States may be less effective at serving the real needs of trafficking victims than the more specialized and local activities of NGOs.[46] In addition to using this policy as an opportunity for statecraft, the United States (even though it has withdrawn from international conventions prohibiting trafficking) also exercises its prerogative to impose sanctions on other countries, notably North Korea and Cuba, that fail to comply with the conventions.[47] The sanctions are largely symbolic measures imposed to shame countries unfriendly to the United States, but when attached to restrictions in foreign aid they may have adverse domestic impact on women and children in those countries.[48]

Overall, the VAWA has not been a focal point for improving the conditions of women in the United States. As a civil rights measure, even when implemented on a state-by-state basis, it provides a problematic foundation for litigation in that it puts an unrealistic burden of proof on victims to show animus as the motivation for violence. Moreover, as a source of funding it has largely been co-opted by more organized and established criminal justice agencies while grassroots battered women's programs are left to falter due to federal and state cuts in social service programs across the board.

the human rights standard

Another way to evaluate the effects of human rights policies is to look at their role in setting national and international standards for the prevention of violence against women. Such standards, at their very best, set the minimum responsibility of the state to affirm anti-discrimination principles and to provide resources for women and their families (including reproductive services, health care, education, and social services). The legal scholar Elizabeth Schneider has argued that the introduction of the human rights framework is useful for not only affirming international standards but also for pointing out the failure of U.S. policies to live up to those standards.[49] Comparative analysis of human rights records may also provide insight into the narrowness of American methods of addressing the problem. Juley Fulcher, an American policy expert for the National Coalition against Violence who has studied Japanese systems to combat domestic violence, recently concluded that although the record of the United States in improving the status of women is more impressive than that of Japan, the United States lags in systems addressing domestic violence.[50] Fulcher attributes the success of the Japanese system to not only more serious attention to the issue at the national level but also an understanding of domestic violence rooted neither in a crisis of family values nor a criminal justice problem.[51]

Alternatives to criminalization are rare in the United States. One option that moves away from punitive state responses is a "restorative justice" procedure that aims to heal rather than punish incidents of domestic violence.[52] This approach is offered by the social work scholar Linda Mills, who proposes "intimate abuse circles" to resolve situations of domestic violence.[53] The possible advantage of this approach is that by employing community-based groups to sort through the situation and devise solutions it accepts the pluralism of perspectives and the need for victims and perpetrators to live within the same communities.

In the United States, there is another example of a locally formed "human rights" movement, a Massachusetts organization called the Women's Rights Network. Its founders participated in the UN Fourth World Conference on Women in Beijing in 1995 and were inspired to "bring Beijing home."[54] Their strategy is twofold: first to identify specific human rights violations in the U.S. context and then to encourage local, community-based activism stemming from forms of testimony about battering (reminiscent of truth commissions).[55] Among the human rights violations they have identified are failure to protect women and children from abuse; allowing the batterer to continue the abuse; denial of due process to battered women; discrimination and bias against battered women; and failure to respect the economic rights of battered women and their children.[56] This organization has attempted to "confront the state" with these violations, by individually and collectively calling into question the discriminatory treatment of battered women in local courts.

While both of these human rights practices move away from employing the power of the state to punish, each leaves the individual vulnerable either to the wider interests of the community or to possible retaliation by officials. The leaders of the Women's Rights Network, for example, worry that making strong claims about human rights violations makes officials very angry, and women who point out abuses on these terms may be subject to backlash by courts. Similarly, the restorative justice solution may leave women in risky situations, especially when they choose to stay (and are supported by the community) in violent families. Without addressing larger issues of structural change, restorative justice may not facilitate women finding more security and safety in their domestic lives.[57]

reconceptualizing the ideal of human rights

The most powerful means to enlarge the ideal of human rights is to frame it in terms of dignity. In this regard, the American view of rights is particularly lacking. The specific phrase "human dignity" has been mostly absent from the American discourse on rights. The language of dignity, especially as applied to individuals rather than the role functioning of institutions, first entered into American constitutional discourse after World War II.[58] Since that time, it has been used in a variety of fashions, including a view of personal dignity linked to autonomy (like the ability to control one's own body). In the antidiscrimination context, dignity stands for the ability to exercise fundamental liberty rights. American equality doctrines have yet to incorporate the fuller scope and interpretation of personal dignity that is expressed in international law and treaty. In these limited applications in American constitutional discourse, moreover, dignity is treated as a status rather than as a guarantee of the capacity for all persons to be part of and engage in a political community.[59]

This more expanded version of human rights is seen in Arendt's political theorizing. She was deeply concerned with protecting citizens from intrusions of both private and public violence and with the propensity under conditions of modernity for there to be an erosion of basic human rights and freedoms. For Arendt, this was a problem of guaranteeing freedom and dignity rather than creating a static guarantee granted by supragovernmental powers.[60] The guarantee of basic human rights emerges from the active commitment of citizens to take risks and claim a stake in the formation of political community.[61] This view of human rights prevents the privileging of one group over another (based on race, class, religion, or nation) and acknowledges the plurality of the human world.

However, Arendt was quite skeptical of world government, which she saw as a centralized authority over the whole globe that could potentially hold a monopoly on all means of violence and problematic as a federalist form of political organization.[62] For Arendt, the protection of human rights could not come through formal legal means or the institutional structure of federalism. The rights that protect women against violence, as currently formulated by the United Nations in CEDAW, are an example of this kind of global federalism. As a form of politics designed to resolve conflicts among states, federalism is often inadequate for resolving complex problems among individuals and groups. The nation-state (and its later refashioning into global government) was originally the eighteenth-century political solution for creating a context for the self-determination of individuals and peoples, but modern conditions have often turned this form of government into an obstacle to achieving the dignity that individuals and communities seek.

In contrast to global federalism, the conditions for the expression of meaningful human rights are found when there is an active commitment to such principles by individuals participating in a political community. In the context of everyday political participation, the guarantee of freedom and dignity emerges when citizens give full respect to the plurality of individual and group interests. This emerges when the discourse of rights is conceived of as contingent, fluid, and grounded in the deliberation of diverse individuals and groups rather than derived from universal principles.

Such theories of human rights ultimately ground the power to protect human dignity in the sovereignty of individual citizens rather than in the enforcement of the monopoly on violence held by the state. In this view, it is the growth of bureaucracy and unresponsive large institutions that makes violence look like an attractive possibility to the citizenry.[63] When citizens take hold of their rights to sovereignty, it opens up the potential for individuals and groups to withdraw from forms of authority invested in the instrumental use of violence. In such a world, it would be possible to promote forms of political organization that would respond to the problem of sexual violence without the reproduction of violence by the state. We should ask: What kinds of solutions are more or less violent? What would make law less arbitrary and less violent? How do we counteract sexual violence in ways that do not merely displace violence onto others who are a perceived threat to the social order?

This reconceptualization of human rights discourse suggests new possibilities but does not provide assurances about its realization or specifics about the necessary conditions for its ripening. Most importantly, it underscores the potential role of nongovernmental organizations in setting the course for new solutions to violence against women, particularly those that promote civic engagement. A model organization that incorporates the potential to capture this sense of political activism is Incite!, a nationally based movement. Incite! is explicitly a social justice movement, but unlike most feminist and women's rights organizations, it addresses both state and interpersonal violence.[64] It stresses the importance of integrating responses to state violence, including anti-prison, anti–prison brutality, and anti-war issues, with responses to domestic and sexual violence. Also, Incite! recognizes the disproportionate burden of both state and interpersonal violence on women of color.[65] Some of their major tenets include a call to "build movements that not only end violence, but that create a society based on radical freedom, mutual accountability, and passionate reciprocity. In this society, safety and security [would] not be premised on violence or the threat of violence."[66]

This organization's objectives go along with the basic premise of this book—that responding to sexual violence in American society requires a critical understanding of the power of the state to both reproduce violence and to isolate victims. Moreover, these activists seek to cross the divide between public and private violence by demanding social justice both for victimized individuals and for communities. Finally, the movement is inspired by a passionate vision of participatory democracy and the desire to preserve "safety and security" through the affirmation of human dignity. Through Incite! we can see the foundations for a feminist activism that is firmly based on strategies of nonviolence and the foundation of a larger agenda for social justice.

activism in context

The "Incite!" strategy for activism, however, emerges from the American context, where despite a highly developed prison-industrial complex and persistent forms of institutional racism, there are guarantees of fundamental political and civil rights for women. Their call for action is, in a sense, an invitation to use these rights as part of a collective social response to counteract violence in intimate relationships. In other local and national contexts, activist strategies must emerge from the particular conditions of politics and culture. As Uma Narayan argues, "Transnational cooperation among feminists depends on all of us better understanding . . . issues of "context" . . . as well as attending to the asymmetries in 'cultural explanations.' "[67] For Narayan, to compare policies about domestic violence between the United States and other countries (such as India) we need to be open to questioning our attributions to cultural difference as well as our tendency to overlook culture as an explanation within Western contexts. In her comparison, she examines how Western attention to "dowry deaths" may create the impression that "domestic violence" in India is far more prevalent and horrific than the domestic violence murders in the United States. After gathering the available data she shows that the murder rates are actually quite similar, but more to her point, Narayan suggests that it is the manner in which Western feminists employ the concept of culture that makes these dowry deaths appear exotic and murders in the United States inexplicable in terms of the unique characteristics of American culture.[68] These attributions to cultural difference certainly have enormous influence on the human rights agenda as it pertains to gender violence. As a result, international programs focus on issues such as genital mutilation, Muslim honor killings, and dowry deaths.[69]

In terms of the design and implementation of strategies to improve women's lives, "differences in culture" are more important than "cultural explanations" for the causes of violence. The agenda for activism from the vantage point of groundbreaking feminists working for NGOs in individual countries looks very different from an international human rights agenda. For example, Majlis, an NGO providing legal assistance to women in India, has had success with an innovative use of injunctive relief. The group uses the civil law to protect battered women's access to their matrimonial home or to "put the man out," which then improves their bargaining position in either cases where the man returns or the woman seeks a divorce.[70] These advocates find this inventive use of the civil law to be far more productive than relying on the newly provided provisions of the Indian Penal Code that criminalizes domestic violence. Another program in Uganda, the Mifumi Project, has approached the problem of domestic violence by working toward criminalizing bride price and discouraging child marriages.[71] Both of these factors create the conditions for bad treatment of women in their homes. These activists in Uganda deftly distinguish that bride price customs have not always contributed to the frequency of domestic violence, but became a dangerous practice for women as a result of their standardization under colonial rule. The problem with the bride price custom in terms of furthering domestic violence is not its role in solidifying marriage as a "gift" but its demand as an essential requirement of marriage and in disputed situations, its demand for return. In this case, local activists believe it is important to criminalize this practice, but with clear recognition of the difficulties of enforcement within the cultural and administrative conditions of local governments. The activities of both of these local domestic violence projects demonstrate how empowering women involves working through the conditions of culture rather than staunch opposition to cultural practices based on universal standards.

Each example shows that the issue at hand is not whether criminalization is an inherently dangerous strategy but rather the importance of considering alternatives other than criminal sanctions against perpetrators and understanding how the effectiveness of such sanctions are dependent on the complexities of governance at the local and/or national level. In both cases, it is more important for activists to support women's basic civil rights to property and personal autonomy than to focus energies on criminalizing the actions of perpetrators. This is yet another reason for feminists to focus their attentions directly on the welfare of women as situated in given societies.

Whereas Narayan cautions against oversimplifying how the meaning and significance of culture is translated across borders, it is also important to raise questions about how the "domestic" is perceived from the vantage point of the international arena. When human rights abuses are characterized as originating out of local contexts, like civil war, ethnic conflicts, and religious fundamentalism, it may encourage a way of looking at the problems as arising from the actions of bad men acculturated by hatred toward women in local situations. As demonstrated in the historian Mary Renda's analysis of how domestic imagery influenced the discourse about the American occupation of Haiti, the forces that influence the perpetration of atrocities, such as the indiscriminate killing of "natives" by American soldiers, may originate from the structure of domination, like colonialism and the patriarchal configuration of militarism.[72] Or more directly, the patriarchal structure allows for the erasure of violence from official reports of the intervention. In this sense, the domestic scene is not local or private but actually constructed within an international arena that has assigned familial roles (such as patriarchal fathers, beaten-down wives, and enslaved children) to nations, leaders, soldiers, and occupied peoples. A chilling replication of this kind of military violence has occurred more recently under the occupation of Iraq. The release of sexually explicit photographs of American military personnel torturing Iraqi prisoners in Abu Ghraib brought attention to sexual abuse as a form of interrogation.[73] Yet coming to terms with the significance of these photographs as documents of human rights violations will require looking beyond how sexual violence is used instrumentally as a means of torture or the ostensive perversity of the torturers. In order to conceptualize how such events constitute a fundamental denial of human rights it will be important to recognize how sexual exploitation was made possible by systematic forms of domination. This domination is essentially an internationalized form of "family violence" that occurs locally (within prisons) and follows from the rationale of the American occupation.

On the other hand, it is problematic for conceptions of human rights to be based on global proscriptions for "gender justice" without looking at the meaning of violence in domestic contexts. Such tendencies arise in human rights activism focused on expanding the definition of sexual crimes into concepts such as genocidal rape. Although the recognition of rape as a crime against humanity in international tribunals gives weight to the effects of sexual brutality as an instrument of warfare, it is also critical to see how this framework and its pursuit in high-profile cases should not be of highest priority on the feminist agenda. As political trials, international tribunals considering rape cases face the classic dilemma between delivering a message, in this case about the human rights of women, and legitimating their authority through conformance with legal procedures. In practice, the effectiveness of such prosecutions depends upon narrowing their objectives to laying blame on individual perpetrators. In addition, the enormous cost of these proceedings is cause to consider whether these trials are diverting resources better spent on helping victims to recover and improving the general welfare of women. It is also not clear what is symbolically achieved by such human rights victories (and they may have many of the elements of "expressive justice" discussed in chapter 3). These trials may make us look at Bosnian rape victims, for example, as women experiencing an extreme form of rape, a mere variant of the same crime that occurs in times of peace and under democratic social conditions. However, there is nothing ordinary about these rapes, in that they are fundamentally an act of ethnic hatred designed to deny these women their rights to exist as Muslims in their homeland. These kinds of insights are obviously not lost on those close to the issue of genocidal rape. Nevertheless, it is still worth reiterating that applying a theory of gender animus, especially when introduced for instrumental political purposes, often works to the detriment of understanding the deeper roots of violence.

CONCLUSION

As chapter 6 reveals, reframing the feminist campaign against sexual violence in terms of human rights policies raises new complexities in terms of the feminist alliance with the state. To some degree, it re-affirms the feminist agenda by emphasizing how sexual violence is a form of gender discrimination and a product of women's oppression. Yet the theory of gender-based animus also reproduces one of the most problematic aspects of feminist ideology by positing gender identity as the "cause" of violence and the privileging of that identity over race and culture. Since human rights policies are implemented, both nationally and internationally, within a federalist structure, they create a system that often relies upon coercive enforcement (often in opposition to local practices) and criminalization. Only human rights projects that genuinely empower citizens and resist state violence can counteract the growing danger of social control.

Moreover, the present trend to internationalize American policies against sexual violence relies upon an invidious distinction between the conditions of privilege for women in the first world versus the third world, and how economic, social, and cultural disadvantage is the root cause of gender violence.[1] Although disadvantageous conditions play some role in the disparate treatment of women across societies, one problem with this comparison is that it holds out the American model as ideal, especially as a system capable of uniformly enforcing strict and punitive sanctions against perpetrators of violence against women. Not only is this model an undesirable export, but this comparison inaccurately portrays both the successes and failures of forty years of anti-violence activism within the United States.

In order to put this discussion of national and international sexual violence policies in perspective, this conclusion puts forth an assessment of the current state of affairs in the movement to address sexual violence. Even though this book has offered a cautionary tale about the movement's involvement with the state, it is not intended to fuel a "backlash" against feminism or to be taken primarily as a critique of the feminist movement.[2] Rather, it moves toward acknowledging the injustices that are brought about not only by the persistence of sexual violence but by the unfortunate conditions under which women seek help. As described throughout *In an Abusive State*, the movement has encountered countervailing forces of criminalization and social control. This has created detours from the primary goals of women's empowerment. There are many questions worth broaching, therefore, about how feminists should effectively form alliances with the state and promote progressive social change.

Fundamentally, this effort must begin with addressing the issue of excessive criminalization. This would be easy if it were wise or practical to advocate for a wholesale effort to decriminalize sexual violence, but violence against women poses special concerns. Social policies regarding rape and domestic violence must take into consideration the real risks for injury or fatality and keep avenues open for police action and prosecution of serious offenses. Yet it is also important to bring together the enduring elements of the original feminist movement with a constructive vision of how women might negotiate their empowerment within a highly regulated state and a dismantled social welfare system. This is crucial to integrating the campaign against sexual violence into a vision of progressive citizenship that is fundamental to the feminist politics of the new century.

demographics of violence

Sexual violence continues to be a serious and chronic problem. Although there is enormous controversy over definitional questions and survey techniques,[3] both domestic violence and sexual assault persist as significant threats to women's health and safety in the United States.[4] No scholarly study has fully measured the influence of movements against sexual violence and their effects on the actual incidence rate.[5] Even if such a study existed, the gradual introduction of reforms

and contravening variables would make such an evaluation indetermi-
nate. Even so, the aggregate data does reveal that gender violence
(men perpetrating against women) is a significant factor in the overall
violent crime rate and that sexual violence (both rape and intimate
partner abuse) is most likely to be committed by known perpetrators
rather than strangers. It is also apparent that people do not equally
experience this kind of violence across the social spectrum; it dispro-
portionately affects women, the poor, and racial minorities. Much of
the early consciousness raising about the issue placed a great deal of
emphasis on every woman's risk for violence despite her circumstances. There were important reasons why some feminist advocates
made these claims. In spearheading recognition of violence against
women as a public problem and in recruiting a broad base of support
from both women and men, it was advantageous to emphasize that
the next victim could be your daughter, sister, wife, or mother. Also,
feminists were breaking through old stereotypes that associated "wife-
beating," in particular, with the lifestyle of lower-class families. It
was crucial to establish, then and now, that the dynamics of intimate
abuse evolve from domination and control that occur in relationships
among people across the economic spectrum.[6] But this rhetorical
framing of the problem obfuscates the reality that a woman's risk for
sexual violence in all forms is highly dependent on her social identity,
status, and circumstances: the most likely victim is female, black,
unmarried, poor, and living alone or with children in an urban area.

Looking back to chapter 2, it becomes apparent that the notion of
"everywoman" as a potential victim may have contributed to American cultural tendencies to become distressed about rape and other
forms of sexual violence when it is associated with the threat of racially
marked strangers disrupting the social order.[7] Consequently, a clear
pattern was established at the beginning of these campaigns and continues to the present day in which cases of rape and domestic violence
that gain significant media and public attention usually involve male
perpetrators who are identified as black or ethnic.[8] In turn, cases in
which the victim fits the "iconic" image of whiteness, innocence, and
high status are more likely to be the focus of media representations of
the crime (both in positive and negative terms). The public discourse
about rape, domestic violence, and their celebrated trials has, in part,
undermined the original feminist impulse to raise the victim's plight
to an issue of public concern. This has occurred because interest
in the victim's experience has been displaced by an outcry focused on

controlling the threat of dangerous men. Moreover, when the victim emerges as relevant to the public drama, it is usually in ways that call into question her innocence and integrity by uncovering and shaming her private actions.

These constraining media and legal representations of victims may to some degree be counteracted by overall trends (confirmed in survey data) toward viewing women as deserving of equal treatment in the home and the workplace and the increasing acceptance of women in nontraditional roles.[9] Second wave feminism and the specific goals of the violence against women movement have played a powerful role in eroding these discriminatory views about women. These changes are potentially critical to reducing the prevalence of rape. Studies of general attitudes toward rape victims and the perceptions about rape among men in general all show that the less likely the person is to maintain rigid sex stereotypes and believe in rape myths, the more likely to acknowledge rape and take responsibility for his or her own behavior.[10] Both convicted rapists and women-batterers often demonstrate a high degree of acceptance of traditional sex roles and gender stereotypes.

On the other hand, these repetitive cultural events are likely to have a cumulative impact on the popular consciousness about sexual violence.[11] Scholars in media studies and political psychology have long recognized that stereotypical motifs of victims and perpetrators are more powerful if they become the exclusive or dominant representation that most people are exposed to. For the victims in these trials, and potentially any victim of rape or intimate violence, the perpetuation of these stereotypes means that any failure to fit into the role of the ideal complainant will cause them to be subjected to scrutiny about the appropriateness of their behavior as women and the validity of their claims.

institutional change

These kinds of victim typifications are routinely applied by prosecutors who process ordinary sexual assault cases. The situation of women who experience intimate violence has not vastly improved despite reforms targeted at improving the treatment of victims (victim "shield" laws, victim advocacy, support and counseling, and improving the attitudes of police, prosecutors, and judges); the expansion of the definition of rape (redefining assault, modifying consent requirements, graduation of offenses); and increasing the levels of reporting, prosecution, and conviction (police sensitivity training, improvement in emergency room procedures and collection of forensic evidence, evidentiary reforms, and stricter penalties).[12] Since 1970, there has been extensive state-by-state change in rape law, resulting, in part, from the advocacy and lobbying of feminist groups. Studies that have attempted to measure the actual results of these reforms in terms of reporting and conviction rates have shown small improvements.[13] Most commentators attribute the lack of significant impact to the persistence of cultural stereotypes about rape and the difficulty of prosecuting nonaggravated cases. The rate of attrition (the dropping out of cases between reporting and conviction) remains extremely high, with only a small percentage of cases leading to the actual punishment of the defendant.[14]

These disappointments in the instrumental consequences of rape reform legislation amount to even more dismal news when considering how the reforms actually operate in a courtroom setting. As illustrated in chapter 3, rape trials, despite formal protections for victims, continue to provide a forum to construct misogynist theories about women and pornographic stories about defendants' motivations. These social constructions of sexual violence not only play a central role in the high-profile trials considered in this book but studies have also shown this to be the case in the trials of more routine cases of sexual assault.[15] Overall, rape law reform has brought about limited change in regard to increasing the likelihood that a victim will be vindicated by the courts, while increased demand on the courts for "expressive justice" in celebrated cases has perpetuated negative stereotypes about victims and perpetrators.

The battered women's movement has encountered similar challenges. Now, shelters and hotlines, some specifically catering to target populations like immigrant women and gays and lesbians, span most areas of the country. Although they lack adequate funding, staff, and bed space, they provide a system of emergency services for thousands of women and their children seeking help each year. While these projects are the most successful elements of the movement and continue to further the original goals of feminist activists, current shelter programs, to varying degrees depending on funding sources, are burdened by their responsibilities to meet guidelines for professional practice. At the same time, the social welfare state turned toward increased forms of regulation and coercive government control. More recently, shelters have faced new challenges in response to increased internal security efforts since 9/11, such as being forced to reveal and report more information about their clients. As discussed in chapters 1 and 4, the battered women's movement has increasingly become embedded in larger systems of control over women, the poor, and racial minorities.[16] Although feminist academics have pointed out the failures of mandatory policies, the effort to introduce new feminist strategies has just begun.[17]

Some recent commentaries about the battered women's movement have defended the feminist movement in response to critiques of mandatory policies and claims that domestic violence is experienced by both women and men.[18] Although these controversies exist, especially within academic circles, this has not resulted in a global assessment of the factors (feminist influences are only one among many) that have contributed to the largely regulatory and criminalized response to sexual violence. Narrowly framed critiques of feminist policymaking often overestimate the power of feminist ideology while underestimating the immense significance of transformations in the relations between the state and individuals and the growing punitive role of the state.

Moreover, some of the negative outcomes of the movement are a direct outgrowth of how the feminist movement initially characterized sexual violence as a social problem. Following the critique in chapter 2, some of the earliest feminist writing created a fateful characterization of the issue as a gender war. Although they provided us an enduring message about the role of patriarchy in promoting violence, such formulations limit our understanding of the problem by focusing on individual victims and perpetrators and exaggerating women's vulnerability to the sadistic exploits of evil men. The accent on the opposition between genders also led to a very slow, and yet incomplete, incorporation into the movement of concerns about women's violence against men[19] and violence between same-sex partners.[20] To move forward with activism on this issue, we need the kind of creative new conceptualization offered by the political scientist Nancy Hirschmann, who sees intimate sexual violence as occurring within a variety of contexts that inhibit freedom. Neither a psychological nor an institutional explanation for women's victimization, considered independently, adequately describes why many women's freedoms are taken away by batterers and not regained by fleeing abusive situations.[21]

In order to understand the constraints on women's freedom more fully, Hirschmann argues that we must recognize how "control at the 'micro' level by individual batterers works interactively and complementarily with the social 'macro' level of courts, police, and medicine to socially construct battered women's choices, desires, and freedom."[22] This kind of reframing moves us beyond a theory of gender animus to a more complex understanding of how violence directed against women is often the direct result of constraints on freedom and agency. In this frame, we can ask questions about women's responsibility (such as in cases in which their children are exposed to violence) and draw connections between the plight of individual women and the larger responsibilities of democratic communities.[23]

beyond criminalization

Moving beyond criminalization is difficult for a movement whose momentum was almost completely dependent on the growth of a law-and-order mentality and increased public support for strategies of coercive control. Most of the law reforms and services designed to address violence against women that were adopted in response to feminist advocacy and lobbying were pushed along by law-and-order forces that reached their peak influence in the United States in the 1980s. As the sociologist Kathy Daly describes, the activism that focused on intimate violence and rape coincided with law-and-order politics that was a response to the perceived failure of the system to get "tough on crime."[24] Another empirical study finds that a political environment focused on law-and-order concerns is the strongest contributing factor in the adoption of state rape reforms.[25] And more generally, studies show that an exaggerated perception of the risk of crime (including aggravated sexual assault) increases the general population's willingness to pay for crime control and punishment.[26] The fairly dramatic and swift response by legislators and criminal justice institutions to all forms of victim-centered advocacy is closely tied to powerful lobbies and public opinion groups supportive of a more repressive law-and-order system. Advocates for reform ended up benefiting from the growing trend to base social policy changes on the avoidance of risk and the widespread exaggeration of perceived risk for sexual assault across the socioeconomic spectrum.[27] This historical connection with "tough on crime" lobbies continues to have major significance, especially to the degree that current funding is dependent on connections to the criminal justice apparatus and criminal justice–based funding. This connection will be costly to break.

What are the possibilities for the reconstruction of social justice for women under the contemporary conditions of governmentality? Any progress in this regard needs to begin with a response to the growth of criminalization. As the number of victims of violence has decreased in the United States in recent years, the number incarcerated, for all types of crimes, has continued the dramatic upward trend that began in the 1970s. These increases are largely due to more severe punishments for drug-related offenses and mandatory sentencing policies, rather than stepped-up enforcement and conviction of perpetrators of sexual violence. Nevertheless, an almost exclusively criminalized response to sexual violence contributes to the increasingly punitive response of the state. For example, men who are arrested for battering are most likely to end up in prison if they have a previous or current history of other criminal offenses. And as noted in chapter 1, battered women often get drawn into the criminal justice system when police follow mandatory arrest policies. The introduction of graduated degrees of sexual assaults and new categories of victims expands the scope of behaviors and age range of persons and activities under criminal surveillance. This means that criminal justice authorities, under the guise of protecting against sexual violence, are able to expand their control over juveniles, homosexuals, and those with prior convictions for sexual offenses. At the same time, the rampant occurrence of sexual abuse within prisons is given little attention or priority as a social problem, except as a significant factor contributing to the high incidence of HIV/AIDS within prison populations and the growing number of poor black women infected through contact with released prisoners.

Given these consequences, is a move toward the abolition of criminal sanctions warranted?[28] In many ways, violence in intimate relationships is uncharacteristic of other behavior that is criminalized, especially in cases of relationship violence where actual physical violence is infrequently employed or is not the primary means of controlling the woman. However, the potential risk of danger to women in all situations of domestic battering is still great and rape is sometimes accompanied by life-threatening physical attacks. In fact, intimate abuse often leads to far more violence than the type of victimless crimes that are the primary focus of abolitionist theorists.[29] Any proposal for lessening the use of sanctions needs to be evaluated in terms of its impact on lessening the prevalence of violence; however, it is not necessarily true that more severe criminal sanctioning actually produces harm reduction.[30] In addition, even though punishment may currently serve a symbolic function, this could be redirected to other means of affirming that violence against women constitutes a fundamental violation of the right to exercise personal autonomy and assure one's own dignity.[31]

The most frequently discussed option for diversion from the criminal justice system is the implementation of community-based or restorative justice programs.[32] These programs may serve as a valuable alternative for a subset of cases where either the threat of continued violence is negligible or the victim desires to continue an intimate relationship with the perpetrator. However, restorative justice systems (like alternative dispute resolution methods) have many liabilities in situations that involve violence and gender oppression, which makes them an unattractive solution for most cases. These approaches may be ineffective at validating the norms against violence and illuminating gender-based dynamics of domination and control. Also, restorative justice programs are only an adequate alternative for women recovering from domestic violence and sexual assault when tangible community support and resources back their processes.

The most desirable solutions are neither perpetrator nor "relationship" focused but directed to addressing the most persistent problems causing and created by sexual violence: the social and economic disadvantage experienced by women and their dependents. The primary goal of a campaign to prevent sexual violence must be to promote the emotional well-being and economic sustainability of women who suffer repeatedly from sexual violence throughout their life span.[33] This certainly involves providing individual women with the emotional, material, and communal support to empower themselves. But this goal is also furthered by pushing for advocacy efforts that focus on systemic issues and unfavorable state action. The transformation of the feminist movement for reproduction rights into "reproductive justice" might serve as a model for redirecting the campaign against sexual violence. Over much of the course of second wave feminism, the constant threat of retreat from the principles in *Roe v. Wade* has put activists on the defense and caused them to narrowly focus on abortion rights. However, for the past ten years this movement has made enormous strides in building coalitions and revisiting their

goals even though these advances have shaken the ideological foundations of what was once a single-issue rights-based campaign. Hopefully, we are on the cusp of a similar revamping of the campaign
against sexual violence which would demand justice not only in individual cases but for the collectivity. Such a movement would call attention not only to the harm of sexual violence but also to the role of
government in preventing the full exercise of women's autonomy and
freedom, and it would encourage action against the state when it fails
to recognize the consequences of violence in women's lives.

An example of such a movement is the emergent grassroots organizing that is stimulated by battered women's treatment in family
courts. This movement has come together as a response to the injustices done by the failure to take into account partner violence in
divorce proceedings and also in response to judicial bias against battered women.[34] Another way to depict this new agenda is to see it
inscribed in the actions of individual women who effectively negotiate
with the state in ways that assert their rightful places in both the public
and private spheres. As illustrated by Donna's story in chapter 6,
when women reject the psychological construction of victimhood,
romantic notions of returning to the confines of private patriarchy,
and unending war with hostile state agencies, they open up possibilities for demanding respect and autonomy in all aspects of their lives.
As in Donna's case, successful reemergence from situations of domestic violence requires clients of shelters or of welfare bureaucracies
to demand the rights to fair treatment that are taken for granted
by "ordinary" citizens who are not in dependent relations with the
welfare state.[35] Feminist activists can also do more to reinstate the
original impulses of the movement that were focused on grassroots
organizing and the founding of shelters and other organizations with
a politicized understanding of the problem. This involves drawing
connections to other broadly based anti-violence movements both locally and globally, including those that raise concerns about the state
as perpetrators of violence in the form of police brutality, discrimination against immigrants, racism in all aspects of crime enforcement
and in foreign wars.

These shifts are deterred, however, by the close links between
advocacy and services for victims and the criminal justice apparatus.
Under the auspices of the Violence against Women Act, the most
common funding model is "community coordination" which involves
cooperation among a network of community-based organizations and

criminal justice personnel. Many in the field see community coordination as the "answer" because it improves the quality and scope of services, and it is urgently needed in rural areas where no specialized services to treat victims exist.[36] Since the programs are designed to encourage cooperation among agencies, this allows for more direct influence of feminist-designed rape crisis centers and battered women's shelters on mainstream organizations. Although these programs have opened up new sources of funding for shelters and direct services for women, they also make increased prosecution rates the first priority of community intervention and the measure of program success. These initiatives further entrench local feminist organizations within systems of punitive justice and the professionalization of victim support.[37]

There are important differences in perspective, however, about the desirability of community coordination. Some argue that the success of the violence against women's movement is in fact contingent on improving victims' treatment within mainstream organizations. In a multidecade analysis of rape crisis organizations and their communities, Patricia Yancey Martin explores why, despite years of reform, women are revictimized at the hands of agencies designated to process their complaints.[38] Her analysis points to the failure of workers in mainstream organizations, like hospitals, police departments, and the courts, to "own rape" and their tendency to mistreat victims, not usually out of hostility but in the process of fulfilling other work objectives. Her conclusions call for a reaffirmation of the feminist vision of rape work and more integration of feminist practices within mainstream institutions. This vision would support continued efforts for community coordination, with the condition that rape crisis centers and other feminist organizations take a more active role. The analysis in *In an Abusive State*, however, is instructive regarding the potential pitfalls of this renewed feminist campaign. As chapter 4 demonstrates, even when feminist methodology has been integrated into mainstream professional practice it does not necessarily yield a system that is supportive and empowering of women. The push for other objectives, often countervailing to feminist purposes, is initiated not only by individual personnel but from external pressures on organizations, often derived from a neoliberal political agenda. It would be a mistake to assume that feminist practices would prevail in mainstream institutions without concerted and intrusive interventions designed to transform these institutions. Feminists must move ahead with an expansive agenda that challenges systems of social control while also being prepared to work outside existing institutional structures.

This book starts this process of moving ahead by presenting a more accurate portrayal of the consequences of the social movement and by calling attention to lessons learned from the history of activism. Although there is piecemeal recognition of many of the counterproductive effects of criminalization, it is imperative to recognize that dramatic instances of injustice, like the Central Park Jogger verdict, are the direct consequence of expressive demands for justice fueled by violence against women activism. The injustices that resulted from this trial are not an aberration but indicative of the kind of excesses that come from controlling sexual violence in the modern state. *In an Abusive State* has also shown that those who are likely to be marked as dangerous are not the only ones at risk. The risk is much broader because the regulation of sexual violence has gradually become integral to a wide range of forms of social control. In this way, the good intentions of social reform were swept up in larger processes that diminish our personal autonomy and freedom. As efforts continue and new approaches are adopted in the United States and internationally, these effects can be mitigated by a more conscious reformulation of the nature of sexual violence and a recognition of the dangers of counteracting it primarily through the punitive and regulatory mechanisms of the modern state.

preface

1. In the 1991 Central Park Jogger trials five young black and Hispanic men—Antron McCray, Kevin Richardson, Raymond Santana, Yusef Salaam, and Khary Wise—were convicted of the rape and brutal attack on a twenty-eight-year-old white woman. The attack occurred while she was jogging in New York's Central Park and is commonly referred to as the "Central Park Jogger" case. The case was reopened in 2002 after another man serving a sentence for unrelated crimes, including the rape of another woman in Central Park two days before the attack on the jogger, confessed to the crime. Three of the defendants successfully vacated the verdict following a hearing on December 5, 2002. Both the original case and the reversal of the convictions are discussed in detail in chapter 3.

2. Like the Central Park trial, the Scottsboro trial drew national attention and raised concerns about racism and court systems. A group of nine black teenagers was riding on the train with a group of whites (including two women millworkers) when a fight ensued between the black and white boys. A white boy forced off the train complained to the stationmaster, who wired ahead about the trouble to the next stop in Paint Rock, Alabama. When the authorities intervened, the two white women accused the black teenagers of rape. Nine black boys were captured and taken to a jail in Scottsboro. After immediate lynching was averted, the first trial was held within twelve days. For a narrative history of the events, the trial, and its aftermath, see Carter, *Scottsboro*.

3. Arendt, *Eichmann in Jerusalem*, 26–27.

4. For a similar analysis, see Gavey, *Just Sex?* 17–49.

5. Despite these differences in interpretation, and ultimately in the framing of solutions, Mills provides a valuable rethinking of the objectives of the movement against domestic violence. See her *Insult to Injury.*

1 the sexual violence agenda

The epigraph to this chapter is from Dale and Robertson, "Interview with Boaventura de Sousa Santos," 151, 153.

1. For an important discussion of the complexities of feminist grassroots organizing and its relation to the state, see Ackelsberg, "Reconceiving Politics?" 391. For an articulation of the position that feminists should be "wary" in their relations with the state, see Mansbridge, "Anti-statism and Difference Feminism in International Social Movements," 355–60.

2. Bevacqua, *Rape on the Public Agenda,* 31.

3. Ibid., 32.

4. Gordon, *Heroes of Their Own Lives,* 251.

5. See, in general, Pizzey, *Scream Quietly or the Neighbors Will Hear;* Schechter, *Women and Male Violence.*

6. This hope for personal liberation through participation in shelter life is described in Beaudry, *Battered Women.*

7. Ibid., 66–70.

8. Ibid., 51–54.

9. See Ferree and Hess, *Controversy and Coalition;* Riger, "Challenges of Success"; Ferguson, *The Feminist Case against Bureaucracy.*

10. Reinelt, "Moving onto the Terrain of the State."

11. For analysis of this trend and its consequences, see Kendrick, "Producing the Battered Woman"; Loseke, *The Battered Woman and Shelters;* Westlund, "Pre-Modern and Modern Power."

12. For a discussion of how feminist service organizations responded to this challenge and a generally positive view of these organizations' ability to maintain their integrity, see Kravetz, *Tales from the Trenches.*

13. For a comprehensive cross-cultural comparison of the results of this activism and an argument for the autonomy of women's movements, see Weldon, *Protest, Policy, and the Problem of Violence against Women.*

14. For similar analysis, see Laurie and Bondi, *Working in the Spaces of Neoliberalism.*

15. See Mink, "Violating Women."

16. For an empirical analysis of the consequences of devolution, see Rodgers, "Evaluating the Devolution Revolution."

17. Garland, *The Culture of Control,* 184. See also Simon, *Governing Through Crime.*

18. Wacquant, "The New 'Peculiar Institution.'"

19. According to Bureau of Justice statistics, "women are now the most

rapidly increasing segment of the population of U.S. prisons" (Comey, "Fastest Growing Prison Population,"15). For a discussion of the intersection between women's victimization and offending, see the studies in Heimer and Kruttschnitt, *Gender and Crime.*

20. See, in general, for an illuminating discussion of neoliberalism's cultural project, Duggan, *The Twilight of Equality?*

21. Jenkins, *Moral Panic*, 226–29.

22. Ibid., 125.

23. For an elaboration of this argument, see Cocca, *Jailbait*, and Cocca, "From 'Welfare Queen' to 'Exploited Teen.' "

24. Corrigan, "Making Meaning of Megan's Law," 301, 308.

25. For a discussion of the politicized context of prosecution and its persistence despite reform efforts, see McCoy, "Prosecution."

26. Chancer, *High Profile Crimes*, 252.

27. For a general discussion of how this polarization is furthered by media presentation, see Wilcox, "Beauty and the Beast."

28. See Moorti, *The Color of Rape.*

29. For an analysis of the effects of the backlash campaign on the feminist movement, see Faludi, *Backlash.*

30. Richardson, "Desiring Sameness?"

31. Bevacqua, *Rape on the Public Agenda*, 170.

32. For a discussion of the growth of penal-welfare systems and their impact on women, see Silliman and Bhattacharjee, *Policing the National Body.*

33. For a study of how prosecutors weed out rape cases by discrediting victims' allegations of sexual assault, see Frohmann, "Discrediting Victims' Allegations of Sexual Assault,"

34. See Frohmann, "Convictability and Discordant Locales."

35. For an empirical study of the effect of mandatory policies on conviction rates, see Peterson and Dixon, "Court Oversight and Conviction under Mandatory and Non-Mandatory Domestic Violence Case Filings." For an interpretation of this study, see Garner, "What Does 'Prosecution' of Domestic Violence Mean?" See also Dobash, "Domestic Violence."

36. See Buzawa and Buzawa, *Do Arrests and Restraining Orders Work?*

37. Fleury, "Missing Voices"; Pearlman, "Neighborhood Environment, Racial Position, and Risk of Police-Reported Domestic Violence"; Weis, "Race, Gender and Critique."

38. Coker, "Race, Poverty, and the Crime-Centered Response to Domestic Violence," 1332.

39. Miller, *Victims as Offenders*, 141.

40. For a discussion of the growth of coercive government control, see O'Malley, "Social Justice after the 'Death of the Social,' " 92, 101; Rose, *Powers of Freedom.*

41. For analysis of the consequences of welfare reform, see Mink and Solinger, *Welfare*.

42. See Abramovitz and Withorn, "Playing by the Rules."

43. This analysis of how political language is used to rationalize chronic social problems is drawn from Edelman, *Political Language*.

44. Bauman, *Modernity and the Holocaust*, 65.

45. For an excellent development of this critique, see Schultz, "Reconceptualizing Sexual Harrassment."

46. Dunlap, "Sometimes I Feel Like a Motherless Child," 565.

47. For a recent article that draws the connection between domestic policy and security politics, see Grewal, "'Security Moms' in the Early Twentieth-Century United States."

48. See Scraton, *Beyond September 11*. And for an analysis that links together the construction of "terror" and the modern conditions of punitive carcerality, see Rodriguez, "State Terror and the Reproduction of Imprisoned Dissent."

2 gender war

The epigraph to this chapter is from Girard, *Violence and the Sacred*, 318.

1. For example, a recent Associated Press story reports, "A woman who was critically burned in an explosion set off by her boyfriend over her unplanned pregnancy has given birth to a son. Gloria Busch was burned over 70 percent of her upper body and lost 12 pints of blood in the explosion in her home March 12. She had three skin-graft operations during a 21-day hospital stay. . . . Authorities said Elersic, who was married, had planned to kill Busch and himself by disconnecting her gas stove and sealing the kitchen with plastic. Elersic forced Busch into a chair and tied her hands and feet with duct tape. He threw a photo of her oldest child, Anthony, 21, in his Marine uniform, taken before he went to the Middle East. 'Look at that picture,' he told her. 'You'll be dead, but you'll never know if he'll make it back home alive.' The house exploded when he lit a cigarette. Busch was blown into her garage." August 20, 2003, Wednesday, Dateline: Buffalo, N.Y.

2. The war metaphor is found in Stevi Jackson's prototypical feminist position on rape: "If sexuality was not bound up with power and aggression, rape would not be possible. When these attributes of masculinity are accentuated, as in war, rape reaches epidemic proportions" ("The Social Context of Rape," 19). Jackson deploys the metaphor to suggest that the condition of war, as a form of masculine aggression, unleashes the propensity of men to rape. Brownmiller in her classic study *Against Our Will* reverses the logic of the metaphor by implying that the act of rape is synonymous with the tools of warfare: "men who commit rape have served in effect as front line masculine shock troops, terrorist guerillas in the longest sustained battle the

world has ever known" (209). Both conceptions of the metaphor imply that all interactions between women and men run the risk of inviting danger whether a woman chooses, as Stevi Jackson puts it, to "walk along a dark street at night" or "negotiate a socio-sexual relationship"(Jackson, "The Social Context of Rape," 26). Rape is seen as simply an extreme manifestation of culturally accepted patterns of male aggression. This war imagery is also found in Judith Herman's *Trauma and Recovery* in which she presents a distinctively feminist interpretation of the psychological model of sexual abuse. Her clinical work and writing are focused on the survivors of psychological trauma and demonstrate a commitment to telling the often unspoken stories of the victims of sexual atrocities. She articulates a feminist argument for remembering the forgotten history of sexual abuse and reawakening it in the individual and social consciousness (Herman, *Trauma and Recovery*, 1).

3. Gordon and Riger, *The Female Fear*, 26.

4. Stanko, *Everyday Violence*, 145.

5. Eroticism does not exist in opposition to violence but is an element of it. In the words of Georges Bataille, "in essence the domain of eroticism is the domain of violence, of violation" (Bataille, *Eroticism*, 16). From his perspective, violence is the inevitable consequence of human beings confronting the states of flux, discontinuity, and fear of annihilation that make erotic impulses possible and raise questions about the core of our existence. Therefore, violence is not an aberration of "peaceful" sexuality but a condition created by the expression of erotic impulses. The forms and meaning of this violence, and its possibilities for pleasure or pain, are contingent upon how these erotic impulses manifest themselves in human relationships.

6. The abject, therefore, can be named as the inescapable presence that haunts and produces the horrors against women. Julia Kristeva, a French theorist who elaborates the theory of abjection in feminist terms, describes the power the abject holds on the social landscape: "There looms, within abjection, one of those violent, dark revolts of being, directed against a threat that seems to emanate from an exorbitant outside or inside, ejected beyond the scope of the possible, the tolerable, the thinkable. It lies there, quite close, but it cannot be assimilated. It beseeches, worries, and fascinates desire, which, nevertheless, does not let itself be seduced" (Kristeva, *Powers of Horror*, 1). In this passage, the abject is written about as if it were a presence, not quite human or supernatural, but a force that society must reckon with. Kristeva evokes the image of the abject as at the boundaries between what is tolerable and intolerable, and this liminality, moreover, is the very source of its power to seduce its audience without being seduced (and therefore tamed) by society. Yet despite its projection as almost beyond what we know to be human, the abject is significant to everyday reality; indeed, the forces of abjection are "eminently productive of culture." In

other terms, abjection is a state of being in which we live; a "something" out there that remains hidden and unknown, yet on the edge of nonexistence it also produces the fear of self-annihilation. See also Singer, *Erotic Welfare*.

7. This dissociation has historical roots. Nineteenth-century feminist movements were formed in connection with crusades against racial oppression. The abolition movement and later anti-lynching campaigns were taken up by feminist activists as part of an appeal to universal human rights. Although the dominant strain of these movements was driven by middle-class philanthropic impulses, the anti-lynching campaigns brought about a short-lived radical politics that recognized how the portrayal of white women as innocent victims of black male sexuality perpetuated a system of white supremacy by rule of terror. These early radicals were keenly aware of the links between racial and sexual terrorism. The efforts of these activists—Ida B. Wells was one of them—were met largely with complacency among American audiences, and ultimately nineteenth-century feminists failed to make a connection between issues of racism, class, and gender. See Ware, *Beyond the Pale*.

8. Morrison, *Race-Ing Justice, En-Gendering Power*, xix.

9. The possibility of black retaliation is called for in the infamous statements of Eldridge Cleaver in the late 1970s in which he advocated the raping of white women by black men as a symbolic affirmation of the latter's growing empowerment.

10. For Kristeva the prohibition that founds society, and where the threat of abjection comes from, is the prohibition directed against the maternal body. On the level of personal history, this means that for the child to achieve a sense of identity as an autonomous subject he or she must reject the mother. Through this form of abjection of the maternal object the child gains separation from her body and distance from the mother's regulation of basic wants and needs. But this abjection constitutes a crisis without resolution, in that one never ceases looking within the maternal body of something "desirable and terrifying, nourishing and murderous." In the other, we incorporate a "devouring mother, for want of having been able to introject her and take joy in what manifests her, for want of being able to signify her: urine, blood, sperm, excrement." The risk of losing oneself through the demands of abjection eroticizes abjection, as the drive to stop the "wound" or "hole in the psyche" is compelled by the endless need to separate from and be renewed by the maternal body. Abjection is the cultural dynamic, therefore, that fuels the targeting of women as objects of desire and disgust and energizes the repulsion of the dangerous or outlaw other, who becomes the abject through the displacement of the maternal body onto the object of dread.

11. Kristeva, *Powers of Horror*, 68.

12. Ibid., 4.

13. Exemplifed, for example, by the phenomenon of victims of brutal rapes sometimes referring to themselves as having died in the attack. See Brison, *Aftermath*, 45–46.

14. Caputi, *The Age of Sex Crime*, 8.

15. The concept of icon has been used extensively and loosely in postmodern discourse analysis and media studies. See, for example, Žižek, "Risk Society and Its Discontents," and Bennett and Lawrence, "News Icons and Social Change." In a more general sense, art historians use the term "iconography" to refer to the branch of art history concerned with the themes in the visual arts and their deeper meaning or content. See Van Straten, *An Introduction to Iconography*. For a discussion of the religious use of the concept as employed here, see Barasch, *Icon*.

16. See the analysis of the heroic imagery of rape in Wolfthal, *Images of Rape*.

17. This painting was part of an exhibit at the University Gallery of the University of Massachusetts at Amherst. The painting is commented on in the University Gallery publication *The Culture of Violence*, 2002. Cole's artwork on rape has been analyzed for its religious qualities in Meyer, "Profane and Sacred," 4.

18. A similar representation is found in popular poetry (easily accessible on the Internet). For example, note the less than subtle Christ imagery in this 1993 poem by Joneve McCormick, which was found online at http://www.cornerpoetry.com/poetry/mccormick/central.html (accessed September 19, 2007):

> *For the Central Park Jogger*
> Spreading your heart
> to fly in the night
> becoming all you could
> in April, the cruelest month,
> you were thrown to the ground
> your head smashed
> with pipe and brick
> your body raped to destroy your light
>
> then, refusing to change
> into something less, you showed us
> what is possible with love
> so that we, too,
> are healed in the spring
> of your resurrection.

19. Faure, "The Buddhist Icon and the Modern Gaze."

20. Ibid.

21. This notion of a predatory landscape is found in T. Mitchell's scholarship. He suggests: "But even the most highly formulaic, conventional, and stylized landscapes represent themselves as true to some sort of nature, to universal structures of an ideal nature, or to codes that are wired in to the visual cortex and to deeply instinctual roots of visual pleasure associated with scopophilia, voyeurism, and the desire to see without being seen." Mitchell, *Landscape and Power*, 16.

22. This is symbolically manifested in a pagodalike structure that has been placed by the side of the road near where the jogger was found.

23. Barasch, *Icon*.

24. Faure, "The Buddhist Icon and the Modern Gaze."

25. Gelb and Hart, "Feminist Politics in a Hostile Environment," 169.

26. Woliver, *From Outrage to Action*.

27. For a discussion of the problems feminists have faced in regard to disbelief about the prevalence of rape, see, for example, Russell and Bolen, *The Epidemic of Rape and Child Sexual Abuse in the United States*, 1–17.

28. Chancer, *High Profile Crimes*, 143.

29. For a critique of Freud from a feminist perspective on trauma, see Herman, *Trauma and Recovery*.

30. See Marecek, "Trauma Talk in Feminist Clinical Practice."

31. MacKinnon, *Only Words*, 3.

32. Adams, *The Emptiness of the Image*, 64–66.

33. Anti-rape activism has brought attention to cases of rape which reach the trial stage, so that possibly the most frequent public ritual in which sexual violence is watched is the notable criminal trial. Activists have attempted to use the trial forum as an opportunity to send a message about sexual abuse and to increase public concern about brutality toward women and children. These reformers have focused on transforming language by redefining sexual assault, limiting verbal assault against women in the courtroom (the so-called second rape), and affirming women's strength by renaming victims as survivors. Yet inevitably the way sexual abuse is seen in the courtroom is strongly determined by the language of forensic medicine. Through this professional language the harm of sexual abuse is translated into evidence. In the courtroom the sexual violence is reenacted in a ritualized fashion according to the narrative conventions used by professionals fulfilling their roles in the legal process: prosecutors, defense attorneys, judges, doctors, therapists, and police officers. See, for example, Matoesian, *Reproducing Rape*.

34. Kemp, "Sexual Abuse, Another Hidden Pediatric Problem," 282–289.

35. Finkel, "Technical Conduct of the Child Sexual Abuse Medical Examination," 557.

36. Ibid., 557.

37. Ibid., 558.

38. Ibid., 560.

39. Ibid., 560.

40. Foucault, The History of Sexuality, 27.

3 expressive justice

The epigraph to this chapter is from Garland, *Culture of Control*, 110.

1. Pressure on police departments has been stimulated by their liability if they fail to respond to domestic violence; see *Thurman v. Torrington.*

2. Garland, *Culture of Control*, 10.

3. See, for example, Cuklanz, *Rape on Prime Time.*

4. Kirchheimer, *Political Justice.*

5. Arnold, *The Symbols of Government.*

6. See Cuklanz, *Rape on Trial.* She argues that recent notable rape trials, including the New Bedford trial, have had an educative effect on the mass public and have popularized the new feminist understanding of rape.

7. For an analysis of gang-rape trials that assumes they serve an educative function, see Benedict, *Athletes and Acquaintance Rape.*

8. See Bumiller, "Rape as a Legal Symbol," and Pitch, "Critical Criminology, the Construction of Social Problems and the Question of Rape."

9. This chapter draws from two previously published articles, Bumiller, "Fallen Angels," and Bumiller, "Spectacles of the Strange."

10. The New Bedford trial was loosely the subject of the 1988 film *The Accused.* The movie does not draw from the media or court presentation of events and most conspicuously does not represent the ethnic dimension of the case.

11. Four of the six defendants were convicted. See *Commonwealth v. Rapozo, Cordeiro, Silva, and Vieira.* A summary of the case is recounted in the appellate decisions; see Commonwealth v. Cordeiro, 519 N.E.2d 1328, 1329 (Mass. 1988), and Commonwealth v. Vieira, 519 N.E.2d 1320, 1321 (Mass. 1988).

12. For a discussion of the representation of the trial, see Horeck, *Public Rape,* 67–90.

13. In the sense that Kristeva uses this psychoanalytic term in reference to the stranger in *Strangers to Ourselves,* 168–92.

14. Toni Morrison in *Playing in the Dark* suggests that race has assumed a complex metaphorical life embedded in daily discourses. She says that images of blackness hold "ambivalences": "[They] can be evil and protective, rebellious and forging, fearful and desirable. . . . Whiteness alone is mute, meaningless, unfathomable, pointless, frozen, veiled, curtained, dreaded, senseless, implacable" (59). While Morrison locates these metaphors in the textual body of classic American literature, this analysis locates blackness

and whiteness in the textual body of the trial and in the urban geography that it replicates. The trial is played out on a landscape both real and imagined. It is narrated so that blackness is seen as movement, or the residues of a fleeting presence, and whiteness is seen as space sullied on the landscape that represents it.

15. Didion, "New York," 46.

16. For a recent critique of rape law along these lines and from a comparative perspective, see Menon, *Recovering Subversion*.

17. This is analogous to Scarry's representational analysis of torture; see *The Body in Pain*, 45–46.

18. The New York City District Attorney's office provided me with copies of the videotaped confessions.

19. Moreover, the motif of strangeness is particularly useful in reinforcing a way of viewing in which we are not conscious of ourselves looking. The narrative protects the viewers from projecting the strangeness within. Kristeva argues that we can protect ourselves from encountering the other and facing our cosmopolitanism by locating the other outside the familiar; in her words, we can "perceive its existence by means of sight . . . but we do not frame within our consciousness." See *Strangers to Ourselves*, 187.

20. The case has been reopened due to the confession of Matias Reyes, who is currently serving a life sentence for unrelated crimes including the rape of another woman in Central Park two days before the attack on the jogger. He has been linked to the rape by DNA evidence. Three of the defendants have successfully vacated the verdict following a hearing on December 5, 2002.

21. Bach, "True Crime, False Confession"; Carter, "Lawsuits by Innocent Youths Target Central Park, Jogger Fiasco"; Dwyer, "Verdict That Failed the Test of Time"; Maddox, "The Ghost of Scottsboro Resurfaced in 1989."

22. See, in general, Garland, *The Culture of Control*.

23. Yusef Salaam did not consent to a videotaped interview. For an explanation of the circumstances, see *People v. Salaam*.

24. For an analysis that focuses on this situation as a case of "false confessions," see Davis, "The Reality of False Confessions—Lessons of the Central Park Jogger Case."

25. See, for example, Krzewinski, "But I Didn't Do It"; Ofshe and Leo, "Symposium on Coercion"; Westervelt and Humphrey, *Wrongly Convicted*. Also see the dissenting opinion of Judge Titone in *People v. Salaam*.

26. Although, as a narrative form, legal confessions are problematic; see, for example, Brooks, "Storytelling without Fear?"

27. The report of this special panel also claims to defend police practices on the grounds that these five defendants are likely to be guilty of the crimes, including the rape of the jogger. The report states: "We adopt the view that the most likely scenario for the events of April 19, 1989 was that the defen-

dants came upon the jogger and subjected her to the same kind of attack, albeit with sexual overtones, that they inflicted upon the other victims in the park that night. Perhaps attracted to the scene by the jogger's screams, Reyes either joined in the attack as it was ending or waited until the defendants had moved on to their next victims before descending upon her himself, raping her and inflicting upon her the brutal injuries that almost caused her death." Executive Summary, Central Park Jogger Case Panel Report, 41. Available online at http://news.findlaw.com/hdocs/docs/cpjgr/nypd12703jgrrpt.pdf (accessed September 19, 2007).

4 administrative justice

The epigraph to this chapter is from Bauman, *Modernity and the Holocaust*, 113.

1. See, for example, Bondi, "Working the Spaces of Neoliberal Subjectivity."

2. This view is expressed by a leading researcher in the field: "The question of what to do about men who batter their female partners has haunted the domestic violence field since its emergence in the late 1970s. Many advocates working with battered women felt—and many still feel—that few batterers could be changed given the social reinforcement and tolerance of violence against women. Trying to counsel or educate these men might, in fact, raise false hopes in battered women and worsen their already difficult circumstances. Protection for women and separation from their male batterers, therefore, became the overarching intervention objective" (Gondolf, "Evaluating Batterer Counseling Programs"). For the official criminal justice position on batterer intervention, see Healy, *Batterer Intervention*.

3. For a similar perspective, see Hacking, *The Social Construction of What?*

4. This chapter draws on a previously published article, Bumiller, "Law at the Margins, 151–168.

5. Beaudry, *Battered Women*, 102–4.

6. Fraser, *Unruly Practices*, 144–60.

7. Ibid., 146.

8. Ibid., 156.

9. Gordon, *Heroes of Their Own Lives*, 257–64.

10. Ibid., 286.

11. Some of the earliest examples of professional literature on battered women are politically informed; see, for example, Dobash and Dobash, *Violence against Wives*.

12. Brook and Davis, *Women, the Family, and Social Work*, 3–50.

13. Davis, "Battered Women," 306–11.

14. This theory was first developed by Lenore Walker; see *The Battered Woman*. The most recent textbooks in the field still see it as the generally accepted theory, e.g., Wallace, *Family Violence*, 194–95.

15. In fact, in terms of "therapeutic" treatment it appears that there is a merging of rape and battering because of the high prevalence of rape of young girls by a member of their household.

16. See, for example, Gondolf, "The Effect of Batterer Counseling on Shelter Outcome."

17. Bergman, "Battered Women—Their Susceptibility to Treatment," 159.

18. See, for example, Nunnally, *Troubled Relationships*, 163–91.

19. Roberts, "Crisis Intervention with Battered Women."

20. Curnow, "The Open Window Phase."

21. Cohen, Forjuoh, and Gondolf, "Injuries and Health Care Use in Women with Partners in Batterer Intervention Programs," 84.

22. Yassen and Glass, "Sexual Assault Survivors Groups," 252.

23. Roberts, "Crisis Intervention with Battered Women," 69.

24. Ibid.

25. Bergman et al., "Battered Women—Their Susceptibility to Treatment."

26. Symes, "Arriving at Readiness to Recover Emotionally After Sexual Assault."

27. Roberts, "Crisis Intervention with Battered Women," 71.

28. Ibid., 74.

29. Martin, "The Historical Roots of Domestic Violence," 16.

30. Roberts, "Crisis Intervention with Battered Women," 74.

31. Geller and Wasserstrom, "Conjoint Therapy for the Treatment of Domestic Violence," 33.

32. Roberts, "Crisis Intervention with Battered Women," 75.

33. Ibid., 76.

34. Ibid., 77.

35. Campbell, "Assessing Dangerousness in Domestic Violence Cases."

36. Gondolf, "Evaluating Batterer Counseling Programs," 617. This researcher disputes the overall conclusion that these programs "do not work" and argues that they have a modest effect as part of a comprehensive "intervention system."

37. Firestone, "Hostility and Recidivism in Sexual Offenders," and Craissati and Beech, "Risk Prediction and Failure in a Complete Urban Sample of Sex Offenders."

38. Contrary to the conclusions reached here, Peter Conrad suggests the political history of the battered women's movement has resulted in less "medicalization" of services for battered women; see Conrad, "Medicalization and Social Control."

39. See, for example, Taft, Brown, and Legge, "General Practitioner Management of Intimate Partner Abuse and the Whole Family."

40. Thomas and Lowitt, "A Traumatic Experience."

41. Purvin, "Unilateral Headache and Ptosis in a 30-Year-Old Woman."

42. Ibid. See also Muelleman, "Battered Women."

43. Sadovsky, "Presentation of Abuse-Related Injuries among Women," 981.

44. Sadovsky, "Patterns of Injury Type and Location in Battered Women," 1379.

45. McCauley, "The 'Battering Syndrome'."

46. Walker, "Assessing Abuse and Neglect and Dental Fear in Women."

47. Beck, "Ocular Injuries in Battered Women," 149.

48. Drossman, "Health Status by Gastrointestinal Diagnosis and Abuse History," 1001.

49. Ibid., 999–1007.

50. Drossman, "Sexual and Physical Abuse and Gastrointestinal Illness," 787.

51. Talley and Boyce, "Abuse and Functional Gastrointestinal Disorders," 1303.

52. Diaz-Olavarieta, "Domestic Violence against Patients with Chronic Neurological Disorders."

53. Webster, "Pregnancy Outcomes and Health Care Use." For more recent commentary on domestic violence and pregnancy, see Gazmararian, "Violence and Reproductive Health," and Melhado, "Women Who Report Abuse during Pregnancy Have an Elevated Risk of Adverse Birth Outcomes," 204.

54. Campbell, "Addressing Battering during Pregnancy," 301.

55. Ibid., 301–6.

56. Dietz, "Delayed Entry into Prenatal Care."

57. Lachs, "Screening for Family Violence."

58. Schafer, Caetano, and Clark, "Rates of Intimate Partner Violence in the United States."

59. Mason, "The Dimensions of an Epidemic of Violence."

60. Biroscak, "Intimate Partner Violence against Women," and Koziol-McLain and Campbell, "Universal Screening and Mandatory Reporting."

61. Schafer, Caetano, and Clark, "Rates of Intimate Partner Violence in the United States."

62. New York Behavioral Risk Factor Surveillance System, "Physical Injuries in Intimate Relationships."

63. Miles-Doan and Kelly, "Geographic Concentration of Violence between Intimate Partners."

64. Gazmararian, "Prevalence of Violence against Pregnant Women";

Mezey and Bewley, "Domestic Violence and Pregnancy." However, see a recent study that finds only an increase in nonphysical abuse during pregnancy: Martin, "Changes in Intimate Partner Violence during Pregnancy."

65. "Severity of Spousal and Intimate Partner Abuse to Pregnant Hispanic Women."

66. Donovan Westby et al., "Frontal Lobe Deficits in Domestic Violence Offenders."

67. Weaver and Clum, "Interpersonal Violence."

68. Michael and Zumpe, "An Annual Rhythm in the Battering of Women."

69. Edinburgh, "Sexual Exploitation of Very Young Hmong Girls."

70. Lemon, Verhoek-Oftendahl, and Donnelly, "Preventative Health Care Use, Smoking, and Alcohol Use among Rhode Island Women Experiencing Intimate Partner Violence."

71. Brown, "Development of the Woman Abuse Screening Tool for Use in Family Practice."

72. Alpert, "Violence in Intimate Relationships and the Practicing Internist," 776.

73. Ibid.

74. Hartzell, "Orbital Fractures in Women Due to Sexual Assault and Domestic Violence," 957.

75. Wright, "Responses to Battered Mothers in the Pediatric Emergency Department."

76. Ibid. See also Spath, "Child Protection Professionals Identifying Domestic Violence Indications."

77. Ibid.

78. Erickson, Hill, and Siegel, "Barriers to Domestic Violence Screening in the Pediatric Setting"; Siegel and Hill, "Screening for Domestic Violence in the Community Pediatric Setting," 847–851.

79. Hartzell, "Orbital Fractures in Women Due to Sexual Assault and Domestic Violence," 957.

80. Beck, "Ocular Injuries in Battered Women," 151.

81. The alternative trend, not discussed here, is the therapeutic approach to the treatment of the male batterer; see, for example, Sonkin, Martin, and Walker, *The Male Batterer*.

82. The conjoint model is still recommended in some of the most recent literature on therapy and domestic violence. However, the recommendation is accompanied by the caveat that this model is most appropriate for relationships with low and moderate levels of violence (and therefore linked up to the process of clinical "risk assessment"). See La Taillade, "Conjoint Treatment of Intimate Partner Violence." Another recent study suggests that conjoint therapy may be useful as an adjunct to other treatment approaches; see Harris, "Conjoint Therapy and Domestic Violence."

83. More recently some social workers and psychologists have raised strong objections to couples therapy if violence is a factor in the relationship. See, for example, Hattendorf and Tollerud, "Domestic Violence."

84. The contention among scientists who examine neurological factors is that "normal males are more liable to physical conditions that often spell pathological aggression—the episodic dyscontrol syndrome, the attention deficient disorder, and the antisocial personality disorder." Elliott, "Neurological Factors," 262.

85. Morrison, "Assessment of Assertion and Problem-Solving Skills in Wife Abusers and Their Spouses," 229.

86. Launius and Jensen, "Interpersonal Problem-Solving Skills in Battered, Counseling, and Control Women," 160.

87. Morrison, "Assessment of Assertion and Problem-Solving Skills in Wife Abusers and Their Spouses," 235.

88. Ibid., 236.

89. Geller and Wasserstrom, "Conjoint Therapy for the Treatment of Domestic Violence," 34.

90. Ibid. The dialogue is reported on 35–46.

91. Recent research within the social work field has challenged these approaches; see, for example, Forte, "Asymmetrical Role-Taking." He argues that the differences in responses to violence between battered women and nonbattered women are accounted for by oppressive social situations, social isolation, and economic dependency.

92. Margolin, "Wife Battering," 94.

93. There is controversy within the scientific literature about the degree to which battered women resemble "ordinary" women. See, for example, Okun, *Woman Abuse.*

94. Cotroneo, "Families and Abuse," 422–424.

95. See, for example, Fineman, "Dominant Discourse, Professional Language, and Legal Change in Child Custody Decision-Making."

96. Beaudry, *Battered Women*, 64.

97. Margolin, "Wife Battering," 95–99.

98. Ibid., 99.

99. Elliott, "Neurological Factors," 363.

100. Linda Gordon's theory of the hyperdevelopment of the verbal is different but may be considered problematic for similar reasons: "Women's verbal skills were honed to sharpness precisely to do battle against men's superior power, including violence. . . . This superiority . . . was a collective characteristic developed as a result of the structural position of gender." Gordon, *Heroes of Their Own Lives*, 286.

101. Launius and Jensen, "Interpersonal Problem-Solving Skills in Battered, Counseling, and Control Women," 161.

102. Gelles and Straus, *Intimate Violence*, 160–67.

103. Ibid., 164.

104. See, for example, Brook and Davis, *Women, the Family, and Social Work*, 46.

105. Gelles and Straus, *Intimate Violence*, 167.

106. Douglas, "The Battered Women's Syndrome," 52–53.

107. For an exception within social scientific approaches, see Denzin, "Toward a Phenomenology of Domestic Violence."

108. Gelles and Cornell, *Intimate Violence in Families*, 22.

109. Nakhaie, "Asymmetry and Symmetry of Conjugal Violence," 549.

110. Thyfault et al., "Battered Women in Court," 57.

111. Douglas, "The Battered Women's Syndrome," 45.

112. See Browne, *When Battered Women Kill*.

113. Douglas, "The Battered Women's Syndrome," 40.

114. Rosewater, "The Clinical and Courtroom Application of Battered Women's Personality Assessments," 86.

115. Preston, "The Sexual Assault Nurse Examiner and the Rape Crisis Advocate."

116. Wasco, "Conceptualizing the Harm Done by Rape."

117. Resnick et al., "Emergency Evaluation and Intervention with Female Victims of Rape and Other Violence."

118. Littel, *Sexual Assault Nurse Examiner* (SANE) Programs.

119. Ibid., 4

120. Martin, "Controversies Surrounding the Rape Kit Exam in the 1980s."

121. Lewis-O'Conner, "Limitation of the National Protocol for Sexual Assault Medical Forensic Examinations."

122. Ibid., 269.

123. Sugar, "Physical Injury after Sexual Assault: Findings of a Large Case Series," and Rossman, "Genital Trauma Associated with Forced Digital Penetration."

124. McGregor et al., "Sexual Assault Forensic Medical Examination."

125. Fanslow, "Indicators of Assault-Related Injuries among Women Presenting to the Emergency Department."

126. Adams et al., "Adolescent Sexual Assault," and Biggs et al., "Genital Injuries Following Sexual Assault of Women with and without Prior Sexual Intercourse Experience."

127. Parnis and DuMont, "Examining the Standardized Application of Rape Kits."

128. The terminology is from Max Weber. Professionals who "appropriate violence" in the production of social science "let [themselves] in for the diabolical forces lurking in all violence." Weber, *Politics as a Vocation*, 125–26.

129. Campbell, "Community Services for Rape Survivors."

130. O'Connor, "Rape Crisis," 28–47.

131. Yassen and Glass, "Sexual Assault Survivors Groups."

5 victim insurgency

1. Fraser, *Unruly Practices*, 158.

2. Fraser and Gordon, "A Genealogy of 'Dependency.'"

3. For an analysis of discourse strategies in routine rape hearings, see Ehrlich, *Representing Rape*.

4. Martin, *Rape Work*, 51; see also Hodgson and Kelley, *Sexual Violence*.

5. Martin, *Rape Work*, 65.

6. The racial composition of the women interviewed included two black, one Hispanic, and three white.

7. I spoke with Patricia about her experiences and also read her fictional writings about battered women, which are loosely autobiographical.

8. For an analysis of the limits and possibilities of choice for battered women from a law reform perspective, see Chiu, "Confronting the Agency in Battered Mothers."

6 universalizing gender justice

This chapter is a revised version of Bumiller, "Freedom from Violence as a Human Right." The epigraph to this chapter is from Kaufman, "To Cut Too Deeply and Not Enough," 14.

1. UN General Assembly, *Convention on the Elimination of All Forms of Discrimination against Women*.

2. Ibid.

3. *Violence against Women Act*.

4. See, generally, Merry, "Constructing a Global Law—Violence against Women and the Human Rights System," and Merry, "Rights, Religion, and Community," 3.

5. Hirsch, "Globalization and the State: Problems of Cross-Cultural Comparison," 1009.

6. See Feinstein and Slaughter, "A Duty to Prevent," 137.

7. Lazarus-Black, "The Politics of Gender Violence."

8. Arendt, *On Violence*, 83.

9. Ibid., 56.

10. Narayan, *Dislocating Cultures*, 88–94.

11. Ibid., 94.

12. Merry, "Constructing a Global Law—Violence against Women and the Human Rights System," 973–74.

13. Ibid., 966.

14. See, Hajjar, "Religion, State Power, and Domestic Violence in Muslim Societies."

15. Ibid., 21.

16. Ibid.

17. MacKinnon, "Disputing Male Sovereignty," 145–46.

18. Resnik, "Citizenship and Violence," 62.

19. Ibid., 63.

20. Resnik and Suk, "Adding Insult to Injury."

21. *United States v. Morrison.*

22. Mackinnon, "Disputing Male Sovereignty," 136.

23. Ibid., 148.

24. See Bauman, "On Postmodern Uses of Sex."

25. Schneider, "Symposium."

26. Ibid., 342.

27. Ibid., 342–43.

28. Picart, "Rhetorically Reconfiguring Victimhood and Agency."

29. Ibid., 116.

30. Ibid., 116–17.

31. Ibid., 118.

32. Byrd, "Specific Provisions of the Violence against Women Act," 598.

33. See Bonner, "Reconceptualizing VAWA's 'Animus' for Rape in States' Emerging Post-VAWA Civil Rights Legislation."

34. Ibid., 1446.

35. Luban, "A Theory of Crimes against Humanity," 105.

36. Bonner, "Reconceptualizing VAWA's 'Animus' for Rape,"1439.

37. Ibid., 1448.

38. Wilson, "Police and the Sexual Assault Examination," 15–16.

39. See, for example, the "STOP Violence against Women Formula Grant," available online at http://egov.oregon.gov/OOHS/CJSD/vawa_org_assessment.shtml (accessed September 19, 2007).

40. Meyer-Emerick, "Policy Makers, Practioners, Citizens."

41. See Uekert, "The Value of Coordinated Community Responses," 134.

42. See *Hernandez v. Ashcroft.*

43. See President Bill Clinton's "Statement on Signing the Victims of Trafficking and Violence Protection Act of 2000" of October 28, 2000, available online at http://www.gpoaccess.gov/wcomp (accessed September 19, 2007).

44. Berman, "(Un)Popular Strangers and Crises (Un)Bounded."

45. Ibid.

46. See, generally, Tzvetkova, "NGO Responses to Trafficking in Women."

47. Mattar, "Monitoring the Status of Severe Forms of Trafficking in Foreign Countries," 160–61.

48. Ibid., 172.

49. Schneider, "Anna Hirsch Lecture," 692–94.

50. Fulcher, "Domestic Violence and the Rights of Women in Japan and the United States."

51. Ibid.

52. Hopkins, "Responding," 294.

53. Mills, *Insult to Injury*, 137–42.

54. *Close to Home.*

55. Cuthbert, *Battered Mothers Speak Out*, 14.

56. Ibid.

57. Hopkins, "Responding," 310–11.

58. Resnik and Suk, "Adding Insult to Injury," 1926–27.

59. See, in general, Nussbaum, *Women and Human Development*, and more recently, Nussbaum, *Frontier of Justice.*

60. Isaac, "A New Guarantee on Earth," 67.

61. Ibid., 68.

62. Parekh, "A Meaningful Place in the World," 48.

63. Arendt, *On Violence*, 84.

64. See "Critical Resistance—Incite! Statement: Gender Violence and the Prison Industrial Complex" on the Incite! Web site, located at http://www.incite-national.org/involve/statement.html (accessed September 19, 2007).

65. Ibid.

66. Ibid.

67. Narayan, *Dislocating Cultures*, 88.

68. Ibid., 113–17.

69. For example, see the Web site of the Open Society Institute's International Women's Program at http://www.soros.org/initiatives/women/focus_areas/h_violence (accessed September 19, 2007).

70. Gowda, address at the conference "Criminalising Gendered Violence."

71. Ndira and Turner, The Mifumi Project and PROMPT Team.

72. See, generally, Renda, *Taking Haiti.*

73. Puar, "Abu Ghraib."

conclusion

1. Abrams, "Feminists in International Human Rights."

2. I write from my ten-year experience of facilitating community learning about issues of sexual violence. Over these years, I have engaged in a partnership with battered women's shelters, police task forces, victim protection units, legal services offices, social services agencies, and feminist activist organizations in my community. This partnership has developed by placing my students in these community settings and inviting professionals and activists to participate in classroom discussions.

3. See Saltzman, "Issues Related to Defining and Measuring Violence against Women."

4. The official data collected by the National Crime Victimization Survey provides an overview of the extent of the violence and demographic variation. These figures most likely underrepresent the actual incidence of crime due to reluctance to report and narrow definitional criteria. Based on the 2002 reports, there were 247,730 victims of rape, attempted rape, and sexual assault. According to 2001 data on "intimate partner violence," there were 691,710 nonfatal violent victimizations. See Rennison, "Intimate Partner Violence, 1993–2001," and Rennison and Welchans, "Intimate Partner Violence." These figures represent an overall decrease in reporting of violent crime since 1993; see Shestack, "Serious Crime Is on a Downward Trend." The data also indicate that persons at the lowest income levels are much more likely to experience intimate partner violence. Black women are victims of domestic violence at a rate 35 percent higher than white women and two-and-a-half times that of women of other races. See Rennison and Welchans, "Intimate Partner Violence," 4.

5. One study attempts to assess the impact of the VAWA on incidence rates and criminal justice intervention. See Cho and Wilke, "How Has the Violence against Women Act Affected the Response of the Criminal Justice System to Domestic Violence?"

6. For a discussion of class and domestic violence, see Hall, "Canal Town Boys," and McKendy, "The Class Politics of Domestic Violence."

7. Cotterill, "Domestic Discord, Rocky Relationships."

8. For a range of perspectives on race, rape, and intimate violence, see Cotterill, "Domestic Discord, Rocky Relationships"; Landwehr, "Racism in Rape Trials"; Lule, "The Rape of Mike Tyson"; Rose, "Crimes of Color"; Wells and Motley, "Reinforcing the Myth of the Crazed Rapist"; Grover and Soothill, "Ethnicity, the Search for Rapists and the Press."

9. "Women Say They've Made Gains but There's Still Work to Do."

10. See Buddie and Miller, "Beyond Rape Myths"; Chiroro et al., "Rape Myth Acceptance and Rape Proclivity"; Peterson, "Was It Rape?"; Whitecotton and Sorenson, "A Sociocultural View of Sexual Assault."

11. See, for example, Projansky, *Watching Rape.*

12. Bachman and Paternoster, "A Contemporary Look at the Effects of Rape Law Reform."

13. Berger, Neuman, and Searles, "The Social and Political Context of Rape Law Reform"; Futter and Mebane, "The Effects of Rape Law Reform on Rape Case Processing"; Gunn and Linden, "The Impact of Law Reform on the Processing of Sexual Assault Cases"; Spohn and Horney, "The Impact of Rape Law Reform on the Processing of Simple and Aggravated Rape Cases."

14. See Frohmann, "Discrediting Victims' Allegations of Sexual Assault."

15. Matoesian, *Law and the Language of Identity*; Smart, *Feminism and the Power of Law*; Taslitz, *Rape and the Culture of the Courtroom*.

16. For a mixed review of progress in the courtroom, see Ptacek, *Battered Women in the Courtroom*.

17. See Chancer, "Rethinking Domestic Violence in Theory and Practice."

18. For example, see Raphael, "Rethinking Criminal Justice Responses to Intimate Partner Violence."

19. See McMahon and Pence, "Making Social Change."

20. See Ristock, *No More Secrets*.

21. Hirschmann, *The Subject of Liberty*.

22. Ibid., 122.

23. For this kind of broad analysis of responsibility and the problem of domestic violence, see Smiley, "Battered Women and Bombed-Out Cities."

24. Daly, "Men's Violence, Victim Advocacy, and Feminist Redress."

25. Berger, Neuman, and Searles, "The Social and Political Context of Rape Law Reform," 243.

26. Cohen, "Willingness-to-Pay for Crime Control Programs."

27. For the description of a "risk society," see Beck, *Risk Society*.

28. There is also discussion about wider use of mechanisms of civil protection for battered women; see, for example, Murphy, "Engaging with the State," 499–521.

29. See, for an example of an American articulation of the abolitionist position, Davis, *Abolition Democracy*.

30. One study, for example, considers whether victims are safer if the abuser receives probation rather than an unlikely jail sentence. See Ames and Dunham, "Asymptotic Justice."

31. "Critical Resistance—Incite!"

32. Hudson, "Restorative Justice."

33. Postmus, "Battered and on Welfare"; Terry, "Poverty Reduction and Violence against Women."

34. Cuthbert et al., *Battered Mothers Speak Out*, and see, in general, Fineman, *The Autonomy Myth*.

35. A recent study finds that poor women who seek help from a legal aid society are satisfied with their treatment, especially if they have minimal expectations. The more pressing question addressed here is whether women in these situations might be inspired to see their problems as situated in a larger context of injustice. See Richman, "Women, Poverty, and Domestic Violence."

36. An example of the successful use of a specialized court is detailed by Mirchandani, "Battered Women's Movement Ideals and Judge-Led Social Change in Domestic Violence Courts."

37. Bell, "Balancing Power through Community Building"; Zweig and Burt, "Effects of Interactions among Community Agencies on Legal System Responses to Domestic Violence and Sexual Assault in STOP-Funded Communities."

38. Martin, *Rape Work*, 3.

BIBLIOGRAPHY

Abramovitz, Mimi, and Ann Withorn. "Playing by the Rules: Welfare Reform and the New Authoritarian State." In *Without Justice for All: The New Liberalism and Our Retreat from Racial Equality*, edited by Adolph Reed, Jr., 151–74. Boulder, Colo.: Westview Press, 1999.

Abrams, Kathryn. "Feminists in International Human Rights: The Changer and the Changed." *Berkeley Journal of International Law* 21:2 (2003): 390–95.

Ackelsberg, Martha. "Reconceiving Politics? Women's Activism and Democracy in a Time of Retrenchment." *Feminist Studies* 27:2 (Summer 2001): 391–429.

Adams, Joyce A., et al. "Adolescent Sexual Assault: Documentation of Acute Injuries Using Photo-coloscopy." *Journal of Adolescent Gynecology* 14 (2001): 175–80.

Adams, Parveen. *The Emptiness of the Image: Psychoanalysis and Sexual Differences*. London: Routledge, 1996.

Alpert, Elaine J. "Violence in Intimate Relationships and the Practicing Internist: New Disease or New Agenda?" *Annals of Internal Medicine* 123:10 (November 15, 1995): 774–81.

Ames, Lynda J., and Katherine T. Dunham. "Asymptotic Justice: Probation as a Criminal Justice Response to Intimate Partner Violence." *Violence against Women* 8:1 (2002): 6–35.

Arendt, Hannah. *Eichmann in Jerusalem: A Report on the Banality of Evil*. New York: Penguin Books, 1963.

——. *On Violence*. New York: Harcourt Brace, 1970.

Arnold, Thurman Wesley. *The Symbols of Government*. New York: Harcourt Press, 1962.

Bach, Amy. "True Crime, False Confession." *Nation* 268:5 (1999): 21–23.

Bachman, Ronet, and Raymond Paternoster. "A Contemporary Look at the Effects of Rape Law Reform: How Far Have We Really Come?" *Journal of Law and Criminology* 84:3 (1993): 554–74.

Barasch, Moshe. *Icon: Studies in the History of an Idea*. New York: New York University Press, 1992.

Bataille, Georges. *Eroticism: Death and Sensuality*. San Francisco: City Lights Books, 1986.

Bauman, Zygmunt. *Modernity and the Holocaust*. Ithaca, N.Y.: Cornell University Press, 2000.

——. "On Postmodern Uses of Sex." *Theory, Culture and Society* 15:3/4 (1998): 19–33.

Beaudry, Micheline. *Battered Women*. Montreal: Black Rose Books, 1985.

Beck, Sylvia R. "Ocular Injuries in Battered Women." *Ophthalmology* 103:1 (January 1996): 148–51.

Beck, Ulrich. *Risk Society: Towards a New Modernity*. London: Sage Publications, 1992.

Bell, Holly, et al. "Balancing Power through Community Building: Setting the Research Agenda on Violence against Women." *Affilia* 19:4 (2004): 404–17.

Benedict, Jeffrey R. *Athletes and Acquaintance Rape*. Thousand Oaks, Calif.: Sage Publications, 1998.

Bennett, W. Lance, and Regina G. Lawrence. "News Icons and Social Change." *Journal of Communication* 45:3 (Summer 1995): 20–39.

Berger, Ronald J. W., Lawrence Neuman, and Patricia Searles. "The Social and Political Context of Rape Law Reform: An Aggregate Analysis." *Social Science Quarterly* 72:2 (June 1991): 221–38.

Bergman, Bo K., et al. "Battered Women—Their Susceptibility to Treatment." *Scandinavian Journal of Social Medicine* 16.3 (1988): 155–60.

Berman, Jacqueline. "(Un)Popular Strangers and Crises (Un)Bounded: Discourses of Sex-Trafficking, the European Political Community and the Panicked State of the Modern State." *European Journal of International Relations* 9:1 (2003): 37–86.

Bevacqua, Maria. *Rape on the Public Agenda: Feminism and the Politics of Sexual Assault*. Boston: Northeastern University Press, 2000.

Biggs, Marleen, et al. "Genital Injuries Following Sexual Assault of Women with and without Prior Sexual Intercourse Experience." *Canadian Medical Association Journal* 159 (1998): 33–38.

Biroscak, Brian J., et al. "Intimate Partner Violence against Women: Findings from One State's ED Surveillance System." *Journal of Emergency Nursing* 32 (February 2006): 12–16.

Bondi, Liz. "Working the Spaces of Neoliberal Subjectivity: Psychotherapeutic Technologies, Professionalisation and Counselling." *Antipode* 37:3 (2005): 497–514.

Bonner, J. Rebekka S. "Reconceptualizing VAWA's 'Animus' for Rape in States' Emerging Post–VAWA Civil Rights Legislation." *Yale Law Journal* III:6 (2002): 1417–57.

Brison, Susan J. *Aftermath: Violence and the Remaking of a Self.* Princeton, N.J.: Princeton University Press, 2002.

Brook, Eve, and Ann Davis. *Women, the Family, and Social Work.* London: Tavistock Publications, 1985.

Brooks, Peter. "Storytelling without Fear? Confession in Law and Literature." In *Law's Stories: Narrative and Rhetoric in the Law*, edited by Peter Brooks and Paul Gewirtz, 114–34. New Haven, Conn.: Yale University Press, 1996.

Brown, Judith Belle. "Development of the Woman Abuse Screening Tool for Use in Family Practice." *Family Medicine* 28 (June 1996): 422–28.

Browne, Angela. *When Battered Women Kill.* New York: Free Press, 1987.

Brownmiller, Susan. *Against our Will.* New York: Simon and Schuster, 1975.

Buddie, Amy M., and Arthur G. Miller. "Beyond Rape Myths: A More Complex View of Perceptions of Rape Victims." *Sex Roles* 45:3/4 (2001): 139–61.

Bumiller, Kristin. "Fallen Angels: The Representation of Violence against Women in Legal Culture." *International Journal of the Sociology of Law* 18 (1990): 125–43.

——. "Freedom from Violence as a Human Right: Toward a Feminist Politics of Nonviolence." *Thomas Jefferson Law Review* 28:3 (Spring 2006): 327–54.

——. "Law at the Margins: The Symbolic Power of Professional Discourse." In *Language, Symbolism, and Politics*, edited Richard Merelman, 151–68. New York: Westview Press, 1992.

——. "Rape as a Legal Symbol: An Essay on Sexual Violence and Racism." *University of Miami Law Review* 42 (1987): 75–91.

——. "Spectacles of the Strange: Envisioning Violence in the Central Park Jogger Trial." In *Media and the Law*, edited by Martha Albertson Fineman and Martha McCluskey, 217–24. New York: Oxford University Press, 1997.

Buzawa, Eve S., and Carl G. Buzawa, eds. *Do Arrests and Restraining Orders Work?* Thousand Oaks, Calif.: Sage Publications, 1996.

Byrd, Richee A. "Specific Provisions of the Violence against Women Act." *Georgetown Journal of Gender and the Law* 3 (2002): 595–608.

Campbell, Jacquelyn C. "Addressing Battering during Pregnancy: Reducing Low Birth Weight and Ongoing Abuse." *Seminars in Perinatology* 19:4 (August 1995): 301–6.

——. "Assessing Dangerousness in Domestic Violence Cases: History, Challenges, and Opportunities." *Criminology and Public Policy* 4:4 (November 2005): 653–72.

Campbell, Rebecca, et al. "Community Services for Rape Survivors: Enhancing Psychological Well-Being or Increasing Trauma?" *Journal of Consulting and Clinical Psychology* 67 (1999): 847–58.

Caputi, Jane. *The Age of Sex Crime.* Bowling Green, Ohio: Bowling Green State University Popular Press, 1987.

Carter, Dan T. *Scottsboro: A Tragedy of the American South.* Baton Rouge: Louisiana State University Press, 1979.

Carter, Richard. "Lawsuits by Innocent Youths Target Central Park Jogger Fiasco." *New York Amsterdam News* 95:6 (2004): 11–42.

Chancer, Lynn. *High Profile Crimes: When Legal Cases Become Social Causes.* Chicago: University of Chicago Press, 2005.

——. "Rethinking Domestic Violence in Theory and Practice." *Deviant Behavior* 25:3 (2004): 266–75.

Chiroro, Patrick, et al. "Rape Myth Acceptance and Rape Proclivity." *Journal of Interpersonal Violence* 19:4 (2004): 427–42.

Chiu, Elaine. "Confronting the Agency in Battered Mothers." *Southern California Law Review* 74 (2001): 1223–74.

Cho, Hyunkag, and Dina J. Wilke. "How Has the Violence against Women Act Affected the Response of the Criminal Justice System to Domestic Violence?" *Journal of Sociology and Social Welfare* 32:4 (December 2005): 125–39.

Close to Home: Case Studies of Human Rights Work in the United States. New York: Ford Foundation, 2004. Available online at http://www.fordfound .org/publications/recent_articles/close_to_home.cfm (accessed September 19, 2007).

Cocca, Carolyn E. "From 'Welfare Queen' to 'Exploited Teen': Welfare Dependency, Statutory Rape, and Moral Panic. *NWSA Journal* 14 (Summer 2002): 56–79.

——. *Jailbait: The Politics of Statutory Rape Laws in the United States.* Albany: State University of New York Press, 2004.

Cohen, Jeffrey H., Samuel N. Forjuoh, and Edward W. Gondolf. "Injuries and Health Care Use in Women with Partners in Batterer Intervention Programs." *Journal of Family Violence* 14:1 (March 1999): 83–94.

Cohen, Mark A., et al. "Willingness-to-Pay for Crime Control Programs." *Criminology* 42:1 (2004): 89–110.

Coker, Donna. "Race, Poverty, and the Crime-Centered Response to Domestic Violence." *Violence against Women* 10:11 (2004): 1331–53.

Comey, Philip. "Fastest Growing Prison Population." *Corrections Today* 68:1 (February 2006): 15.

Conrad, Peter. "Medicalization and Social Control." *Annual Review of Sociology* 18 (1992): 209–32.

Corrigan, Rose. "Making Meaning of Megan's Law." *Law and Social Inquiry* 31 (Spring 2006): 267–317.

Cotroneo, Margaret. "Families and Abuse: A Contextual Approach." In *Family Resources: The Hidden Partner in Family Therapy*, edited by Mark A. Karpel, 413–37. New York: Guilford Press, 1986.

Cotterill, Janet. "Domestic Discord, Rocky Relationships: Semantic Prosodies in Representations of Marital Violence in the O. J. Simpson Trial." *Discourse and Society* 12:3 (2001): 291–313.

Craissati, Jackie, and Anthony Beech. "Risk Prediction and Failure in a Complete Urban Sample of Sex Offenders." *Journal of Forensic Psychiatry and Psychology* 16 (March 2005): 24–40.

"Critical Resistance—Incite! Statement on Gender Violence and the Prison-Industrial Complex." *Social Justice* 30:3 (2003): 141–50.

Cuklanz, Lisa M. *Rape on Prime Time: Television, Masculinity, and Sexual Violence*. Philadelphia: University of Pennsylvania Press, 2000.

Curnow, S. A. "The Open Window Phase: Helpseeking and Reality Behaviors by Battered Women." *Applied Nursing Research* 10 (August 1997): 128–35.

Cuthbert, Carrie, et al. *Battered Mothers Speak Out: A Human Rights Report on Domestic Violence and Child Custody in the Massachusetts Family Courts*. Wellesley, Mass.: Wellesley Centers for Women, 2002.

Dale, Roger, and Susan Robertson. "Interview with Boaventura de Sousa Santos." *Globalisation, Societies and Education* 2:2 (July 2004): 147–60.

Daly, Kathleen. "Men's Violence, Victim Advocacy, and Feminist Redress." *Law and Society Review* 28:4 (1994): 777–87.

Davis, Angela Y. *Abolition Democracy: Beyond Empire, Prisons and Torture*. New York: Seven Stories Press, 2005.

Davis, Liane. "Battered Women: The Transformation of a Social Problem." *Social Work* 32 (1987): 306–11.

Davis, Sharon L. "The Reality of False Confessions—Lessons of the Central Park Jogger Case." *New York University Review of Law and Social Change* 30 (2006): 209–53.

Denzin, Norman K. "Toward a Phenomenology of Domestic Violence." *American Journal of Sociology* 90 (November 1984): 483–513.

Diaz-Olavarieta, Claudia. "Domestic Violence against Patients with Chronic Neurological Disorders." *Archives of Neurology* 56 (June 1999): 681–85.

Didion, Joan. "New York: Sentimental Journeys." *New York Review of Books* (January 17, 1991): 45–57.

Dietz, Patricia. "Delayed Entry into Prenatal Care: Effect of Physical Violence." *Obstetrics and Gynecology* 90 (August 1997): 221–24.

Dobash, R. Emerson, and Russell Dobash. *Violence against Wives: A Case against the Patriarchy.* New York: Free Press, 1979.

Dobash, Rebecca Emerson. "Domestic Violence: Arrest, Prosecution, and Reducing Violence." *Criminology & Public Policy* 2:2 (March 2003): 313–18.

Donovan Westby, Margaret, et al. "Frontal Lobe Deficits in Domestic Violence Offenders." *Genetic, Social, and General Psychology Monographs* 125 (February 1999): 71–102.

Douglas, Mary Ann. "The Battered Women's Syndrome." In *Domestic Violence on Trial: Psychological and Legal Dimensions of Family Violence,* edited by Daniel Jay Sonkin. New York: Springer, 1987.

Drossman, Douglas. "Health Status by Gastrointestinal Diagnosis and Abuse History." *Gastroenterology* 110 (1996): 999–1007.

——. "Sexual and Physical Abuse and Gastrointestinal Illness." *Annals of Internal Medicine* 123:10 (November 15, 1995): 782–94.

Duggan, Lisa. *The Twilight of Equality? Neoliberalism, Cultural Politics, and the Attack on Democracy.* Boston: Beacon Press, 2003.

Dunlap, Justine. "Sometimes I Feel Like a Motherless Child: The Error of Pursuing Battered Mothers for the Failure to Protect." *Loyola Law Review* 50 (Fall 2004): 565–622.

Dwyer, Jim. "Verdict That Failed the Test of Time." *New York Times,* December 6, 2002, A1.

Edelman, Murray J. *Political Language: Words That Succeed and Policies That Fail.* New York: Academic Press, 1977.

Edinburgh, Laurel, et al. "Sexual Exploitation of Very Young Hmong Girls." *Journal of Adolescent Health* 39:1 (July 2006): 111–18.

Ehrlich, Susan. *Representing Rape: Language and Sexual Consent.* New York: Routledge, 2001.

Elliott, Frank A. "Neurological Factors." In *Handbook of Family Violence,* edited by Vincent B. Van Hasselt, 359–82. New York: Plenum Press, 1988.

Erickson, Mary J., Teresa D. Hill, and Robert M. Siegel. "Barriers to Domestic Violence Screening in the Pediatric Setting." *Pediatrics* 108:1 (2001): 98–103.

Faludi, Susan. *Backlash: The Undeclared War against American Women.* New York: Crown, 1991.

Fanslow, Janet I., et al. "Indicators of Assault-Related Injuries among Women Presenting to the Emergency Department." *Annals of Emergency Medicine* 32 (September 1998): 341–48.

Faure, Bernard. "The Buddhist Icon and the Modern Gaze." *Critical Inquiry* 24 (Spring 1988): 768–69.

Feinstein, Lee, and Anne-Marie Slaughter. "A Duty to Prevent." *Foreign Affairs* 83:1 (January–February 2004): 136–61.

Ferguson, Kathy E. *The Feminist Case against Bureaucracy*. Philadephia: Temple University Press, 1984.

Ferree, Myra Marx, and Beth B. Hess. *Controversy and Coalition: The New Feminist Movement*. Boston: Twayne Publishers, 1985.

Fineman, Martha. *The Autonomy Myth: A Theory of Dependency*. New York: New Press, 2004.

——. "Dominant Discourse, Professional Language, and Legal Change in Child Custody Decision-Making." *Harvard Law Review* 101 (February 1988): 724–74.

Finkel, Martin A. "Technical Conduct of the Child Sexual Abuse Medical Examination." *Child Abuse and Neglect* 22: 6 (1998): 555–566.

Firestone, Philip. "Hostility and Recidivism in Sexual Offenders." *Archives of Social Behavior* 34 (June 2005): 277–83.

Fleury, Ruth E. "Missing Voices: Patterns of Battered Women's Satisfaction with the Criminal Legal System." *Violence against Women* 8:2 (2002): 181–206.

Forte, J. A. "Asymmetrical Role-Taking: Comparing Battered and Nonbattered Women." *Social Work* 42 (January 1997): 113–15.

Foucault, Michel. *The History of Sexuality*. New York: Vintage Books, 1980.

Fraser, J. Scott. "Strategic Rapid Intervention in Wife-Beating." In *Troubled Relationships*, edited by Elam Nunnally, 163–91. New York: Sage, 1988.

Fraser, Nancy. *Unruly Practices: Power, Discourse, and Gender in Contemporary Social Theory*. Minneapolis: University of Minnesota Press, 1989.

Fraser, Nancy, and Linda Gordon. "A Genealogy of 'Dependency': Tracing a Keyword of the U.S. Welfare State." In *Justice Interruptus: Critical Reflections on the "Postsocialist" Condition*, by Nancy Fraser, 121–49. New York: Routledge, 1997.

Frohmann, Lisa. "Convictability and Discordant Locales: Reproducing Race, Class, and Gender Ideologies in Prosecutorial Decisionmaking." *Law and Society Review* 31 (1997): 531–56.

——. "Discrediting Victims' Allegations of Sexual Assault: Prosecutorial Accounts of Case Rejections." In *Rape and Society*, edited by Patricia Searles and Ronald J. Berger, 199–214. Boulder, Colo.: Westview Press, 1995.

Fulcher, Juley A. "Domestic Violence and the Rights of Women in Japan and the United States." *Human Rights* 29 (2002): 16–17.

Futter, Stacy, and Walter R. Mebane Jr. "The Effects of Rape Law Reform on Rape Case Processing." *Berkeley Women's Law Journal* 16:72 (2001): 72–140.

Garland, David. *The Culture of Control: Crime and Social Order in Contemporary Society*. Chicago: University of Chicago Press, 2001.

Garner, Joel. "What Does 'Prosecution' of Domestic Violence Mean?" *Criminology and Public Policy* 4:3 (August 2005): 567–73.

Gavey, Nicola. *Just Sex? The Cultural Scaffolding of Rape.* New York: Routledge, 2005.

Gazmararian, Julie A., et al. "Violence and Reproductive Health: Current Knowledge and Future Directions." *Maternal and Child Health Journal* 4:2 (2000): 79–84.

Gazmararian, Julie A., and Suzanne Lazorick. "Prevalence of Violence against Pregnant Women." *Journal of the American Medical Association* 275:24 (June 26, 1996): 1915–20.

Gelb, Joyce, and Vivien Hart. "Feminist Politics in a Hostile Environment: Obstacles and Opportunities." In *How Social Movements Matter,* edited by Marco Giugni et al., 149–81. Minneapolis: University of Minnesota Press, 1999.

Geller, Janet A., and Janice Wasserstrom. "Conjoint Therapy for the Treatment of Domestic Violence." In *Battered Women and Their Families: Intervention Strategies and Treatment Programs,* edited by Albert R. Roberts, 33–48. New York: Springer, 1984.

Gelles, Richard J., and Claire Pedrick Cornell. *Intimate Violence in Families.* Beverly Hills, Calif.: Sage Publications, 1985.

Gelles, Richard J., and Murray A. Straus. *Intimate Violence.* New York: Simon and Schuster, 1988.

Girard, Rene. *Violence and the Sacred.* Baltimore: Johns Hopkins University Press, 1972.

Gondolf, Edward. "The Effect of Batterer Counseling on Shelter Outcome." *Journal of Interpersonal Violence* 3:3 (September 1988): 275–89.

——. "Evaluating Batterer Counseling Programs: A Difficult Task Showing Some Effects and Implications." *Aggression and Violent Behavior* 9 (2004): 605–31.

Gordon, Linda. *Heroes of Their Own Lives: The Politics and History of Family Violence: Boston, 1880–1960.* New York: Penguin Books, 1988.

Gordon, Margaret T., and Stephanie Riger. *The Female Fear: The Social Cost of Rape.* Urbana: University of Illinois Press, 1991.

Gowda, Veena. Address at "Criminalising Gendered Violence: Local, National and International Perspectives," Law School, University of Bristol, September 14–15, 2004.

Grewal, Inderpal. " 'Security Moms' in the Early Twentieth-Century United States: The Gender of Security in Neoliberalism." *Women's Studies Quarterly* 34 (Spring/Summer 2006): 25–39.

Grover, Chris, and Keith Soothill. "Ethnicity, the Search for Rapists and the Press." *Ethnic and Racial Studies* 19:3 (1996): 567–84.

Gunn, Rita, and Rick Linden. "The Impact of Law Reform on the Processing of Sexual Assault Cases." *Canadian Review of Sociology and Anthropology* 34:2 (1997): 155–75.

Hacking, Ian. *The Social Construction of What?* Cambridge, Mass.: Harvard University Press, 1999.

Hajjar, Lisa. "Religion, State Power, and Domestic Violence in Muslim Societies: A Framework for Comparative Analysis." *Law and Social Inquiry* 29:1 (2004): 1–38.

Hall, Julia. "Canal Town Boys: Poor White Males and Domestic Violence." *Anthropology and Education Quarterly* 31:4 (2000): 471–85.

Harris, Gregory E. "Conjoint Therapy and Domestic Violence: Treating the Individual and the Relationship." *Counseling Psychology Quarterly* 19:4 (December 2006): 373–79.

Hartzell, Kathleen. "Orbital Fractures in Women Due to Sexual Assault and Domestic Violence." *Ophthalmology* 103:6 (June 1996): 953–57.

Hattendorf, J., and T. R. Tollerud. "Domestic Violence: Counseling Strategies That Minimize the Impact of Secondary Victimization." *Perspectives in Psychiatric Care* 33 (January–March 1997): 14–23.

Healy, Kerry, et al. *Batterer Intervention: Program Approaches and Criminal Justice Strategies.* Washington, D.C.: U.S. Department of Justice, February 1998.

Heimer, Karen, and Candace Kruttschnitt. *Gender and Crime: Patterns in Victimization and Offending.* New York: New York University Press, 2006.

Herman, Judith Lewis. *Trauma and Recovery: The Aftermath of Violence—From Domestic Abuse to Political Terror.* New York: Basic Books, 1997.

Hirsch, Susan F. "Globalization, and the State: Problems of Cross-Cultural Comparison: Analyzing Linguistic Strategies in Tanzanian Domestic Violence Workshops." *Law and Social Inquiry* 28:4 (Fall 2003): 1009–44.

Hirschmann, Nancy J. *The Subject of Liberty: Toward a Feminist Theory of Freedom.* Princeton, N.J.: Princeton University Press, 2003.

Hodgson, James F., and Debra S. Kelley. *Sexual Violence: Policies, Practices and Challenges in the United States and Canada.* Westport, Conn.: Praeger, 2002.

Hopkins, C. Quince, Mary P. Ross, and Karen J. Bachar. "Responding: Two New Solutions: Applying Restorative Justice to Ongoing Intimate Violence: Problems and Possibilities." *Saint Louis University Public Law Review* 23 (2004): 294–311.

Horeck, Tanya. *Public Rape: Representing Violation in Fiction and Film.* New York: Routledge, 2004.

Hudson, Barbara. "Restorative Justice: The Challenge of Sexual and Racial Violence." *Journal of Law and Society* 25:2 (1998): 616–35.

Irigaray, Luce. *Speculum of the Other Woman.* Translated by Gillian C. Gill. Ithaca, N.Y.: Cornell University Press, 1985.

Isaac, Jeffrey. "A New Guarantee on Earth: Hannah Arendt on Human

Dignity and the Politics of Human Rights." *American Political Science Review* 90:1 (1996): 61–74.

Jackson, Stevi. "The Social Context of Rape: Sexual Scripts and Motivation." In *Rape and Society: Readings on the Problem of Sexual Assault*, edited by Patricia Searles and Ronald J. Berger, 16–27. Boulder, Colo.: Westview Press, 1995.

Jenkins, Philip. *Moral Panic: Changing Concepts of the Child Molester in Modern America*. New Haven: Yale University Press, 1998.

Kaufman, Eleanor. "To Cut Too Deeply and Not Enough: Violence and the Incorporeal." *Parallax* 9:1 (2003): 14–28.

Kemp, C. Henry. "Sexual Abuse, Another Hidden Pediatric Problem: The 1977 C. Anderson Aldrich Lecture." *Pediatrics* 62:3 (September 1978): 282–89.

Kendrick, Karen. "Producing the Battered Woman." In *Community Action and Feminist Practices*, edited by Nancy A. Naples, 151–74. New York: Routledge, 1998.

Kirchheimer, Otto. *Political Justice: The Use of Legal Procedure for Political Ends*. Princeton, N.J.: Princeton University Press, 1961.

Koziol-McLain, Jane, and Jacquelyn C. Campbell. "Universal Screening and Mandatory Reporting: An Update on Two Important Issues for Victim/Survivors of Intimate Abuse." *Journal of Emergency Nursing* 27 (December 2001): 602–6.

Kravetz, Diane. *Tales from the Trenches: Politics and Practice in Feminist Service Organizations*. Lanham, Md.: University Press of America, 2004.

Kristeva, Julia. *Powers of Horror: An Essay on Abjection*. New York: Columbia University Press, 1982.

——. *Strangers to Ourselves*. New York: Columbia University Press, 1991.

Krzewinski, Lisa M. "But I Didn't Do It: Protecting the Rights of Juveniles during Interrogation." *Boston Third World Law Journal* 22 (Spring 2002): 355–87.

Lachs, M. S. "Screening for Family Violence: What's an Evidence-Based Doctor to Do?" *Annals of Internal Medicine* 140 (March 2, 2004): 399–400.

Landwehr, Patricia H., et al. "Racism in Rape Trials." *Journal of Social Psychology* 142:5 (2002): 667–69.

La Taillade, Jaslean J., et al. "Conjoint Treatment of Intimate Partner Violence: A Cognitive Behavioral Approach." *Journal of Cognitive Psychotherapy* 20:4 (Winter 2006): 393–410.

Launius, Margaret H., and Bernard L. Jensen. "Interpersonal Problem-Solving Skills in Battered, Counseling, and Control Women." *Journal of Family Violence* 2:2 (1987): 151–62.

Laurie, Nina, and Liz Bondi. *Working in the Spaces of Neoliberalism*. Malden, Mass.: Blackwell, 2005.

Lazarus-Black, Mindie. "The Politics of Gender Violence: Law Reform in Local and Global Places." *Law and Social Inquiry* 28 (2003): 980–81.

Lemon, S. C., W. Verhoek-Oftendahl, and E. F. Donnelly. "Preventative Health Care Use, Smoking, and Alcohol Use among Rhode Island Women Experiencing Intimate Partner Violence." *Journal of Women's Health and Gender-Based Medicine* 11 (July–August 2002): 555–62.

Lewis-O'Conner, A., et al. "Limitation of the National Protocol for Sexual Assault Medical Forensic Examinations." *Journal of Emergency Nursing* 31 (June 2005): 267–70.

Littel, Kristin. *Sexual Assault Nurse Examiner (SANE) Programs: Improving the Community Response to Sexual Assault Victims.* Washington, D.C.: U.S. Department of Justice, April 2001.

Loseke, Donileen R. *The Battered Woman and Shelters: The Social Construction of Wife Abuse.* Albany: State University of New York Press, 1992.

Luban, David. "A Theory of Crimes against Humanity." *Journal of International Law* 29 (Winter 2004): 85–162.

Lule, Jack. "The Rape of Mike Tyson: Race, the Press and Symbolic Types." *Critical Studies in Mass Communication* 12:2 (1995): 176–96.

MacKinnon, Catharine A. "Disputing Male Sovereignty: On *United States v. Morrison.*" *Harvard Law Review* 114:135 (2000): 135–77.

———. *Only Words.* Cambridge, Mass.: Harvard University Press, 1993.

Maddox, Alton H., Jr. "The Ghost of Scottsboro Resurfaced in 1989." *New York Amsterdam News* 93:25 (2002): 12.

Mansbridge, Jane. "Anti-Statism and Difference Feminism in International Social Movements." *International Feminist Journal of Politics* 5 (November 2002): 355–60.

Marecek, Jeanne. "Trauma Talk in Feminist Clinical Practice." In *New Versions of Victims: Feminist Struggle with the Concept,* edited by Sharon Lamb, 158–82. New York: New York University Press, 1999.

Margolin, Gayla, et al. "Wife Battering." In *Handbook of Family Violence,* edited by Vincent B. Van Hasselt et al., 89–117. New York: Plenum Press, 1988.

Martin, Del. "The Historical Roots of Domestic Violence." In *Domestic Violence on Trial: Psychological and Legal Dimensions of Family Violence,* edited by Daniel Jay Sonkin, 3–20. New York: Springer, 1987.

Martin, Patricia Yancey, et al. "Controversies Surrounding the Rape Kit Exam in the 1980s: Issues and Alternatives." *Crime and Delinquency* 31 (April 1985): 223–46.

Martin, Patricia Yancey. *Rape Work.* New York: Routledge, 2003.

Martin, Sandra L., et al. "Changes in Intimate Partner Violence during Pregnancy." *Journal of Family Violence* 19:4 (August 2004): 201–10.

Mason, James O. "The Dimensions of an Epidemic of Violence." *Public Health Reports* 108 (1993): 1–3.

Matoesian, Gregory M. *Law and the Language of Identity: Discourse in the William Kennedy Smith Rape Trial.* New York: Oxford University Press, 2001.

———. *Reproducing Rape: Domination through Talk in the Courtroom.* Chicago: University of Chicago Press, 1993.

Mattar, Mohamed Y. "Monitoring the Status of Severe Forms of Trafficking in Foreign Countries: Sanctions Mandated under the U.S. Trafficking Victims Protection Act." *Brown Journal of World Affairs* 10:1 (2003): 159–78.

McCauley, Jeanne. "The 'Battering Syndrome': Prevalence and Clinical Characteristics of Domestic Violence in Primary Care Internal Medicine Practices." *Annals of Internal Medicine* 123 (November 1995): 737–46.

McCoy, Candace. "Prosecution." In *The Handbook of Crime and Punishment,* edited by Michael Tonry, 457–73. New York: Oxford University Press, 1998.

McGregor, Margaret J., et al. "Sexual Assault Forensic Medical Examination: Is Evidence Related to Successful Prosecution?" *Annals of Emergency Medicine* 39 (2002): 639–47.

McKendy, John P. "The Class Politics of Domestic Violence." *Journal of Sociology and Social Welfare* 24:3 (1997): 135–55.

McMahon, Martha, and Ellen Pence. "Making Social Change." *Violence against Women* 9: 1 (2003): 47–75.

Meili, Trisha. *I Am the Central Park Jogger: A Story of Hope and Possibility.* New York: Scribner, 2003.

Melhado, L. "Women Who Report Abuse during Pregnancy Have an Elevated Risk of Adverse Birth Outcomes." *International Family Planning Perspectives* 4 (December 2005): 204.

Menon, Nivedita. *Recovering Subversion: Feminist Politics beyond the Law.* Urbana: University of Illinois Press, 2004.

Merry, Sally Engle. "Constructing a Global Law—Violence against Women and the Human Rights System." *Law and Social Inquiry* 28:4 (2003): 941–77.

———. "Rights, Religion, and Community: Approaches to Violence against Women in the Context of Globalization." *Law and Society Review* 35 (2001): 39–89.

Meyer, Jerry D. "Profane and Sacred: Religious Imagery and Prophetic Expression in Postmodern Art." *Journal of American Academy of Religion* 65:1 (Spring 1997): 19–46.

Meyer-Emerick, Nancy. "Policy Makers, Practitioners, Citizens: Perceptions of the Violence against Women Act of 1994." *Administration and Society* 33 (2003): 657–58.

Mezey, Gillian C., and Susan Bewley. "Domestic Violence and Pregnancy." *British Medical Journal* 314:7090 (1997): 1295.

Michael, Richard P., and Doris Zumpe. "An Annual Rhythm in the Battering of Women." *American Journal of Psychiatry* 143 (May 1986): 637–40.

Miles-Doan, Rebecca, and Susan Kelly. "Geographic Concentration of Violence between Intimate Partners." *Public Health Reports* (1977): 135–41.

Miller, Susan L. *Victims as Offenders: The Paradox of Women's Violence in Relationships.* New Brunswick, N.J.: Rutgers University Press, 2005.

Mills, Linda G. *Insult to Injury: Rethinking Our Responses to Intimate Abuse.* Princeton, N.J.: Princeton University Press, 2003.

Mink, Gwendolyn. "Violating Women: Rights Abuses in the Welfare Police State." In *Lost Ground: Welfare Reform, Poverty, and Beyond,* edited by Randy Albelda and Ann Withorn, 95–112. Cambridge, Mass.: South End Press, 2002.

Mink, Gwendolyn, and Rickie Solinger. *Welfare: A Documentary History of U.S. Policy and Politics.* New York: New York University Press, 2003.

Mirchandani, Rekha. "Battered Women's Movement Ideals and Judge-Led Social Change in Domestic Violence Courts." *The Good Society* 13 (2004): 32–37.

Mitchell, W. J. T. *Landscape and Power.* Chicago: University of Chicago Press, 1994.

Moorti, Sujata. *The Color of Rape: Gender and Race in Television's Public Spheres.* Albany: State University of New York Press, 2002.

Morrison, Randall L. "Assessment of Assertion and Problem-Solving Skills in Wife Abusers and Their Spouses." *Journal of Family Violence* 2:3 (1987): 227–38.

Morrison, Toni. *Playing in the Dark: Whiteness and the Literary Imagination.* Cambridge, Mass.: Harvard University Press, 1992.

——, ed. *Race-ing Justice, En-gendering Power: Essays on Anita Hill, Clarence Thomas, and the Construction of Social Reality.* New York: Pantheon Books, 1992.

Muelleman, R. L. "Battered Women: Injury Location and Types." *Annals of Emergency Medicine* 28 (November 1996): 486–92.

Murphy, Jane C. "Engaging with the State: The Growing Reliance on Judges and Lawyers to Protect Battered Women." *American University Journal of Gender, Social Policy and the Law* 11 (2003): 499–521.

Nakhaie, M. Reza. "Asymmetry and Symmetry of Conjugal Violence." *Journal of Comparative Family Studies* 29:3 (Autumn 1998): 549–67.

Narayan, Uma. *Dislocating Cultures: Identities, Traditions, and Third-World Feminism.* New York: Routledge, 1997.

Ndira, Patrick, and Atuki Turner. "The Mifumi Project and PROMPT Team, Bristol, UK and Tororo, Uganda." Address at "Criminalising Gendered Violence: Local, National and International Perspectives," Law School, University of Bristol, September 14–15, 2004.

New York Behavioral Risk Factor Surveillance System. "Physical Injuries in Intimate Relationships." *Morbidity and Mortality Weekly Report* 45 (1996): 765–67.

Nunnally, Elam W., et al., eds. *Troubled Relationships*. New York: Sage, 1988.

Nussbaum, Martha. *Frontier of Justice: Disability, Nationality, Species Membership*. Cambridge, Mass.: Harvard University Press, 2006.

——. *Women and Human Development: The Capacities Approach*. Cambridge: Cambridge University Press, 2000.

O'Connor, Jennifer. "Rape Crisis: The Debate over Professionalized Services." *Herizons*, 18 (Winter 2005): 28–47.

Ofshe, Richard J., and Richard A. Leo. "Symposium on Coercion: An Interdisciplinary Examination of Coercion, Exploitation, and the Law: Coerced Confessions." *Denver University Law Review* 74 (1997): 979–1122.

Okun, Lewis. *Woman Abuse: Facts Replacing Myths*. Albany: State University of New York Press, 1986.

O'Malley, Pat. "Social Justice after the 'Death of the Social.'" *Social Justice* 26:2 (1999): 92–101.

Parekh, Serena. "A Meaningful Place in the World: Hannah Arendt on the Nature of Human Rights." *Journal of Human Rights* 3:1 (2004): 41–53.

Parnis, Deborah, and Janice DuMont. "Examining the Standardized Application of Rape Kits: An Exploratory Study of Post-Sexual Assault Professional Practices." *Health Care for Women International* 23 (2002): 846–53.

Pearlman, Deborah N., et al. "Neighborhood Environment, Racial Position, and Risk of Police-Reported Domestic Violence: A Contextual Analysis." *Public Health Reports* 118:1 (2003): 44–59.

Peterson, Richard R., and Jo Dixon. "Court Oversight and Conviction under Mandatory and Nonmandatory Domestic Violence Case Filings." *Criminology & Public Policy* 4:3 (August 2005): 535–57.

Peterson, Zoë D. "Was It Rape? The Function of Women's Rape Myth Acceptance and Definitions of Sex in Labeling Their Own Experiences." *Sex Roles* 51:3/4 (2004): 129–44.

Picart, Caroline Joan (Kay) S. "Rhetorically Reconfiguring Victimhood and Agency: The Violence against Women Act's Civil Rights Clause." *Rhetoric and Public Affairs* 6:1 (2003): 97–126.

Pitch, Tamar. "Critical Criminology, the Construction of Social Problems, and the Question of Rape." *International Journal of the Sociology of Law* 13 (1985): 35–46.

Pizzey, Erin. *Scream Quietly or the Neighbors Will Hear*. Short Hills, N.J.: R. Enslow Publishers, 1977.

Postmus, Judy L. "Battered and on Welfare: The Experiences of Women with the Family Violence Option." *Journal of Sociology and Social Welfare* 31:2 (2004): 113–23.

Preston, Lee D. "The Sexual Assault Nurse Examiner and the Rape Crisis

Advocate: A Necessary Partnership." *Topics in Emergency Medicine* 25 (2003): 243–46.

Projansky, Sarah. *Watching Rape: Film and Television in Postfeminist Culture.* New York: New York University Press, 2001.

Ptacek, James. *Battered Women in the Courtroom: The Power of Judicial Responses.* Boston: Northeastern University Press, 1999.

Puar, Jasbir. "Abu Ghraib: Arguing against Exceptionalism." *Feminist Studies* 30:2 (2004): 522–34.

Purvin, Valerie. "Unilateral Headache and Ptosis in a 30-Year-Old Woman." *Survey of Ophthalmology* 42 (1997): 163–68.

Raphael, Jody. "Rethinking Criminal Justice Responses to Intimate Partner Violence." *Violence against Women* 10:11 (2004): 1354–66.

Reinelt, Claire. "Moving onto the Terrain of the State: The Battered Women's Movement and the Politics of Engagement." In *Feminist Organizations: Harvest of the New Women's Movement,* edited by Myra Marx Ferree and Patricia Yancey Martin, 84–104. Philadelphia: Temple University Press, 1995.

Renda, Mary A. *Taking Haiti: Military Occupation and the Culture of U.S. Imperialism, 1915–1940.* Chapel Hill: University of North Carolina Press, 2001.

Rennison, Callie Marie. "Intimate Partner Violence, 1993–2001." *Crime Data Brief.* Washington, D.C.: Bureau of Justice Statistics. NCJ 197838, U.S. Department of Justice, Office of Justice Programs, 2003.

Rennison, Callie Marie, and Sarah Welchans. "Intimate Partner Violence." *Special Report.* Washington, D.C.: Bureau of Justice Statistics, NCJ 179247, U.S. Department of Justice, Office of Justice Programs, 2000.

Resnick, Heidi, et al. "Emergency Evaluation and Intervention with Female Victims of Rape and Other Violence." *Journal of Clinical Psychology,* 56 (2000): 1317–33.

Resnik, Judith. "Citizenship and Violence." *The American Prospect* 10 (March 27–April 10, 2000): 62–63.

Resnik, Judith, and Julie Chi-hye Suk. "Adding Insult to Injury: Questioning the Role of Dignity in Conceptions of Sovereignty." *Stanford Law Review* 55 (2003): 1921–62.

Richardson, Diane. "Desiring Sameness? The Rise of a Neoliberal Politics of Normalisation." *Antipode* 37:3 (2005): 515–35.

Richman, Kimberly D. "Women, Poverty, and Domestic Violence: Perceptions of Court and Legal Aid Effectiveness." *Sociological Inquiry* 72:2 (2002): 318–44.

Riger, Stephanie. "Challenges of Success: Stages of Growth in Feminist Organization." *Feminist Studies* 20 (Summer 1994): 275–301.

Ristock, Janice L. *No More Secrets: Violence in Lesbian Relationships.* New York: Routledge, 2002.

Roberts, Albert R. "Crisis Intervention with Battered Women." In *Battered Women and Their Families: Intervention Strategies and Treatment Programs,* edited by Albert R. Roberts, 65–83. New York: Springer, 1984.

Rodgers, Harrell. "Evaluating the Devolution Revolution." *Review of Policy Research* 22 (May 2005): 275–99.

Rodriguez, Dylan. "State Terror and the Reproduction of Imprisoned Dissent." *Social Identities* 9 (2003): 183–203.

Rose, Nikolas S. *Powers of Freedom: Reframing Political Thought.* Cambridge: Cambridge University Press, 1999.

Rose, William. "Crimes of Color: Risk, Profiling, and the Contemporary Racialization of Social Control." *International Journal of Politics* 16:2 (2002): 179–206.

Rosewater, Lynne Bravo. "The Clinical and Courtroom Application of Battered Women's Personality Assessments." In *Domestic Violence on Trial: Psychological and Legal Dimensions of Family Violence,* edited by Daniel Jay Sonkin, 86–94. New York: Springer, 1987.

Rossman, Linda, et al. "Genital Trauma Associated with Forced Digital Penetration." *American Journal of Emergency Medicine* 22 (March 2004): 101–4.

Russell, Diana E. H., and Rebecca M. Bolen. *The Epidemic of Rape and Child Sexual Abuse in the United States.* Thousand Oaks, Calif.: Sage Publications, 2000.

Sadovsky, Richard. "Patterns of Injury Type and Location in Battered Women." *American Family Physician* 55:4 (March 1997): 1379–80.

——. "Presentation of Abuse-Related Injuries among Women." *American Family Physician* 59:4 (February 15, 1999): 976–78.

Saltzman, Linda E. "Issues Related to Defining and Measuring Violence against Women." *Journal of Interpersonal Violence* 19:11 (2004): 1235–43.

Scarry, Elaine. *The Body in Pain: The Making and Unmaking of the World.* New York: Oxford University Press, 1985.

Schafer, John Raul Caetano, and Catherine L. Clark. "Rates of Intimate Partner Violence in the United States." *American Journal of Public Health* 88:11 (November 1998): 1702–4.

Schechter, Susan. *Women and Male Violence: The Visions and Struggles of the Battered Women's Movement.* Boston: South End Press, 1982.

Schneider, Elizabeth M. "Anna Hirsch Lecture: Transnational Law as a Domestic Resource: Thoughts on the Case of Women's Rights." *New England Law Review* 38 (2004): 689–723.

——. "Symposium: Battered Women and Feminist Lawmaking: Author Meets Readers, Elizabeth M. Schneider, Christine Harrington, Sally Engle Merry, Renee Romkens and Marianne Wesson." *Journal of Law and Policy* 10 (2002): 313–72.

Schultz, Vicki. "Reconceptualizing Sexual Harassment." *Yale Law Journal* 107 (1998): 1683–1805.

Scraton, Phil. *Beyond September 11: An Anthology of Dissent.* London: Pluto Press, 2002.

"Severity of Spousal and Intimate Partner Abuse to Pregnant Hispanic Women." *Journal of Health Care for the Poor and Underserved* 9 (August 1998): 248–61.

Shestack, Jerome J. "Serious Crime Is on a Downward Trend." *Human Rights: Journal of the Section of Individual Rights and Responsibilities* 25:1 (1998): 13.

Siegel, Robert M., and Teresa D. Hill. "Screening for Domestic Violence in the Community Pediatric Setting." *Pediatrics* 104:4 (October 1999): 874–77.

Silliman, Jael, and Anannya Bhattacharjee. *Policing the National Body: Sex, Race, and Criminalization.* Cambridge, Mass.: South End Press, 2002.

Simon, Jonathan. *Governing Through Crime: How the War on Crime Transformed American Democracy and Created a Culture of Fear.* New York: Oxford University Press, 2007.

Singer, Linda. *Erotic Welfare: Sexual Theory and the Politics of the Epidemic.* New York: Routledge, 1993.

Smart, Carol. *Feminism and the Power of the Law.* New York: Routledge, 1989.

Smiley, Marion. "Battered Women and Bombed-out Cities: A Question of Responsibility." In *Midwest Studies in Philosophy*, volume 20: *Moral Concepts*, edited by Peter A. French et al., 15–35. Notre Dame, Ind.: University of Notre Dame Press, 1995.

Sonkin, Daniel Jay Del Martin, and Lenore E. Walker. *The Male Batterer: A Treatment Approach.* New York: Springer, 1985.

Spath, Robin. "Child Protection Professionals Identifying Domestic Violence Indications: Implications for Social Work Education." *Journal of Social Work Education* 39:3 (Fall 2003): 497–516.

Spohn, Cassia C., and Julie Horney. "The Impact of Rape Law Reform on the Processing of Simple and Aggravated Rape Cases." *Journal of Criminal Law and Criminology* 86:3 (1996): 861–87.

Stanko, Elizabeth Anne. *Everyday Violence: How Women and Men Experience Sexual Danger.* London: Pandora/Unwin Hyman, 1990.

Straten, Roelof van. *An Introduction to Iconography.* Amsterdam: Gordon and Breach, 1994.

Sugar, N. F., et al. "Physical Injury after Sexual Assault: Findings of a Large Case Series." *American Journal of Obstetrics and Gynecology* 190 (2004): 71–76.

Symes, Lene. "Arriving at Readiness to Recover Emotionally After Sexual Assault." *Archives of Psychiatric Nursing* 1 (February 2000): 30–38.

Taft, Angela, Dorothy H. Brown, and David Legge. "General Practitioner Management of Intimate Partner Abuse and the Whole Family: Qualitative Study." *British Medical Journal* 328:7440 (March 13, 2004): 618–21.

Talley, Nicholas J., and Philip Boyce. "Abuse and Functional Gastrointestinal Disorders: What Is the Link and Should We Care." *Gastroenterology* 110:4 (1996): 1301–4.

Taslitz, Andrew E. *Rape and the Culture of the Courtroom.* New York: New York University Press, 1999.

Terry, Geraldine. "Poverty Reduction and Violence against Women: Exploring Links, Assessing Impact." *Development in Practice* 14:4 (2004): 469–80.

Thomas, Patricia, and Nancy Ryan Lowitt. "A Traumatic Experience." *New England Journal of Medicine* 333:5 (August 3, 1995): 307–11.

Thyfault, Roberta K., Cathy E. Bennett, and Robert B. Hirschhorn. "Battered Women in Court: Jury and Trial Consultants and Expert Witnesses." In *Domestic Violence on Trial: Psychological and Legal Dimensions of Family Violence,* edited by Daniel Jay Sonkin, 55–70. New York: Springer, 1987.

Tzvetkova, Marina. "NGO Responses to Trafficking in Women." *Gender and Development* 10:1 (2002): 60–68.

Uekert, Brenda K. "The Value of Coordinated Community Responses." *Criminology and Public Policy* 3:1 (2003): 133–36.

UN General Assembly. *Convention on the Elimination of All Forms of Discrimination against Women.* Resolution. 34/180. U.N. Doc. A/34/46. December 18, 1979.

Violence against Women Act. Pub. L. No. 103–322, 108 Stat. 1902–55 (1994).

Wacquant, Loic. "The New 'Peculiar Institution': On Prison as the Surrogate Ghetto." *Theoretical Criminology* 4 (August 2000): 377–90.

Walker, E. A. "Assessing Abuse and Neglect and Dental Fear in Women." *Journal of the American Dental Association* 127 (April 1996): 485–90.

Walker, Lenore E. *The Battered Woman.* New York: Harper and Row, 1979.

Wallace, Harvey. *Family Violence: Legal, Medical, and Social Perspectives.* Boston: Pearson, 2005.

Ware, Vron. *Beyond the Pale: White Women, Racism, and History: Questions for Feminism.* London: Verso, 1993.

Wasco, Sharon M. "Conceptualizing the Harm Done by Rape: Applications of Trauma Theory to Experiences of Sexual Assault." *Trauma, Violence and Abuse* 4 (October 2003): 309–22.

Weaver, T. L. and G. A. Clum. "Interpersonal Violence: Expanding the Search for Long-Term Sequelae within a Sample of Battered Women." *Journal of Traumatic Stress* 9 (October 1996): 783–803.

Weber, Max. *Politics as a Vocation.* Minneapolis: Fortress Press, 1965.

Webster, Joan. "Pregnancy Outcomes and Health Care Use: Effects of

Abuse." *American Journal of Obstetrical Gynecology* 174 (February 1996): 760–67.

Weis, Lois. "Race, Gender and Critique: African-American Women, White Women, and Domestic Violence in the 1980s and 1990s." *Signs: Journal of Women in Culture and Society* 27:1 (2001): 139–69.

Weldon, S. Laurel. *Protest, Policy and the Problem of Violence against Women: A Cross-National Comparison*, Pittsburgh: University of Pittsburgh Press, 2002.

Wells, Christina E., and Erin E. Motley. "Reinforcing the Myth of the Crazed Rapist: A Feminist Critique of Recent Rape Legislation." *Boston University Law Review* 81:127 (2001): 127–98.

Westervelt, Saundra D., and John A. Humphrey. *Wrongly Convicted: Perspectives on Failed Justice.* New Brunswick, N.J: Rutgers University Press, 2001.

Westlund, Andrea. "Pre-Modern and Modern Power: Foucault and the Case of Domestic Violence." *Signs: Journal of Women in Culture and Society* 24:4 (Summer 1999): 1045–67.

Whitecotton, Jacquelyn W., and Susan B. Sorenson. "A Sociocultural View of Sexual Assault: From Discrepancy to Diversity." *Journal of Social Issues* 48:1 (1992): 187–95.

Wilcox, Paula. "Beauty and the Beast: Gendered and Raced Discourse in the News." *Social and Legal Studies* 14 (2005): 515–32.

Wilson, Craig R. "Police and the Sexual Assault Examination." *FBI Law Enforcement Bulletin* 71:1 (January 2002): 14–17.

Wolfthal, Diane. *Images of Rape: The "Heroic" Tradition and Its Alternatives.* New York: Cambridge University Press, 1999.

Woliver, Laura. *From Outrage to Action.* Urbana: University of Illinois Press, 1993.

"Women Say They've Made Gains but There's Still Work to Do." *Marketing to Women: Addressing Women and Women's Sensibilities* 16:8 (August 1, 2003).

Wright, Rosalind J. "Responses to Battered Mothers in the Pediatric Emergency Department: A Call for an Interdisciplinary Approach to Family Violence." *Pediatrics* 99 (February 1977): 186–92.

Yassen, Janet, and Lois Glass. "Sexual Assault Survivors Groups: A Feminist Practice Perspective." *Social Work* 29:3 (May–June 1984): 252–57

Žižek, Slavoj. "Risk Society and Its Discontents." *Historical Materialism: Research in Critical Marxist Theory* 2 (Summer 1998): 143–64.

Zweig, Janine M., and Martha R. Burt. "Effects of Interactions among Community Agencies on Legal System Responses to Domestic Violence and Sexual Assault in STOP-Funded Communities." *Criminal Justice Policy Review* 14: 2 (2003): 249–53.

cases cited

Commonwealth v. Rapozo, Cordeiro, Silva, and Vieira, Mass. Super. Ct. (March 17, 1984).

Hernandez v. Ashcroft, 345 F.3d 824 (9th Cir. 2003).

People v. Salaam, 83 N.Y.2d 51; 629 N.E.2d 371; 607 N.Y.S.2d 899 (1993).

Thurman v. Torrington, 595 F.Supp. 1521 (D. Conn. 1984).

United States v. Morrison, 529 U.S. 598 (2000).

Luban, David, 144
Lynching, 10, 21, 172 n. 7

MacKinnon, Catherine, 31
Mandatory arrest, xiii, 11–12, 142, 160
Mandatory sentences, xii, 169 n. 35
Martin, Patricia Yancy, 165
Masochist hypothesis, 67, 85
Maternal body, 172 n. 10
Media reports, 23, 158, 170 n. 1; race in, 30; of New Bedford case, 39–40, 41; of Central Park case, 42
Medicaid, 107
Medical examination, 32, 44; in trials, 33
Medical journals, 73–74
Medical profession, 74–79
Megan's Laws, 8
Meili, Trisha, 100. *See also* Central Park jogger
Merry, Sally, 139
Mills, Linda, xiii, 147, 168 n. 5 (Preface)
Minimization, 91
Miranda protections, 57
Moral panics, 8
Morrison, Toni, 22
Mothers: single, 13; charged with failure to protect, 14; murder of, 23; welfare, 97; battered women as, 114–20

Narayan, Uma, 151, 152
Narratives, 102, 110
National Association for the Advancement of Colored People (NAACP), xi
National Organization for Women (NOW), 2
Neoliberalism, xv, 1, 6–7, 11, 13, 15; growth of, 5; expressive justice and, 37; penal and welfare system influenced by, 64–65

New Bedford trial, xv, 39, 41, 44–45; artistic representations of, 25; media reports of, 39–40; moment of transgression in, 46–47; bystanders in, 47–48; homo-erotic scene in, 48; victim's testimony at, 100–109
New York City, 24, 43, 99
New York City Police Department, 61, 176–77 n. 27
Neurological disorders, 77–78, 79

Parentification, 86
Patriarchy, 95, 97, 110
Perpetrators, 1, 7, 158; segregation from society of, 2; castigation of, 9; victims turned into, 13–14; sadistic motives of, 35; hostility toward, 40; stereotypes of, 63; rehabilitation of, 64; programs for, 73; ethnicity of, 157; treatment of, 177 n. 2. *See also* Defendants; Strangers
Picart, Caroline, 143
Police harassment, 111–13
Police interrogations, 57, 61
Pornographic images, 31
Portuguese community, 41
Posttraumatic stress disorder (PTSD), 91. *See also* Trauma
Poverty, 14, 131; as context for battering, 187 n. 35
Predatory landscape, 174 n. 21
Prison, xii, xv, 10, 162, 168–69 n. 19
Prison abolitionists, 162–63
Professional norms, xvi
Professionals: education of, 65; clients helped by, 67, 78–79, 88; therapeutic language used by, 68; medical, 73–79; case study method and, 74–75; social science methodology and, 89–90; violence confronted by, 94, 182 n. 128; rhetoric of, 129
Prosecutorial power, xii

KRISTIN BUMILLER is professor of political science and women's and gender studies at Amherst College.

Library of Congress Cataloging-in-Publication Data
Bumiller, Kristin, 1957–
In an abusive state : how neoliberalism appropriated the feminist
movement against sexual violence / Kristin Bumiller.
p. cm.
Includes bibliographical references and index.
ISBN-13: 978-0-8223-4220-5 (cloth : alk. paper)
ISBN-13: 978-0-8223-4239-7 (pbk. : alk. paper)
1. Sex crimes—Political aspects. 2. Sexual abuse victims—Political aspects.
3. Feminism—Political aspects. 4. Neoliberalism. 5. Criminal justice,
Administration of. I. Title.
HV6566.B86 2008
364.15'3—dc22   2007043975

94786864R10139

Made in the USA
Middletown, DE
21 October 2018